PANIC PLAN

for the

ACT
ASSESSMENT®

THOMSON

PETERSON'S

Australia • Canada • Mexico • Singapore • Spain • United Kingdom • United States

About The Thomson Corporation and Peterson's

With revenues approaching US$6 billion, The Thomson Corporation (www.thomson.com) is a leading global provider of integrated information solutions for business, education, and professional customers. Its Learning businesses and brands (www.thomsonlearning.com) serve the needs of individuals, learning institutions, and corporations with products and services for both traditional and distributed learning.

Peterson's, part of The Thomson Corporation, is one of the nation's most respected providers of lifelong learning online resources, software, reference guides, and books. The Education Supersite℠ at www.petersons.com—the Internet's most heavily traveled education resource—has searchable databases and interactive tools for contacting U.S.-accredited institutions and programs. In addition, Peterson's serves more than 105 million education consumers annually.

An American BookWorks Corporation Project

For more information, contact Peterson's, 2000 Lenox Drive, Lawrenceville, NJ 08648; 800-338-3282; or find us on the World Wide Web at www.petersons.com/about.

ISBN 0-7689-0858-2

Printed in Canada

10 9 8 7 6 5 4 3   04 03

CONTENTS

CONTENTS

PLAN OF ATTACK

WEEK ONE

WO WEEK STUDY PLAN

WEEK TWO

DAY 1

ABOUT THE ACT ASSESSMENT

The ACT Assessment is a multiple-choice test that is required for admission by many colleges throughout the United States and Canada. Taking this test can be an anxious time for many students, but by its very nature of being a multiple-choice test, you can prepare for this examination by learning some of the tricks and approaches to answering this type of question format.

The ACT Assessment tests are offered five times during the school year: October, December, February, April, and June. Check your state's schedules, however, since the test may not be offered in your state during a particular month. If you are planning to take the test, you can obtain a registration packet in your school, or write directly to: ACT, P.O. Box 168, Iowa City, Iowa 52243.

This book has been written for you—the student—to help you prepare for the examination. It will give you an understanding of the overall test and guide you, step by step, through each of the four areas covered on the exam. There is a logical approach to this process, exemplified by the content and format of this book. Let's take a moment to look at what you will find in this book.

INTRODUCTION

This section of the book presents an overview of the exam. It is designed to help you understand the nature of the test, what you have to know, and how to go about preparing for it.

Part I—Diagnostic Pretest

The Diagnostic Pretest is a full-length ACT Assessment examination, similar in content to the one you will eventually take. The purpose of this test is to help you diagnose your strengths and weaknesses. After you have taken the test and marked your scores, you will quickly be able to zero in on those specific subjects or question types that give you trouble. Armed with this knowledge, you can then focus only on those areas that need additional work. After all, why spend weeks reviewing material that you already know? Make sure, however, that you read the analysis of each answer. This will help you understand more fully what will be required of you on the actual examination.

Part II—Review Section

The ACT Assessment consists of four subject areas: English, Mathematics, Reading, and Science Reasoning. This section contains review material and practice questions for each of these subjects. Once you have taken the diagnostic pretest and have determined what areas require further study, you can go right to the specific section in Part II to concentrate your time and energy on reviewing the appropriate material.

Part III—Evaluation Tests

Once you have studied and reviewed the necessary subject areas or question types, it's time to evaluate your progress. Part III contains two full-length ACT Assessment exams to afford you further practice and determine if there are any additional areas that need to be studied. Take the first exam, grade yourself, and read through the explanations of the answers. Go back and review anything that requires further studying. Then take the second examination. The more you practice, the more you increase your chances for a higher score on the actual examination.

THE EXAM

The actual examination is composed of four sections:

English Test	75 questions	45 minutes
Mathematics Test	60 questions	60 minutes
Reading Test	40 questions	35 minutes
Science Reasoning Test	40 questions	35 minutes

ENGLISH TEST

This portion of the examination will test your understanding of the basics of standard written English. It will cover punctuation, basic grammar and usage, and sentence structure. In addition, you will be tested on rhetorical skills—strategy, organization, and style. You will not be tested on things like spelling or vocabulary, nor do you have to worry about reciting the rules of grammar.

The test will present five prose passages accompanied by about fifteen multiple-choice questions. These questions will test your basic understanding of writing and rhetorical skills.

The following chart will give you an idea of the actual types of questions you will encounter:

Content/Skills	Number of Items	Percentage of English Test
Usage/Mechanics	**40**	
Punctuation	10	13%
Basic Grammar and Usage	12	16%

Content/Skills	Number of Items	Percentage of English Test
Sentence Structure	18	24%
Rhetorical Skills	**35**	
Strategy	12	16%
Organization	11	15%
Style	12	16%

Although the question content will be fairly evenly presented on the English test, you can see that the greatest number of questions will be in the area of sentence structure. It becomes important, then, to concentrate a little more of your studying on that type of question.

MATHEMATICS TEST

The mathematics you will be tested upon is material that you have probably already learned and covers the content of mathematics courses given from the ninth through eleventh grades. The test includes pre-algebra, elementary algebra, intermediate algebra, coordinate geometry, plane geometry, and some trigonometry.

The following is a chart that gives the breakdown of the Mathematics Test:

Content	Number of Items	Percentage of Mathematics Test
Pre-Algebra	14	23%
Elementary Algebra	10	17%
Intermediate Algebra	9	15%
Coordinate Geometry	9	15%
Plane Geometry	14	23%
Trigonometry	4	7%

This chart should give you a good idea on where to focus your study efforts. Pre-algebra and plane geometry will require the most effort.

READING TEST

The subjects covered on this portion of the test include topics that usually appear in books and magazines read by high school seniors and college freshmen and cover the following areas: social studies, prose fiction, humanities, and natural science. Rather than test specific facts or your vocabulary knowledge, the test focuses on your skills in "referring" and "reasoning." This means that you will be required to derive meaning from the passages by referring to what is specifically stated in them, and to draw conclusions and other meanings based on reasoning.

The following is a table of the different types of questions you will encounter on the Reading Test. There will normally be one passage covering each of the four content areas, and each passage will contain ten questions. Although there are four different content areas, only one skill is really being tested—reading comprehension.

Reading Content	Number of Items	Percentage of Reading Test
Social Studies	10	25%
Natural Science	10	25%
Prose Fiction	10	25%
Humanities	10	25%

SCIENCE REASONING TEST

The Science Reasoning Test will present seven sets of scientific information covering four major areas of study—biology, chemistry, physical science, and earth and space science. It is primarily a test of reasoning and problem-solving skills. The information is presented in three different forms of questions:

1. Data Representation (graphs, charts, tables, illustrations, etc.)

2. Research Summaries (one or more related experiments)

3. Conflicting Viewpoints (two or more hypotheses or views that are inconsistent with one another)

This test contains 40 questions, usually spread out over seven sets of scientific information or passages. The following chart will give you an idea of the types of questions that you can expect.

Format	Number of Items	Percentage of Science Test
Data Representation	15	38%
Research Summaries	18	45%
Conflicting Viewpoints	7	17%

These four subject areas will be covered and explained in greater detail later in each of the specific chapters in Part II.

SCORING

It is probably not that important to understand the scoring procedure. What is obvious is that the better you do on the examination, the higher your score. The higher your score, the better chance you have of being accepted to the school of your choice. The ACT Assessment bulletin will give you the tables and charts to help you understand how your score is computed. You will probably be better served by spending your time studying for the test.

STRATEGIES

1. Know How Much Time You Have

From the preceding information, you can quickly determine how much time you will be allocated to answer each question and know why you will have to be familiar with the material on the test.

English Test	About ½ minute per question
Math Test	1 minute per question
Reading Test	Less than 1 minute per question
Science Reasoning Test	Less than 1 minute per question

This shouldn't intimidate you at all. Instead, it should give you a goal toward which to aim. The more you practice, the faster you will become, until you are able to breeze through the material that you know even faster than the allotted time and give yourself a few extra minutes to concentrate on the material you don't know.

2. Understand the Directions

By understanding the directions for each examination, you will save time on the actual ACT Assessment test. Since you have only a limited amount of time for each section and each question, don't waste time reading and rereading directions when you can learn them here and now, commit them to memory, and never have to look at them again. Each section in Part II will give you the directions. Memorize them!

3. Understand the Question Formats

Each section of the exam presents the material in different formats. However, there will be no surprises. Learn the different formats for each of the four sections. If you are comfortable with that knowledge, it will eliminate some test anxiety.

The good news, however, is that all of the questions in all of the areas are multiple-choice. This gives you an advantage when you have to guess (see #7). Later on in this book you will encounter strategies for answering multiple-choice questions.

4. Fill in the Blanks Carefully

Nothing would be worse than getting to the end of almost three hours of testing to find out that you have run out of little answer ovals because you skipped one. Make sure you are careful about filling in the blanks, especially if you decide to skip some questions so you can come back to them after you have answered the easier questions. Check the blanks every few questions on the Mathematics Test, or every time you begin a new passage in the English, Reading, or Science Reasoning Tests.

5. Erase Completely

If you have skipped an oval and need to go back, or you have answered a question incorrectly, make sure you erase the incorrect answer completely. If you don't, there is a good possibility that the machine reading your answer page may mark it as incorrect.

6. Start with the Easy Questions, Then Try the Harder Ones

As with most tests, it makes sense to answer the easiest questions first. These should take less time to answer, thus giving you some extra time for those that are more difficult. This is especially important for any test that is timed. If there is actually time left when you have filled in all of the blanks, try to review your work.

7. Answer Every Question

This topic is highlighted because it is vitally important. Your ACT score is based on the number of questions you have answered correctly, and you are not penalized for wrong answers. Therefore, it is worth your while to guess. One technique that is recommended is as follows:

- Answer the easy questions first.

- Check your time.

- Then try the more difficult ones.

- Check your time.

- Try those questions that are most difficult.

- Fill in the remaining blanks.

- Check your time again and review if you can.

Some test experts recommend a different approach. They suggest filling in all of the answers consecutively, just in case you run out of time. If you are not confident that you will be able to get through the easier questions quickly and have enough time left over to go back, fill in the answers as you come to them. Also, if you are concerned that by skipping some of the answers you may forget to leave the appropriate questions blank, then it is also better to work consecutively. Practicing with the three full-length tests in this book will help you decide which technique is best for you.

8. **Practice Under Simulated Situations**

As you practice with the tests in this book, time yourself. Make believe you are in the room where you are actually taking the test. Use a stopwatch, if you can, to time each section. Since you are only practicing for the test, it is probably more realistic to take one section at a time, and take them on separate days. It is often difficult to set aside three full hours during a school week, or even on a busy weekend, to take the entire test. After all, the purpose of practicing with this book is to improve your speed on each test. Obviously, as you improve the timing of each test, your total time will also decrease.

9. **Prepare Yourself for the Actual Test**

HOW TO ANSWER THE ENGLISH GRAMMAR QUESTIONS

You have studied the English language for many years. Some of you have mastered the basic usage of our language, some of you have a refined and professional ability to use and understand our language, and some of you may find yourselves struggling with this portion of the ACT Assessment test. In order to better equip you to succeed in this part of the test, several suggestions are offered:

1. Read this overview very thoroughly.

2. Study the two categories and all of the subjects that fall under them.

3. Do the practice passages.

4. Study the manner in which the questions are worded.

5. Try to write a passage yourself, and then write questions and answers in the style of this section. Going through the exercise of writing a passage will help you learn the style of the test.

The ACT Assessment tests your knowledge of standard English usage and mechanics and your rhetorical skills. The questions focus on your knowledge of proper punctuation, sentence structure, and basic grammar and usage. Your understanding of style, organization, and strategy will also be examined. The ACT Assessment will test your knowledge of ALL aspects of our language. Here is a description of the two large categories of questions that will be on the ACT Assessment:

I. USAGE AND MECHANICS

There are three sections in this category:

1. Sentence Structure—Approximately 24 percent of the questions will be from this section. These questions are concerned with how to properly construct a sentence with regard to modifiers, phrases, clauses, and general logic.

2. Basic Grammar and Usage—Approximately 16 percent of the questions will be from this section. These questions test your knowledge of pronoun case, parts of speech, verb formation, use of idioms, noun-pronoun agreement, and proper use of modifiers.

3. Punctuation—Approximately 13 percent of the questions will be from this section. These questions test your ability to properly use internal and end-of-sentence punctuation.

II. RHETORICAL SKILLS

There are three sections in this category:

1. Style—Approximately 16 percent of the questions will be from this section. These questions focus on your ability to make appropriate word and phrase choices and your ability to avoid the problems of wordiness, redundancy, clichés, and ambiguous references.

2. Organization—Approximately 15 percent of the questions will be from this section. These questions test your ability to understand how ideas are organized, ordered, and unified. Here are some typical questions you may find in this section:

   • Which sentence does not belong in the above paragraph?

   • Which is the best topic sentence for the paragraph?

   • Unscramble the above paragraph and choose the correct sequence of sentences from the following choices:

3. Strategy—Approximately 16 percent of the questions will be from this section. These questions focus on your ability to choose appropriate transitions and strong opening and closing sentences and to understand which words and expressions reflect the purpose and meaning of the passage. Here are some typical questions from this section of the ACT Assessment:

   • Which of these statements best expresses the author's intentions?

   • The main point the author is concerned with is . . .

- Which of the following titles would be appropriate for the preceding passage?

How to Effectively Handle the Questions

1. Pace yourself.

You will have 45 minutes to answer seventy-five questions. You have about 30 seconds to answer each question. Do not linger over a question you do not understand. If you are confused, move on to the next question. After you have completed the questions that are easier for you to understand, then go back and answer any you have omitted.

2. Carefully examine the underlined portion of the passage as it relates to the question.

Look closely at the answer choices. From them, you will be able to tell what you are being tested for (grammar, punctuation, word choice, and so on).

3. Select the best answer.

At first glance, more than one answer may seem to be correct. Eliminate answer choices one at a time. There is always a best answer.

4. Check your answer in context.

Reread the sentence with your selected answer substituted for the underlined portion. As time permits, check your work.

5. Become familiar with the style of the passages.

You MUST study these practice passages in order to learn the language of the test questions. Some of the questions focus on underlined sections that ask you to change the words. Other questions require that you read and understand the whole paragraph in context. Often, questions that test your rhetorical skills will not refer to an underlined word or phrase. Instead, you will need to answer questions about the passage in general. Begin thinking about the ways in which you can successfully answer these typical questions:

- The main point of the paragraph is . . .

- Which of the following is an appropriate title for the passage?

- Which sentence does not belong in the above passage?

At this point, study the review section with practice passages. Read the passages, answer the questions, and then check your answers. If you do not understand the question, read the explanation in the answer section. The explanation is there to help you differentiate between the answer options that you are given.

Do not skip over this section. It is imperative that you become familiar with the style of the questions if you want to be successful in the English portion of the ACT Assessment.

PRACTICE QUESTIONS—USAGE AND MECHANICS

Passage 1

In order to write an effective movie review, several elements must be explained for the reader being that they need it. The plot should be explained, but not too thoroughly, thus ruining any surprises that the audience prefers to experience firsthand. The rating of the movie should be explained, so that readers can use the review to help them make decisions regarding their childrens attendance of the movie. Actors in the movie under review may deserve praise or criticism. Finally, a good reviewer needs to adopt a rating system to indicate their personal judgment regarding the possible success of the movie. Siskel and Ebert have their "thumbs up/thumbs down" system, and other reviewers use stars or other symbols. When a reviewer uses a personal rating system the system should be easily understood. Graphics might help the viewer to understand the reviewer's intent.

1. (A) NO CHANGE
   (B) reader, because they need it.
   (C) reader.
   (D) reader since they can use the help.

2. (F) NO CHANGE
   (G) not too thoroughly, not ruining any surprises
   (H) not too thoroughly, to prevent ruining any surprises
   (J) not too thoroughly, so as not to be ruining any surprises

3. (A) NO CHANGE
   (B) children's attendance
   (C) childrens' attendance
   (D) childs' attendance

4. (F) NO CHANGE
   (G) to indicate their own personal judgment
   (H) to indicate his/her personal judgment
   (J) to indicate everyone's personal judgment

5. (A) NO CHANGE
   (B) rating system, the system
   (C) rating system; the system
   (D) rating system it

Passage 2

Both the play *Romeo and Juliet* and the musical *West Side Story* contain the same famous forbidden love story. In *Romeo and Juliet*, the main characters and lovers Romeo and Juliet come from feuding families. In *West Side Story*, the main characters and lovers Maria and Tony come from feuding gangs. In both stories, the <u>lovers plot</u> to find times to meet, and despite the
                                      1
difference in time periods in the two works, both stories contain a "balcony" scene in which the female is on a <u>balcony, in</u> Maria's case, the balcony is a
                                                              2
fire escape, and her male <u>lover, which is</u> below on the ground, professes his
                              3
undying love. In both stories, death occurs for the male lover. In *Romeo and Juliet*, both lovers appear to die, until Juliet awakens from a deathlike sleep to discover that Romeo had taken poison <u>when thinking that</u> Juliet was dead. In
                                               4
West Side Story, Tony dies after he is stabbed in a gang fight.

1. (A) NO CHANGE
   (B) lover's plot
   (C) lovers' plot
   (D) lovers plots

2. (F) NO CHANGE
   (G) balcony which in
   (H) balcony as in
   (J) balcony. In

3. (A) NO CHANGE
   (B) lover, who is
   (C) lover, that is
   (D) lover that could be

4. (F) NO CHANGE
   (G) when he thought
   (H) when he is thinking
   (J) when they are thinking

PRACTICE QUESTIONS—
RHETORICAL SKILLS

Passage 3

Music has been called the universal language. People from all walks of

life have attempted to interpret and explain this statement. Clearly, music

possesses a universal notation system. If an individual can read music in one

country, he/she can read music in another country as well. The sheets of

music do not need to be translated for musicians. A second reason that music

is considered the universal language is because of the effect that music has on

human emotions. Music can both express and generate feeling. Many people
                                                                        1
who perform music are affected as they play or sing. Classical, gospel,
___
1
country, rock, rap, popular, and all other types of music lend the same

opportunity for emotional reaction in the performer and in the audience.

Some people are moved by song lyrics, others by instrumental music, and

others by the mood established by music. Music can unite and alienate

generations of people. Music can inspire action—even revolution. The youth

of any culture frequently identify themselves separately from their parents and

guardians by their music listening preferences. Adults who did the same thing

in their youth seem to forget that music is a bonding part of adolescence for

many people. Perhaps the best advice for adults who do not enjoy the

musical tastes of their children is to "turn a deaf ear."

1. This underlined phrase is written poorly. The weakness is attributed to which of the following writing problems?

   (A) Ambiguous reference
   (B) Cliché
   (C) Redundancy
   (D) Wordiness

2. Which is the best topic sentence for the paragraph?

   (F) Music has been called the universal language.
   (G) People from all walks of life have attempted to interpret and explain this statement.
   (H) Music can both express and generate feeling.
   (J) Music can inspire action— even revolution.

3. The main point the author is concerned with is:

   (A) Adults should let their children listen to any type of music.
   (B) Music can generate emotion.
   (C) Music provides a universal experience in several ways.
   (D) Performers experience more emotion than audience members.

4. The author offers two explanations for the phrase "music is the universal language." What is the author's first explanation?

   (F) Music has been called the universal language.
   (G) People from all walks of life have attempted to interpret and explain this statement.
   (H) Clearly, music possesses a universal notation system.
   (J) The sheets of music do not need to be translated for musicians.

Passage 4

[1] If the speech is well-researched and well-organized and presents

                                                    2

content clearly in a style which is easy to follow, the speaker will feel more

                  2

confident. [2] When preparing to deliver a speech to an audience, the best approach is to first realize that many people are highly fearful of public speaking. [3] The art of public speaking improves with practice and experience. [4] The best methods to avert stage fright are good preparation, rehearsal, and fervor. [5] Additionally, if the speaker possesses fervor—a genuine desire for the message to be heard—the speaker has a higher chance of overcoming stage fright and delivering the message with success. [6] The speaker must rehearse the speech orally prior to the actual presentation.

1. Unscramble the above paragraph and choose the correct sequence of sentences from the following choices:

   (A) NO CHANGE
   (B) 4, 1, 2, 6, 5, 3
   (C) 2, 4, 1, 6, 5, 3
   (D) 3, 6, 5, 4, 2, 1

2. This underlined phrase is poorly written. The weakness is attributed to which of the following writing problems?

   (F) Wordiness
   (G) Redundancy
   (H) Ambiguous reference
   (J) Cliché

3. Which of the following titles would be appropriate for the preceding passage?

   (A) Everything You Need to Know About Public Speaking
   (B) How to Overcome Stage Fright in Public Speaking
   (C) How to Organize a Speech
   (D) How to Approach Public Speaking

4. Which of these statements best expresses the author's intent?

   (F) Speaking is fearful but manageable.
   (G) You are not alone in your fear to speak publicly.
   (H) Don't be afraid to speak.
   (J) Speaking gets easier the older you get.

NOW CHECK YOUR ANSWERS

Answers to Passage 1

1. **The correct answer is (C).** The original, choice (B), and choice (D) contain excessive words and break the specific guidelines to avoid usage of "being that" and the words "since" and "because." **(Sentence Structure)**

2. **The correct answer is (H).** Any other answer creates faulty sentence structure. **(Sentence Structure)**

3. **The correct answer is (B).** This answer alone uses the proper possessive form of the word children. **(Punctuation)**

4. **The correct answer is (H).** The singular word reviewer requires a singular pronoun, not the plural pronoun as offered in the original. This is called proper pronoun reference. **(Basic Grammar and Usage)**

5. **The correct answer is (B).** An introductory clause must be set aside from the rest of the sentence by a comma. **(Punctuation)**

Answers to Passage 2

1. **The correct answer is (A).** Both choices (B) and (C) are incorrect because there is no need for a possessive form. "Lovers" is simply plural. Choice (D) is illogical. **(Punctuation)**

2. **The correct answer is (J).** All other answers allow for a run-on sentence or a comma splice to occur. One sentence needs to end and a new one begin at this point. **(Sentence Structure)**

3. **The correct answer is (B).** The word "who" refers to people. The word "that" refers to animals or objects. **(Basic Grammar and Usage)**

4. **The correct answer is (G).** The problem here lies in the correct tense. Romeo took the poison in the past, so a past tense is necessary for correct sentence structure. All other answers utilize an incorrect tense. **(Sentence Structure)**

Answers to Passage 3

1. **The correct answer is (D).** While it might at first appear that redundancy is in operation in this grouping of words, the actual problem is wordiness. Too many words are used. The simpler, more direct way to say this is: "Many musical performers . . ." **(Style)**

2. **The correct answer is (G).** While this is not a clearly written thesis, this is the only possible answer. Choices (C) and (D) are subordinate points that the author makes in the effort to interpret what the phrase, stated in choice (A), "music is a universal language," means to him/her. **(Organization)**

3. **The correct answer is (C).** Choices (A) and (D) are merely opinions that might be concluded from the passage, but neither statement appears in the passage. These conclusions may not reflect the author's intent in any manner. Choice (B) is one of the points the author attempts to make, but this is not the main point the author attempts to make. **(Strategy)**

4. **The correct answer is (H).** Choice (A) simply restates the phrase, choice (B) establishes the author's intent to do what others before have attempted to do, and choice (D) is an example of the first explanation offered by the author. **(Organization)**

Answers to Passage 4

1. **The correct answer is (C).** This sequence is the most orderly and logical of the options. **(Organization)**

2. **The correct answer is (G).** While wordiness and redundancy are similar, there is a distinct difference between the two. This exemplifies redundancy, for all of the words following the word "well-organized" further define the word "well-organized" and are not necessary. **(Style)**

3. **The correct answer is (B).** While the content suggested by the title in choice (C) is contained briefly within the passage, this title is too limiting. Likewise, the content suggested by the titles in choices (A) and (D) is too broad to match the content presented in this passage. **(Strategy)**

4. **The correct answer is (F).** The content in choices (B) and (C) is too limited to fit the passage, and the content in choice (D) is not inferred in the passage. **(Strategy)**

At this point you should be able to recognize the different types of questions in the following practice passage, the question types are combined.

PRACTICE PASSAGE—
USAGE AND MECHANICS AND
RHETORICAL SKILLS

The nonverbal behaviors that occur in a courtroom have been studied by people from many professions for many purposes. One group in <u>particular</u>
1
<u>communication experts are</u> extremely interested in synthesizing the nonverbal
1
behavior <u>that occurs</u> in the courtroom. The facial expressions of judges are
2
noted, scrutinized, and observed with intensity. Attorneys, judges, and defendants each <u>watch the movements of the jury like a hawk.</u> Many commu-
3
nication experts believe that much of the nonverbal behavior in the <u>courtroom as opposed to facts and evidence, determines and indicates the</u>
4
eventual outcome of the trial. Other communication experts are more skeptical of making predictions based solely on nonverbal behavior in the courtroom.

The event most widely scrutinized by the communication experts who believe that nonverbal behavior can be "read" in the courtroom is the moment when the verdict has been reached by the jury. The experts tell us that if upon filing back into the courtroom, the jury does not look at the defendant, the verdict is "Guilty." In contrast, if at least one member of the jury looks at the defendant, <u>the verdict is not yet known by nonverbal</u>
6
<u>behavior at that point.</u> The next action that is purported to let the communi-
6
cation experts "know" the verdict is the behaviors that occur when the spokesperson for the jury hands the verdict written on paper to the bailiff to give to the judge. The experts predict that if the spokesperson for the jury

looks at the defendant, the verdict is "Not Guilty." In contrast, if the spokes-person avoids the defendant, the verdict is "Guilty."

In cases of multiple defendants, there is much that communication experts believe about observing the relationship and behaviors between each defendant and their attorney. If there is a high substantial amount of
7   8
verbal interaction and a high level of exchange, the attorney supposedly has a high regard for the client, and for the client's hope of being found "Not Guilty." In contrast, if there are few interactions between defendant and attorney, then the experts tell us that either the attorney does not feel confident about the future of the client, or the attorney feels that he/she has
9
not done a good job of representing the client and, as a result, feels guilty
9
about possibly losing the case, so he/she limits contact with the defendant.
9
These assumptions are especially viewed as the trial nears conclusion.
11
    Finally, the overall atmosphere in the courtroom is examined by the communication experts, and as the plaintiffs address the jury, the judge, each
12
other, and others seated in the courtroom, special attention is placed on eye contact and ambient movement. Nonverbal behavior accounts for the
13
difference between a lawyer who has the entire courtroom on the edge of its
13
seats and the lawyer who lulls the members of the courtroom to a peaceful
13
state of inattention.
13

1. (A) NO CHANGE
   (B) particular communication experts is
   (C) particular, communication experts, are
   (D) particular, communication experts, is

2. (F) NO CHANGE
   (G) in and of
   (H) of
   (J) that occur in

3. This underlined phrase is weakly written. This error is called:
   (A) Ambiguous reference
   (B) Cliché
   (C) Redundancy
   (D) Wordiness

4. (F) NO CHANGE
   (G) courtroom, as opposed to facts, and evidence, determines and indicates
   (H) courtroom as opposed to facts, and evidence, determines and indicates
   (J) courtroom, as opposed to facts and evidence, determines and indicates

5. Which of these statements best expresses the author's intentions?
   (A) Some communication experts view nonverbal behavior in the courtroom as predictive.
   (B) Skeptical communication experts should remain silent.
   (C) Some communication experts enjoy observing the nonverbal behavior in the courtroom.
   (D) Nonverbal behavior in the courtroom is interesting, but should not receive any importance.

6. The awkward quality of this sentence is caused by:
   (F) subject-verb agreement error
   (G) shift in verb tense
   (H) weak sentence construction
   (J) pronoun reference

7. (A) NO CHANGE
   (B) each defendants and their attorney
   (C) each defendant and his/her attorney
   (D) each defendant and they're attorney

8. (F) NO CHANGE
   (G) high amount
   (H) substantial amount
   (J) high, substantial

9. What is the problem with this underlined portion of the passage?

   (A) Word choice
   (B) Ambiguous reference
   (C) Wordiness
   (D) Redundancy

10. The main point the author is concerned with is:

    (F) Nonverbal behavior may affect the outcome of a trial.
    (G) Nonverbal behavior is unpredictable in a courtroom.
    (H) Some people believe in nonverbal behavior.
    (J) Nonverbal behavior in a courtroom may tell us how people have made decisions.

11. What is the problem with this word?

    (A) Word choice
    (B) Ambiguous reference
    (C) Wordiness
    (D) Redundancy

12. (F) NO CHANGE
    (G) plaintiff's
    (H) plaintiffs'
    (J) plaintiffs's

13. (A) NO CHANGE
    (B) This sentence needs to be shortened.
    (C) This sentence does not seem to follow the rest of the passage logically.
    (D) This sentence contains a subject-verb agreement error.

14. Which is the best topic sentence for the first paragraph?

    (F) The nonverbal behaviors that occur in a courtroom have been studied by people from many professions for many purposes.
    (G) One group in particular, communication experts, are extremely interested in synthesizing the nonverbal behavior that occurs in the courtroom.
    (H) The facial expressions are noted, scrutinized, and observed with intensity.
    (J) Attorneys, judges, and defendants each watch the movements of the jury like a hawk.

15. Which of the following titles would be appropriate for the preceding passage?

    (A) "How to Predict the Verdict in the Courtroom"
    (B) "Don't Believe What you See in the Courtroom"
    (C) "Judge, Jury, and Attorney Behavior in the Court-room"
    (D) "Nonverbal Behavior in the Courtroom"

NOW CHECK YOUR ANSWERS

1. **The correct answer is (D).** The special group needs to be set aside by commas. This is an appositive. A subject-verb agreement error is also present. The word "group" is singular and requires the singular verb "is." **(Punctuation and Basic Grammar and Usage)**

2. **The correct answer is (H).** The construction "nonverbal behaviors that occur" has already appeared in the first sentence of the passage. To repeat that same construction is evidence of unimaginative writing. **(Sentence Structure)**

3. **The correct answer is (B).** To "watch like a hawk" is a cliché. Using this cliché is also not wise in the potentially politically charged context of a courtroom. **(Style)**

4. **The correct answer is (J).** Setting aside the qualifying information "as opposed to facts and evidence" requires the appropriate use of commas. **(Punctuation)**

5. **The correct answer is (A).** All of the other options are opinions based on information found in the passage. **(Strategy)**

6. **The correct answer is (H).** The sentence is weakly written. Nonverbal behavior is not able to "know" something. Poor word choice is also part of the problem. None of the other answers is logical. **(Sentence Structure and Style)**

7. **The correct answer is (C).** This is a common pronoun reference problem. The pronoun "each" is singular and must have a singular antecedent. His/her is the only appropriate antecedent because "their" is plural. **(Basic Grammar and Usage)**

8. **The correct answer is (G).** Choice (D) offers correct punctuation, but to maintain parallelism with the subsequent usage of the word "high," the only appropriate response is to omit "substantial" from the sentence. **(Sentence Structure)**

9. **The correct answer is (B).** While this portion of the sentence contains many words, the problem does not occur with wordiness, redundancy, or word choice. The ambiguity occurs with the usage of the words "client" and "defendant." Both words refer to the same person although the sentence structure suggests there are two people. This may confuse the reader. **(Style)**

10. **The correct answer is (J).** Choice (H) is never discussed in the passage. While choices (F) and (G) are present within the content of the passage, both answers are too limiting to function as the main point for the author. The majority of the passage clearly discusses how experts observe nonverbal behavior after reaching decisions. **(Strategy)**

11. **The correct answer is (A).** "Viewed" is clearly the wrong word to convey the appropriate meaning for the sentence. The words "apparent" or "observable" would better suit the sentence. The other options are illogical. **(Style)**

12. **The correct answer is (F).** The word as written is the correct plural form as required by the sentence. There is no requirement for the possessive form in this construction. **(Basic Grammar and Usage)**

13. **The correct answer is (C).** This sentence is neither too long, nor does it contain a subject-verb agreement error. The sentence does not logically fit the rest of the passage. In the discussion of nonverbal behavior, the concept of effectiveness or the quality of the nonverbal behavior has not occurred. A discussion of which lawyer can hold the attention of the courtroom strays from the flow of the passage as it stands. **(Organization)**

14. **The correct answer is (G).** Choice (F) is introductory in nature, with no indication of direction. Choices (H) and (J) contain specific details and do not conceptualize the point of the paragraph as does the sentence in choice (G). **(Organization)**

15. **The correct answer is (D).** While titles in choices (A), (B), and (C) contain information present in the passage, only the title in choice (D) is inclusive enough to be appropriate. **(Strategy)**

HOW TO ANSWER ACT ASSESSMENT QUESTIONS

GENERAL SUGGESTIONS

Much of the success in test-taking comes from being comfortable both physically and mentally with the test you are taking. Physical comfort is very easy to achieve. Just remember a few important points:

1. **Be on time.** Actually, to be a few minutes early doesn't hurt. No one is helped by feeling rushed when beginning a test.

2. **Have a supply of pencils (#2) with good erasers.** There will be no time for borrowing or sharpening a pencil once the test begins.

3. **Wear comfortable clothing.** Layers of clothing are best, since they can be removed or put on, depending upon the temperature of the room. Don't wear shoes that pinch or a too-tight belt!

4. **Get a good rest the night before.** Cramming right before an ACT Assessment is not helpful and can sometimes lead to panic and confusion.

Mental comfort is a little more difficult to achieve. *Preparation* is the key and comes with study and practice in the weeks and months before the test. Mental comfort is gained by becoming familiar with the test format, instructions, and types of problems that will appear.

MATH TEST STRATEGIES

The math section of the ACT Assessment consists of a total of sixty questions. Forty percent of the test (twenty-four questions) is made up of questions from pre-algebra and elementary algebra. Thirty percent of the test (eighteen questions) is drawn from intermediate algebra and coordinate geometry. Finally, 30 percent of the test (eighteen questions) consists of plane geometry and trigonometry questions. All questions are in the multiple-choice format, with five answer choices. Remember that on the ACT Assessment there is no penalty for wrong answers, so you should answer every question, even if you have to guess.

You will receive four scores for the mathematics portion of the ACT Assessment: a total test score based on all 60 questions and subscores for pre-algebra/elementary algebra, intermediate algebra/coordinate geometry, and plane geometry/trigonometry.

Be sure that you have taken enough sample tests to be thoroughly familiar with the instructions. The instructions are part of the timed test. Do not spend valuable time reading them as if you had never seen them before. Of course, you can read them quickly to refresh your memory each time you start a new section of the test.

TEST-TAKING STRATEGIES

Pace Yourself

You are allowed 60 minutes for the entire math section. If you spend too much time on each question, you will not complete enough questions to receive a good score. Many very intelligent students work too slowly and spend too much time on details or neatness. As a result, they score lower than they should. As you work, put a mark by problems that take too long and a different mark by those you do not know how to solve so you can go back to them later if you have time.

Bring a watch to the test and thus eliminate worry about how much time is left. When time is almost up, you should look over the rest of the problems and work those you know you can do most quickly.

All questions are equally weighted. Allot your time accordingly. Remember that hard questions count the same as easy ones. Don't miss out on one that might be easy for you by stubbornly sticking to one that might be more difficult.

Use the Test Booklet Scratch Area

For many problems, a simple sketch drawn in the scratch area of the test booklet will make the solution readily apparent and will thus save time. Also, do not attempt to do all computation work in your head. Remember to use the scratch area of the test booklet; only mark your answers on the answer sheet.

Specific Suggestions

All of the general suggestions given will not help you if you are not prepared to solve the problems and arrive at the correct answers.

The examination questions require knowledge of pre-algebra, elementary and intermediate algebra, plane and coordinate geometry, and trigonometry. Most of the problems require some insight and originality—that is, you will need to know not only *how* to perform certain operations but also *when* to perform them. Very rarely will you be required to do a plain computation or find a routine solution.

Vocabulary is very important. A problem that asks you to find a *quotient* will be hard to do if you do not know the meaning of this term. Some basic terms you should know:

sum:	the answer to an addition problem
product:	the answer to a multiplication problem
quotient:	the answer to a division problem
difference:	the answer to a subtraction problem
integer:	a whole number, either positive or negative or 0
prime number:	a number with no factors other than 1 and itself
even integers:	2, 4, 6, 8, etc.
odd integers:	1, 3, 5, 7, etc.
consecutive integers:	numbers in order, 1, 2, 3, or 7, 8, 9, etc.

The following suggestions may help you find the correct answer more efficiently.

Look for Shortcuts

Rarely will a problem on the ACT Assessment involve a long, cumbersome computation. If you find yourself caught up in a maze of large numbers, you have probably missed a shortcut.

Example

Which is larger?

$$\frac{5}{23} \times \frac{7}{33} \quad \text{or} \quad \frac{7}{23} \times \frac{5}{31}$$

Solution

Examination of the problem will let you see that after multiplying, in each case the numerators of the resulting fractions will be the same ($5 \cdot 7$ and $7 \cdot 5$). When the numerators of two fractions are the same, the fraction with the smaller denominator will be the larger fraction. In this case, the denominators are $23 \cdot 33$ and $23 \cdot 31$. It is not necessary to do the actual multiplication to see that $23 \cdot 31$ will be the smaller product (or denominator), making the larger fraction.

Estimate

On any timed competitive examination, it is necessary that you are able to estimate. Sometimes it is helpful to round off all numbers to a convenient power of 10 and estimate the answer. This will often enable you to pick the correct answer quickly without performing a lot of time-consuming computations. In some cases it will eliminate one or more of the answers right away, thus improving your chances if you have to guess.

Example

Which of the following is closest to the value of $\dfrac{3654 \cdot 248}{1756}$?

(A) 50   (B) 500   (C) 5,000   (D) 5   (E) 50,000

Solution

3,654 is about 4,000. 248 is about 200 (or 300) and 1,756 is about 2,000. The problem then becomes:

$$\dfrac{\overset{2}{\cancel{4000}} \cdot 200}{\underset{1}{\cancel{2000}}} \cong 400$$

Therefore, choice (B) is correct.

Substitute

Change confusing problems to more meaningful ones by substituting simple numbers for letters. Many students get confused by problems containing letters in place of numbers. These letters are called variables. Just remember that the letters stand for numbers; therefore, the same operations can be performed on them. Just think of how you would do the problem if there were numbers, and then perform the same operations on the letters.

Example

If a man was x years old y years ago, how many years old will he be z years from now?

Solution

Substitute small numbers for the letters. If a man was 20 years old 5 years ago, how many years old will he be 8 years from now? The man is now 25 years old (20 + 5). Eight years from now he will be 20 + 5 + 8, or 33 years old. Back in the original problem, substitute letters for numbers in your solution:

$20 + 5 + 8 = x + y + z$

Work Backward

Some experts advise against this, but in some cases it can be advantageous for you to look at the answers first. You can save valuable time by knowing that all the answers are in common fractional or decimal form. Then you will want to work only in the form in which the answers are given.

Are all the answers the same except for one digit or placement of a decimal? Knowing this can save you time.

Example

The square root of 106.09 is exactly:

(A) .103   **(B)** 1.03   **(C)** 10.3   **(D)** 103   **(E)** 1030

Solution

Don't use your time to find the square root of 106.09. Work backward from the answers, which are all the same except for the placement of the decimal. Using the definition of square root (the number that when multiplied by itself will produce a given number), you can see that choice (C) is the only one that will give an answer of 106.09 when multiplied by itself.

Another type of problem in which it is helpful to work backward is the problem that contains an equation to solve. Try each answer in the equation to see which one fits will help, especially if you are unsure of how to solve the equation.

Answer the Question

Always check to see if you have answered the question asked.

Example

If $3x + 2 = 12$, find $x - \dfrac{1}{3}$

(A) $3\dfrac{1}{3}$ **(B)** 3   **(C)** 10   **(D)** 4   **(E)** $5\dfrac{2}{3}$

Solution

Solving the equation:

Add -2 to both sides
$$3x + 2 = 12$$
$$-2 = -2$$
$$3x = 10$$

Divide by 3
$$x = \dfrac{10}{3} = 3\dfrac{1}{3}$$

Notice that $x = 3\dfrac{1}{3}$, which is choice (A). However, the problem asked us to find $x - \dfrac{1}{3}$. Therefore, the correct answer is (B).

Guess

Remember that there is no penalty for a wrong answer. Thus, you should leave no question unanswered. If you are not sure how to solve a problem, see if you can eliminate two or more answers by any of the previously discussed strategies. Then guess from the remaining possibilities.

READING TEST STRATEGIES

The reading section of the ACT Assessment is a 35-minute, forty-question test of your ability to read and comprehend fiction, social science, natural science, and humanities reading passages. The questions asked in the reading section can be broken down into two main categories: (1) questions that ask you for information specifically presented in the passage; and (2) questions that ask you to draw inferences from the passage—that is, to answer questions based on what is implied rather than stated in the passage.

You will receive an overall reading score for this section of the test plus two subscores: one based on your reading of the social science and physical science sections and one based on your prose fiction and humanities scores.

In the Reading Test, you will read four passages, each of which is followed by ten multiple-choice questions. The passages are selected to represent the level of reading encountered by first-year college students. The reading passages are drawn from the following subject areas:

- **Social Sciences:** history, political science, economics, anthropology, psychology, and sociology.

- **Natural Sciences:** biology, chemistry, physics, and physical sciences.

- **Humanities:** art, music, philosophy, theater, architecture, and dance.

- **Prose Fiction:** intact short stories or excerpts from short stories or novels.

Don't expect the passages to be familiar to you; even the specific subjects may not be familiar to you, but you may feel more comfortable with a natural science passage, for example—even on an unfamiliar topic—if you have focused on science in your high school studies.

Before we look more specifically at the kinds of questions you will encounter on the test, let's discuss certain strategies you will need to practice and use on the reading section of the ACT Assessment.

TEST-TAKING STRATEGIES

Relying on Information Within the Passage

Occasionally you may encounter a reading passage that discusses a subject you have studied. While this can make the passage easier to read, it can also tempt you to rely on your own knowledge about the subject. You must rely solely on the information presented in the passage for your answers—in fact, sometimes the "wrong answers" for the questions are based on true information about the subject not given in the passage. Since the test makers are testing your reading ability (rather than your general knowledge), an answer based on information not contained in the passage is considered incorrect.

Thus, if you are reading a passage discussing Pavlov's famous experiments with dogs (which you have studied), be sure you don't base your answers to the questions on information not presented in the reading passage. Even if it is true of Pavlov's experiments, it will be counted as a wrong answer.

Choosing the Order of the Passages

The test makers have arranged the reading passages in an order that may not be the best order for you. Before you start reading the passages, quickly look through them and choose which order will work best for you. For example, if you find the fiction-reading passage easiest, you may want to start with that passage even though the fiction passage may be placed after the humanities and social sciences passages. Don't forget to do all four passages, however.

If you read the passages out of order, you may want to transfer the answers to the answer sheet after you have finished all the passages since you will be reading the questions in a different order from the one set up on the answer sheet. (You will need to pace yourself so that you have time to transfer the answers at the end.) If you choose to transfer the answers as you go, be sure you're marking the answers for the correct numbers—if the fiction section is third, it will begin with question number 21, not question number 1.

Pacing Yourself

In order to complete the test in 35 minutes, you will need to practice pacing yourself. Make sure you don't spend so much time on some of the passages that you don't have time to complete all four passages. You will have about 8 ½ minutes to read one passage and answer the ten questions—that breaks down to between 2 and 3 minutes to read the passage and between 30 and 40 seconds per question.

Since you need to make every second count, be sure you don't waste any time—by reading the directions, for example. We'll discuss them right now so that you know what they say: "There are four passages in this test. Each passage is followed by several questions. After reading a passage, choose the best answer to each question and fill in the corresponding oval on your answer document. You may refer to the passages as often as necessary."

You also need to avoid working too long on any one question or any one passage—if it's hard, go on. If you have time at the end, go back and work on it some more.

You may need to increase your reading speed in order to complete the test in the allotted time. (Although reading speed doesn't necessarily correspond to intelligence or to reading ability, on a timed test your reading speed will affect your score.) Since you have only 35 minutes to read four passages and answer forty questions, you need to read at least 250 words per minute in order to complete the test.

Annotating

Since you will need to refer back to the reading passages to answer the questions, you need to annotate, or mark up the passage to help you find specific elements in the passage. Many high school students have been taught not to write in their textbooks because they are school property and must be returned in good condition. However, annotation is a skill worth practicing. When you take the test, you will not be able to use highlighter pens, so you should practice using a pencil. You will want to use different kinds of marks to mean different things—if you just use underlining, your marks won't help you quickly find the elements in the passage that you need. Here are some suggestions: circle names of people, historic periods, etc.; underline important words; double-underline words in lists; draw a line down the left-hand margin to mark the line numbers specifically mentioned in a question.

In addition to marking up the passage, especially if you use the reading strategy of reading the question stems first, mark the key words in the question stems, too—they may tell you where in the passage to look for information or which kind of question you are being asked. The question stem is the introductory part of the question, not the possible answers. For example, the question stem might say, "According to the passage, Einstein wanted to prove which of the following theories?" You might mark it like this:

According to the passage, (Einstein) wanted to prove which of the following theories?

If you decide to skip a question and return to it later, mark the question, perhaps by circling the question number, so you can find it easily later—like this:

(2)   Martha Graham's dance style could best be called which of the following?

Eliminating Wrong Answers

If you find that you can quickly and accurately tell which are the right answers when you take the Panic Plan Practice Test, don't change your strategy. However, many students find they are doing poorly on the test because they decide too quickly which is the correct answer without considering all the choices. Also, even students who usually choose correctly find this strategy helpful when they are stumped by a question: eliminate the wrong answers first. As you eliminate each answer, mark it—perhaps with a slash through the letter so that you don't have to remember which ones you've eliminated—like this:

A. Life is for the living.

Often, one of the choices is clearly weaker than another. By eliminating that choice, you increase your chances of making a correct choice by 25 percent. The weakest choice often has nothing to do with the passage or presents a clichéd truism about life—such an answer can be eliminated quickly. Often other wrong answers refer to information listed in the passage in other places. It won't be completely off the topic, but it will not relate to the portion of the passage being discussed in the question.

If you eliminate a second wrong answer, you have increased your chance of answering the question correctly by another 25 percent. Other types of wrong answers to look out for are answers that are partially true, that are too broad, or that rely on information outside the passage.

With practice, you should usually be able to eliminate three wrong answers, leaving you with the right answer. But even if you can't eliminate three wrong answers, eliminate as many as possible—then guess.

Reading Strategies

We will discuss three main reading strategies. You will need to try them all and choose which one works best for you. You may find some work better than others or that certain ones work best for certain types of passages.

The *first strategy* is to read the passage first, annotating as you go; then answer the questions. This strategy will probably be most useful for the fiction passages, but for the other passages it's probably the weakest choice. (However, if you find it works best for you, stick with it.)

For the *second strategy*, read the question stems first, annotating them as you go. After reading the question stems, read the passage.

This method helps guide your reading, so you focus only on those parts of the reading passage that help you answer the questions.

The *third strategy* is often the most useful, though it may take a bit of time to become used to it. We'll call it PQR, which stands for Preview the passage, read the Question stems, then Read the passage. This method is very helpful because you get a brief picture of the passage first, then a look at what the questions will be, and finally, as you read the passage, you can look for the answers to the questions. However, you will need to work quickly to be able to use this method. (Try using it timed so that you don't spend more than 8½ minutes reading and answering the questions for any one passage.)

To preview, quickly skim the first paragraph of the selection—or if the first paragraph is long, read just the first and last sentences. Now quickly read the first sentence of all the subsequent paragraphs and the last sentence of the final paragraph. This preview should give you a sense of the subject of the passage and an idea of what each paragraph is about.

The next step is the Q step—quickly read the question stems, annotating them as needed. Now go back to the passage and read it quickly all the way through, annotating as you find the answers to the questions. Now answer the questions. Although this method is the most difficult to get used to, it is worth practicing since it can be so helpful.

As you take the Practice Tests in this book, try using these three methods to determine which works best for you. For example, you may find that for the fiction passage, you like the first reading strategy, reading the passage first. For passages in subjects in which you feel some familiarity, you might be more comfortable reading the question stems first, then reading the passage. For the passages you feel most unsure of, you may want to use the PQR method.

QUESTION TYPES

Now let's look more specifically at the kinds of questions you will encounter on the test. The natural science, social science, and humanities reading passages are all similar to one another; they are informative passages such as you might expect to encounter in textbooks.

Factual Questions

The first type of questions you might encounter are factual questions: simple fact, complex facts, negative questions, and puzzle questions. With fact questions, the correct answer is stated either in the exact words from the passage or in words that are almost identical to the words in the passage. But note that wrong answers for these questions usually are also taken right from the passage but fail to answer the question.

A simple fact question might ask something like: "According to the passage, the author believes that . . ." The information for this question is specifically stated in the passage. Sometimes fact questions are more complex, requiring you to combine facts or glean information from more than one place in the passage.

Sometimes fact questions are presented as negative questions: you are asked to choose which of the choices *is not correct*. Negative questions can be identified because the question stem usually contains the word EXCEPT, in all caps.

Another tricky fact question is the "logic puzzle" type. This type of question usually presents three or four situations and then asks you to select which situation, or combination of situations, is correct. Although these questions look intimidating, answering them only requires a refinement of the technique of eliminating wrong answers.

Inference Questions

Fact and inference questions can be very similar to each other, but with inference questions, the answer is either stated in different terms from the words used in the passage or is only implied or suggested by the passage.

Another type of inference question asks about the meaning of words or phrases in the passage. Often you will be asked to identify the meaning of a word you don't know at all or that you may have encountered before but can't define. In these cases, you will need to rely on clues provided in the passage to help you identify the best word choice.

Main Idea Questions

Questions about the main idea of a paragraph or the subject of a passage are similar as well. Your task here is to come up with the answer that best summarizes or encompasses what the paragraph or passage says. The main idea of a passage is often stated in the first paragraph. If you are asked to identify the main idea or point of an individual paragraph (rather than the entire passage), look for the answer choices that are mentioned in that particular paragraph. Often you can eliminate several choices that appear in different paragraphs, or those that are not mentioned at all.

READING PRACTICE

Complete the practice passages below. There are additional strategies you should use to help you improve your score on the reading section.

Then analyze what kinds of errors you're making: Do you mostly miss inference questions? Do you have a hard time finding the facts in the passage? Do you struggle with the fiction passages but not with the informative ones? Once you analyze these problems, you can focus your attention on refining your skills with those particular kinds of questions.

Passage 1

Line Despite the modern desire to be easy and
      casual, Americans from time to time give
      thought to the language they use—to
      grammar, vocabulary, and gobbledygook.
5   And, as on other issues, they divide into
      two parties. The larger, which includes
      everybody form the proverbial plain man to
      the professional writer, takes for granted
      that there is a right way to use words and
10   construct sentences, and many wrong ways.
      The right way is believed to be clearer,
      simpler, more logical, and therefore more
      likely to prevent error and confusion. Good
      writing is easier to read; it offers a pleasant
15   combination of sound and sense.
          Against this majority view is the
      doctrine of an embattled minority, who
      make up for their small number by their

20 great learning and their place of authority
in the school system and the world of
scholarship. They are the professional
linguists, who deny that there is such a
thing as correctness. The language, they
say, is what anybody and everybody speaks.

25 Hence, there must be no interference with
what they regard as a product of nature.
They denounce all attempts at guiding
choice; their governing principle is
epitomized in the title of a speech by a

30 member of the profession: "Can Native
Speakers of a Language Make Mistakes?"
Within the profession of linguists
there are, of course, warring factions, but,
on this conception of language as a natural

35 growth with which it is criminal to tamper,
they are at one. In their arguments one
finds appeals to democratic feelings of
social equality (all words and forms are
equally good) and individual freedom (one

40 may do what one likes with one's own
speech). These assumptions further suggest
that the desire for correctness, the very
idea of better or worse in speech, is a
hangover from aristocratic and oppressive

45 times. To the linguists, change is the only
ruler to be obeyed. They equate it with life
and accuse their critics of being clock-
reversers, enemies of freedom, menaces to
"life."

1. The larger of the two groups
mentioned believes that

(A) all language is natural.
(B) good writing must be
grammatical.
(C) language has its right ways
and its wrong ways.
(D) language is democratic.

2. According to the author, the
professional writer is

(F) a scholar.
(G) a professional linguist.
(H) part of the minority.
(J) part of the majority.

3. The professional linguists

   (A) deny there is such a thing as correctness.
   (B) epitomize their profession.
   (C) are at war.
   (D) never write articles.

4. In the phrase "their governing principle is epitomized in" (lines 28–29), the word *epitomized* means

   (F) referred to.
   (G) denied.
   (H) summed up.
   (J) mentioned.

5. The desire for correctness is equated by some with

   (A) liberalism.
   (B) a collapse of standards.
   (C) lack of freedom.
   (D) depression.

6. The only ruler to be obeyed is

   (F) scholarship.
   (G) linguistic heritage.
   (H) scholarly standards.
   (J) change.

Passage 2

Line Early experimenters in chemistry identified
a group of substances having certain
properties in common. These substances,
when dissolved in water, acted as electrical
5   conductors, reacted with metals such as
zinc to liberate gas, were corrosive to the
skin, turned blue litmus to red, and tasted
sour. These substances were called acids.
Further study and experimentation indi-
10   cated that acids release hydrogen ions in
water solution.
      Another group of substances has
properties that contrast strongly with the
properties of acids, with the exception of
15   the property of electrical conductivity.
These substances change red litmus to blue,
and, when added to an acid, cause the
identifying properties of the acid and those
of the added substance to disappear. The
20   one property that remains characteristic of
the mixture is electrical conductivity. The
substances in this second group are called
bases. Again, further study and experimentation indicated that bases combine with

25 hydrogen ions. This combination forms
water. The remaining portion of the acid
and the base form a salt. So, when an acid
and a base are combined, the chemical
reaction results in the production of a salt
30 and water.

In order to understand the behavior of
acids and bases, we have two definitions.
The first comes from the laboratory
determination of what an acid or a base
35 does; that is, how we can recognize the
acid or the base. This is called an operational definition because it gives the
measurements or operations used to classify
a substance. The second type of definition
40 is a conceptual one. It helps to explain. It
tries to answer the question "Why?" Neither
is the complete nor perfect definition. As
chemical systems become more compli-
cated, we have to expand these definitions.

1. It can be inferred that bases

(A) release hydrogen ions in
     small amounts.
(B) use up hydrogen ions.
(C) release hydrogen ions in
     large amounts.
(D) taste sour.

2. The electrical conductivity that
remains as a property of the acid-
base mixture is best explained as
a characteristic of the

(F) acid only.
(G) base only.
(H) acid and base.
(J) salt.

3. Which is a characteristic of an
acid?

I.   It turns litmus blue.
II.   It releases hydrogen ions.
III. Electrical conductivity
IV.   It combines with hydro-
      gen ions.

(A) Only I and III
(B) Only II and IV
(C) Only II and III
(D) Only III and IV

4. Which operational definition of
an acid is most helpful in
explaining why certain chemical reactions occur as they do?

(F) An acid reacts with zinc to
     produce hydrogen gas.
(G) An acid turns litmus red.
(H) An acid tastes sour.
(J) An acid is corrosive to the
     skin.

Passage 3

Line High audience loyalty is characteristic of
radio stations. Often a listener turns on the
same station day after day and keeps it
turned on most of the day. There is little
5   switching. This is because of the programming policies of the stations. Programming
policies determine the audiences. Some
programs appeal to general and diversified
audiences; others are beamed to identifiable
10   groups.
     Most stations are strong on music,
interspersed with newscasts, weather
reports, and similar features. Each, however, is likely to feature a particular type of
15   programming. Stations and programs may
be categorized in several ways. Here are
some typical examples:
     Middle-of-the-road music. This type of
music predominates. It features Broadway
20   and movie numbers, "oldies but goodies,"
and current popular tunes, except rock 'n'
roll, rhythm and blues, country and
western, jazz, classical, and sacred music,
both orchestral and vocal.
25   *"Talk" radio.* These stations devote a
major portion of their programming to
interviews and discussions on a wide
variety of subjects. They often feature
guests who are well-known authorities on
30   food, drama, public affairs, education, and
other subjects. Many of the shows are
interactive, and the public can telephone
the host to express their own views.
     Farm programs. Usually located in
35   rural areas, stations broadcasting this type
of program devote few or many hours to
subjects of interest to rural area families,
including daily stock and crop quotations.
     Ethnic stations. These stations devote
40   the entire broadcasting day or a large
portion of the day to ethnic (African-

American, Hispanic-American, Asian-
American) music and performers. Especially
in large metropolitan areas, they may divide
45   their time between ethnic programming
and foreign language programs.

     Foreign language stations. Programs
on these stations are broadcast in one or
more foreign languages. Some of these
50   stations devote only a few hours to a single
language; others may have programs in as
many as ten different languages.

     Stations often owe their popularity
not just to program content, but to
55   individual disc jockeys, newscasters,
talk-show hosts, sportscasters, announcers,
and other personalities.

1. The author states that audiences
   listen to the same station
   because they

   (A) don't switch stations.
   (B) belong to groups.
   (C) like the programs and
       personalities.
   (D) listen to music.

2. Examples of stations programmed
   for specific groups are

   (F) news, ethnic, and music
       stations.
   (G) farm, music, and talk
       stations.
   (H) foreign language, music,
       and news stations.
   (J) foreign language, farm,
       and ethnic stations.

3. The word *beamed* in paragraph
   1 means

   (A) smiled.
   (B) lit up.
   (C) sent out.
   (D) flashed.

4. In this selection, the author

   (F) disapproves of present
       radio programming.
   (G) approves of present radio
       programming.
   (H) feels audiences are too
       easily satisfied.
   (J) described types of radio
       programming.

5. Many radio listeners

   (A) switch stations constantly.
   (B) also watch television.
   (C) respond to radio advertis-
       ers.
   (D) keep their radios on all
       day.

6. One type of programming not
   mentioned is

   (F) classical music.
   (G) oldies but goodies.
   (H) sacred music.
   (J) opera.

NOW CHECK YOUR ANSWERS

Answers to Passage 1

1. **The correct answer is (C).** This is stated in paragraph 1. Choices (A), (B), and (D) are not mentioned in the passage.

2. **The correct answer is (J).** This is stated in paragraph 1. Choices (F), (G), and (H) are the opposite of the correct answer.

3. **The correct answer is (A).** This is directly stated in paragraph 2. The other choices are not mentioned.

4. **The correct answer is (H).** This is a vocabulary question, and this is the one definition of the word.

5. **The correct answer is (C).** This can be inferred from the tone of the last three sentences in paragraph 3. The use of the phrases "oppressive times," "only ruler to be obeyed," and "enemies of freedom" are the clues.

6. **The correct answer is (J).** The answer is clearly stated in the last paragraph. Choices (F), (G), and (H) are specific "rulers"; therefore, all three choices are the opposite of "change."

Answers to Passage 2

1. **The correct answer is (B).** Since bases combine with hydrogen ions (paragraph 2), and acids release hydrogen ions (paragraph 1), then it can be inferred that bases use up hydrogen ions.

2. **The correct answer is (H).** The selection indicates that in the acid-base mixture, the properties of the acid and the base disappear (except electrical conductivity). It follows that electrical conductivity is a property of the salt that is formed.

3. **The correct answer is (C).** Acids release hydrogen ions and act as electrical conductors. Selection I is incorrect, since the passage states that acid turns blue litmus red, and therefore you can eliminate choice (A). Paragraph 1 states that acids release hydrogen ions in water solution, and thus selection II is correct. That narrows down your choices to (B) and (C). Since selection IV is the opposite of selection II, and paragraph 2 states that bases combine with hydrogen ions, thus you can eliminate selection IV and choice (B).

4. **The correct answer is (F).** An operational definition comes from what a substance does. Obviously, the one choice that best explains chemical reactions of acids is choice (F). Other answers to this question are also operational definitions but do not refer to chemical reactions of acids.

Answers to Passage 3

1. **The correct answer is (C).** The first and last paragraphs indicate that programming policies determine the audiences (paragraph 1), and that various types of radio personalities are responsible for stations' popularity (paragraph 9). Choice (A) is merely a repeat of the question. Choices (B) and (D) do not tell *why* audiences are loyal to one station.

2. **The correct answer is (J).** Foreign language, farm, and ethnic stations are meant for specific groups. News, talk, and music stations are meant for a general audience. Choices (F), (G), and (H) are only partially correct. *Remember:* If part of an answer is incorrect, the entire answer is considered incorrect.

3. **The correct answer is (C).** The word *beamed* in paragraph 1 refers to radio signals sent out to a receiver.

4. **The correct answer is (J).** This selection is descriptive; the author makes no value judgments. Choices (F), (G), and (H) are incorrect, since the questions indicate opinions ("disapproves," "approves," "feels"), which cannot be inferred from the selection.

5. **The correct answer is (D).** Paragraph 1 states that listeners turn on the same station and keep it turned on most of the day.

6. **The correct answer is (J).** This is a good question in which to use the process of elimination. Choices (F), (G), and (H) are all mentioned in paragraph 3. Operas are not mentioned in the selection.

SCIENCE AND MATHEMATICS REVIEW

SCIENCE REASONING TEST STRATEGIES

The science reasoning section requires you to have a basic knowledge of the subject areas. However, this part of the ACT Assessment is not designed to test your ability to recall specific facts. Rather, it is designed to test your ability to recognize and solve problems in a logical and scientific manner.

There are forty questions on the Science Reasoning Test. You will have 35 minutes to answer all forty questions. The questions may be from any science discipline, including astronomy, biology, chemistry, earth science, and physics.

You will be asked to answer questions based on research summaries, graphs and tables, and conflicting viewpoints. Because the Science Reasoning Test is not based on knowledge of facts, cramming to memorize as many facts as possible won't be of much help. Instead, use these strategies.

1. Scan the passage to see what it is about; then reread it carefully.

2. Answer the questions first that simply test to see if you know the facts. Then answer the harder questions.

3. Make sure you read all of the choices carefully.

4. Cross out those choices that are clearly incorrect. The process of elimination is sometimes the best way to arrive at the correct answer. As you consider the choices, make sure you are answering the question that has been asked. Although a choice may contain a true statement, it is the incorrect answer if it does not answer the question asked.

5. Make sure you answer all the questions. There is no penalty for guessing.

In the practice section that follows, there is a series of passages followed by several questions. Answer the questions, and then check your answers with the answer key. Study the explanations given to help you understand the material more fully.

Passage 1

Different strains of the free-living bacterium *Microbiologicus studenticus* showed differences in degree of motility (movement) due to differing numbers of flagella present when each strain of bacterium was grown at 21 percent oxygen, the concentration present in the normal atmosphere. Studies were conducted to determine whether the number of flagella varied depending on the amount of oxygen in the growth medium.

Experiment 1

Twelve cultures of the same strain of bacteria were grown with constant temperature, light, and 21 percent oxygen. The bacteria, upon examination, averaged two polar flagella each, with one at each end of the cells.

Experiment 2

Twelve cultures of the same strain of bacteria were grown with constant temperature and light, but with 18 percent oxygen. The bacteria produced an average of four polar flagella each, with two at each end of the cells.

Experiment 3

Twelve cultures of the same strain of bacteria were grown with constant temperature and light, but with 16 percent oxygen. The bacteria produced an average of six polar flagella each, with three at each end of the cells.

Experiment 4

Twelve cultures of the same strain of bacteria were grown with constant temperature and light, but with 12 percent oxygen. No flagella were produced.

1. Which experiment served as a control?

   (A) Experiment 1
   (B) Experiment 2
   (C) Experiment 3
   (D) Experiment 4

2. Which is a valid conclusion based on Experiment 2 alone?

   (F) Oxygen levels less than those found in the normal atmosphere make this strain of bacterium produce more flagella.

   (G) Oxygen levels less than those found in the normal atmosphere make this strain of bacterium produce fewer flagella than normal.

   (H) This strain of bacterium produces flagella only if exposed to oxygen.

   (J) This strain of bacterium produces flagella in response to changes to temperature.

3. Which of the following was the experimental variable in this series of experiments?

   (A) Temperature
   (B) Nutrients
   (C) Bacterial strain
   (D) Oxygen

4. Which of the following is a valid conclusion based on Experiments 2 and 4?

   (F) Decreasing oxygen levels eliminate flagella production entirely.
   (G) Increasing oxygen levels eliminate flagella production entirely.
   (H) Oxygen has no effect on flagella production.
   (J) Increasing oxygen levels reduce production of flagella.

5. Which of the following is a method for checking to see if a continued decrease in oxygen levels will increase flagella production?

   (A) Grow twelve cultures of different strains of bacteria at the same level of oxygen.
   (B) That was checked in Experiment 4.
   (C) That was done in Experiments 1 through 4.
   (D) This cannot be done.

6. If the investigator wished to study the effects of protein concentration, which of the following would be most helpful?

   (F) Experiment 4 should be repeated with several different levels of protein supplement in the growth medium.
   (G) All four experiments should be repeated, varying both oxygen levels and protein concentrations.
   (H) Protein metabolism occurs only at 21 percent oxygen, so Experiment 1 should be repeated with varied amounts of protein.
   (J) One of the first three experiments should be repeated several times, using different amounts of protein supplement in the growth medium.

Passage 2

In the early part of the eighteenth century, the English scientist John Dalton (1767–1844) proposed an *atomic theory* based on experimentation and chemical laws known at that time. A summary of his proposals is as follows:

Proposal 1: Elements are composed of tiny, discrete, indivisible, and indestructible particles called atoms. These atoms maintain their identity throughout physical and chemical changes.

Proposal 2: Atoms of the same element are identical in mass and have the same chemical and physical properties. Atoms of different elements have different masses and different chemical and physical properties.

Proposal 3: Chemical combinations of two or more elements always occur in whole-number ratios to form a molecule.

Proposal 4: Atoms of different elements can unite in different ratios to form more than one compound.

Later modifications to Dalton's theory included the discovery of the electron in 1879 by Sir William Crookes; the discovery of the proton in 1886 by Eugen Goldstein and J. J. Thompson; and the discovery of the neutron in 1932 by Sir James Chadwick. The electron was described as a subatomic particle with virtually no mass and a negative (-) electric charge. The proton was described as a subatomic particle with a relative mass of 1 and a positive (+) electric charge. The neutron was described as a subatomic particle also with a relative mass of 1 and no electric (neutral) charge. The number of protons in an element's atom was also defined as that element's *atomic number*.

1. If all of the scientists mentioned in the preceding passage could meet today and discuss atomic theory, they would *all* agree that

   (A) the atom is solid and indivisible.
   (B) the atom is indestructible.
   (C) carbon and oxygen can combine in more than one method.
   (D) more than one form of an element is possible.

2. Which of the four major proposals of Dalton's atomic theory described in the preceding passage was essentially disproved when the first nuclear weapon was exploded?

   (F) Proposal 1
   (G) Proposal 2
   (H) Proposal 3
   (J) Proposal 4

3. During the development of the atomic theory, *isotopes* were discovered. Atoms having different atomic masses, but the same atomic number, are called isotopes. Using the preceding description of the history of the atomic theory, predict when the term "isotope" was correctly defined.

(A) Before 1879

(B) After 1879 but prior to 1886

(C) After 1886 but prior to 1932

(D) After 1932

4. Hypothetical element "X" has an atomic number of 81 and an atomic mass of 204. An atom of element "X" will contain how many neutrons?

(F) 81

(G) 204

(H) 123

(J) Impossible to calculate since the number of electrons was not specified

5. The term "allotropy" is used to designate the existence of an element in two or more forms in the same physical state. For example, oxygen (O_2) and ozone (O_3) are called *allotropes*. The concept of allotropy most directly extends which of Dalton's four basic proposals?

(A) Proposal 1

(B) Proposal 2

(C) Proposal 3

(D) Proposal 4

6. Atoms of elements are said to be "electrically neutral." Which of the following statements supports that proposal?

(F) In a neutral atom, the number of protons equals the number of neutrons.

(G) In a neutral atom, the number of electrons equals the number of protons.

(H) In a neutral atom, the number of neutrons equals the number of electrons.

(J) In a neutral atom, the atomic number is the same as the atomic mass.

Passage 3

An experiment is performed on a system consisting of a mass m resting on a horizontal surface attached to a free-hanging mass M as shown in the figure below. The system is originally at rest. When released, the mass m is free to move through some displacement, x. The time, t, it takes to move through this distance, x, is measured. The purpose of this experiment is to determine how various physical variables affect the motion of m.

Experiment 1

In this experiment the system is released from rest and allowed to move through various distances. The masses m and M are held constant. The distances and the times are summarized in Table 1.

Table 1

x	t
20.0 cm	0.404 s
40.0 cm	0.571 s
60.0 cm	0.700 s

Experiment 2

In this experiment mass is transferred from mass m on the horizontal surface to the hanging mass M. The total mass of the system $m + M$ remains constant throughout the experiment. The system is allowed to move through a fixed distance of 60.0 cm. The results are summarized in Table 2.

Table 2

M	t
50.0 g	0.700 s
100.0 g	0.495 s
150.0 g	0.404 s

Experiment 3

In this experiment the hanging mass M is kept constant, but additional mass is added to mass m on the horizontal surface. The system is released from rest and allowed to move through a distance of 60.0 cm. The results are summarized in Table 3.

Table 3

m	t
100.0 g	0.606 s
150.0 g	0.700 s
200.0 g	0.782 s

1. A suspended 50-g mass M is attached to a 100-g mass m and released from rest. Based on the data, one can conclude that

   (A) x will be directly proportional to t.
   (B) x will be directly proportional to t^2.
   (C) x will be inversely proportional to t.
   (D) x will be inversely proportional to t^2.

2. In Experiment 2, a student suspends a mass M of 200.0 g. Based on the results given, he would correctly predict the time taken to travel 60.0 cm is

   (F) 0.831 s.
   (G) 0.568 s.
   (H) 0.350 s.
   (J) 0.158 s.

3. Based on the data presented, one can conclude that

(A) the system is moving at constant velocity.

(B) the system is accelerating.

(C) the time of travel is independent of the mass of the system.

(D) the distance traveled is proportional to the mass M.

4. On the basis of all the experiments, the travel time *must* be *increased* by which of the following conditions?

I. Only the amount of suspended mass M is increased.

II. The total mass of the system $M + m$ is increased.

III. Only the mass m resting on the horizontal surface is increased.

(F) I only

(G) II and III only

(H) I and II only

(J) III only

5. Which of the following variables (x, t, M, m) is dependent on the other three?

(A) x

(B) t

(C) M

(D) m

6. Which of the following conditions would result in the shortest travel time?

(F) $M = 200$ g, $m = 50$ g, $x = 100$ cm

(G) $M = 200$ g, $m = 50$ g, $x = 60$ cm

(H) $M = 50$ g, $m = 200$ g, $x = 60$ cm

(J) $M = 50$ g, $m = 200$ g, $x = 100$ cm

Passage 4

	Mercury	Venus	Earth	Mars	Jupiter
Distance from Sun AU	0.39	0.72	1.00	1.52	5.20
Millions of Kilometers	58	108	150	228	778
Period of Revolution	88^d	225^d	365.25^d	687^d	12^{yr}
Orbital Velocity (km/s)	47.5	35.0	29.8	24.1	13.1
Period of Rotation	59^d	243^d	24^h	24.6^h	$\sim 10^h$
Diameter	4,854	12,112	12.751	6,788	143,000
Relative Mass	0.056	0.82	1.0	0.108	318.00
Average Density (g/cm³)	5.1	5.3	5.5	3.94	1.34
Number of Known Satellites	0	0	1	2	16

	Saturn	Uranus	Neptune	Pluto
Distance from Sun AU	9.54	19.18	30.06	39.44
Millions of Kilometers	1,427	2,866	4,492	5,909
Period of Revolution	29.5^{yr}	84^{yr}	165^{yr}	248^{yr}
Orbital Velocity (km/s)	9.6	6.8	5.3	4.7
Period of Rotation	~10.5^h	10.75^h	16^h	6.4^d
Diameter	121,000	47,000	46,529	~2,400
Relative Mass	95.20	14.60	17.30	~0.01(?)
Average Density (g/cm^3)	0.70	1.55	1.64	~1.5(?)
Number of Known Satellites	17	15	8	1

1. Which planet is most similar to Earth in size and mass?

   (A) Mercury
   (B) Venus
   (C) Jupiter
   (D) Neptune

2. What is the ratio of the period of revolution to the period of rotation in days for Mercury?

   (F) 2/3
   (G) 180
   (H) 3/2
   (J) 1/180

3. Which planet has the greatest mass?

   (A) Venus
   (B) Earth
   (C) Jupiter
   (D) Saturn

4. What is the relationship between a planet's distance from the Sun and its orbital velocity?

   (F) The closer a body is to the S#un, the slower the orbital velocity.
   (G) The greater the distance from the Sun, the greater the orbital velocity.
   (H) The closer a body is to the Sun, the greater the orbital velocity.
   (J) There is no relationship between a body's distance from the Sun and its orbital velocity.

NOW CHECK YOUR ANSWERS

Answers to Passage 1

1. **The correct answer is (A).** Normal growth conditions were used in this experiment.

2. **The correct answer is (F).** The only variable was a decreased level of oxygen.

3. **The correct answer is (D).** The oxygen levels were the only thing changed from one experiment to the next.

4. **The correct answer is (F).** This is the only possible answer of the choices given.

5. **The correct answer is (C).** The level of oxygen was decreased steadily from Experiment 1 to 3.

6. **The correct answer is (J).** Any of the experiments in which flagella actually grew could be used as the experimental design, except that the level of oxygen would then be held constant, and the protein concentration would then be the variable.

Answers to Passage 2

1. **The correct answer is (C).** Dalton recognized that the same elements could combine in more than one method (Proposal #4) to form different compounds. Carbon monoxide (CO) and carbon dioxide (CO_2) would be an example. The other scientists modified his other proposals. Atoms are not solid; they can be changed (atomic warfare). Finally, allotropes have been discovered.

2. **The correct answer is (F).** Dalton noted in his proposal that atoms are indestructible. Nuclear explosions change atoms and produce energy.

3. **The correct answer is (D).** An isotope is a form of an element with a different atomic mass due to a change in the "neutron count." Neutrons were first described in 1932.

4. **The correct answer is (H).** To calculate the number of neutrons from the information given, subtract the atomic number (the number of protons) from the atomic mass (the number of protons and neutrons): $204 - 81 = 123$.

5. **The correct answer is (B).** The concept of *allotropy* is significant here. For example, ozone is an allotrope of oxygen. They are composed of the *same element*, but have significantly different chemical and physical properties.

6. **The correct answer is (G).** The two subatomic particles that have an electric charge are the proton (+) and the electron (−). Hence, to be electrically neutral, the number of protons must equal the number of electrons in an atom.

Answers to Passage 3

1. **The correct answer is (B).** Since $M + m$ is constant, we can use Table 1 to see that x/t^2 is the same for all three entries.

2. **The correct answer is (H).** M is inversely proportional to t^2. For all values in Experiment 2, $M \times t^2 = 24.5$. If $M = 200$ then $t^2 = 0.1225$ and $t = 0.35$.

3. **The correct answer is (B).** The system is accelerating. In all cases the variables x, M, and m are proportional to t^2. This indicates that the velocity must be changing as time changes.

4. **The correct answer is (J).** From the tables, one can see that as M increases, the travel time decreases. As m increases, the travel time increases. For case II the travel time might increase or decrease as $M + m$ increases, depending on where the increased mass is placed.

5. **The correct answer is (B).** A dependent variable is one that is determined by other variables in the relation. The elapsed time was determined by the distance traveled and the masses added.

6. **The correct answer is (G).** From the tables, the greater the mass M the shorter the travel time. The smaller the mass m, the shorter the travel time. The shorter the distance, the shorter the travel time. Choice (B) had the greatest M, smallest m, and shortest distance.

Answers to Passage 4

1. **The correct answer is (B).** Venus has the most similar size and mass to Earth. Earth's diameter is 12,751, and Venus's is 12,112. Earth's mass is 1.0, and the mass of Venus is 0.82. No other planets are as close to Earth's diameter and mass as Venus.

2. **The correct answer is (H).** Mercury has a period of revolution of 88 days and a period of rotation of 59 days. 88 days/59 days $\approx 3/2$ (90/60 = 3/2).

3. **The correct answer is (C).** Jupiter has the greatest mass, 318 $\times$ the Earth's mass.

4. **The correct answer is (H).** Mercury, the planet closest to the Sun, has the greatest orbital velocity. Each planet farther from the Sun is progressively slower.

www.petersons.com
50
Peterson's ■ Panic Plan for
the ACT Assessment

MATHEMATICS REVIEW

WHOLE NUMBERS

Definitions

The set of numbers {1, 2, 3, 4, . . .} is called the set of *counting numbers* and/or natural numbers, and/or sometimes the set of *positive integers*. (The notation, { }, means "set" or collection, and the three dots after the number 4 indicate that the list continues without end.) *Zero* is usually not considered one of the counting numbers. Together the counting numbers and zero make up the set of *whole numbers*.

Odd and Even Numbers

A whole number is *even* if it is divisible by 2; it is *odd* if it is not divisible by 2. Thus, zero is an even number.

Example

2, 4, 6, 8, and 320 are even numbers; 3, 7, 9, 21, and 45 are odd numbers.

Prime Numbers

The positive integer p is said to be a prime number if $p \neq 1$ and the only positive divisors of p are itself and 1. The first ten primes are 2, 3, 5, 7, 11, 13, 17, 19, 23, and 29. All other positive integers that are neither 1 nor prime are *composite numbers*. Composite numbers can be *factored*, that is, expressed as products of their divisors or factors; for example, $56 = 7 \cdot 8 = 7 \cdot 4 \cdot 2$. In particular, composite numbers can be expressed as products of their *prime* factors in just one way (except for order).

Example

Find the prime factors of 210.

$210 = 2 \cdot 3 \cdot 5 \cdot 7$ (written in any order)

Consecutive Whole Numbers

Numbers are consecutive if each number is the successor of the number that precedes it.

Examples

7, 8, 9, 10, and 11 are consecutive whole numbers.

8, 10, 12, and 14 are consecutive even numbers.

The Number Line

A useful method of representing numbers geometrically is the *number line.*

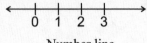

Number line

Ordering of Whole Numbers

On the number line the point representing 8 lies to the right of the point representing 5, and we say $8 > 5$ (read "8 is greater than 5"). One can also say $5 < 8$ ("5 is less than 8"). For any two whole numbers a and b, there are always three possibilities:

$a < b,$ $\qquad$ $a = b,$ $\qquad$ or $\qquad$ $a > b.$

If $a = b$, the points representing the numbers a and b coincide on the number line.

Operations with Whole Numbers

The basic operations on whole numbers are addition (+), subtraction (−), multiplication (· or ×), and division (÷).

Addition

How are three numbers—say, 3, 4, and 8—added? One way is to write:

$(3 + 4) + 8 = 7 + 8 = 15$

Another way is to write:

$3 + (4 + 8) = 3 + 12 = 15$

The parentheses merely group the numbers together. The fact that the same answer, 15, is obtained either way illustrates the *associative property* of addition:

$(r + s) + t = r + (s + t)$

The order in which whole numbers are added is immaterial—that is, $3 + 4 = 4 + 3$. This principle is called the *commutative property* of addition.

If 0 is added to any whole number, the whole number is unchanged. Zero is called the *identity element* for addition.

Subtraction

Subtraction is the inverse of addition. The order in which the numbers are written is important; there is no commutative property for subtraction.

$$4 - 3 \neq 3 - 4$$

The $\neq$ is read "not equal."

Multiplication

Multiplication is a commutative operation:

$$43 \cdot 73 = 73 \cdot 43$$

The result or answer in a multiplication problem is called the *product*.

Multiplication can be expressed with several different symbols:

$$9 \cdot 7 \cdot 3 = 9 \times 7 \times 3 = 9(7)(3)$$

Besides being commutative, multiplication is *associative:*

$$(9 \cdot 7) \cdot 3 = 63 \cdot 3 = 189$$
and
$$9 \cdot (7 \cdot 3) = 9 \cdot 21 = 189$$

A number can be quickly multiplied by 10 by adding a zero at the right of the number. Similarly, a number can be multiplied by 100 by adding two zeros at the right:

$$38 \cdot 10 = 380$$
and
$$100 \cdot 76 = 7600$$

Division

Division is the inverse of multiplication. It is not commutative:

$$8 \div 4 \neq 4 \div 8$$

The parts of a division example are named as follows:

$$\text{divisor} \overline{)\, \text{dividend}}^{\text{quotient}}$$

Division by 0 is not defined (has no meaning). Zero divided by any number other than 0 is 0:

$$0 \div 56 = 0$$

Whole Number Problems:

1. What are the first seven multiples of 9?

2. Express 176 as a product of prime numbers.

3. What are the divisors of 60?

4. Which property is illustrated by the following statement?

   $(9 \times 7) \times 5 = 9 \times (7 \times 5)$

5. Which property is illustrated by the following statement?

   $(16 + 18) + 20 = (18 + 16) + 20$

FRACTIONS

Definitions

The bottom number, *denominator,* indicates into how many parts something is divided. The top number, *numerator,* tells how many of these parts are taken. A fraction indicates division:

$$\frac{7}{8} = 8\overline{)7}$$

If the numerator of a fraction is 0, the value of the fraction is 0. If the denominator of a fraction is 0, the fraction is not defined (has no meaning):

$$\frac{0}{17} = 0 \qquad \frac{17}{0} \quad \text{not defined (has no meaning)}$$

If the denominator of a fraction is 1, the value of the fraction is the same as the numerator:

$$\frac{18}{1} = 18$$

If the numerator and denominator are the same number, the value of the fraction is 1:

$$\frac{7}{7} = 1$$

Equivalent Fractions

Fractions that represent the same number are said to be *equivalent*.

Example

$$\frac{2}{3} = \frac{4}{6} = \frac{6}{9} = \frac{8}{12}$$

Inequality of Fractions

If two fractions are not equivalent, one is smaller than the other.

For the fractions $\frac{a}{b}$ and $\frac{c}{b}$:

$$\frac{a}{b} < \frac{c}{b} \text{ if } a < c$$

That is, if two fractions have the same denominator, the one with the smaller numerator has the smaller value.

If two fractions have different denominators, find a common denominator by multiplying one denominator by the other. Then use the common denominator to compare numerators.

Example

Which is smaller, $\frac{5}{8}$ or $\frac{4}{7}$?

$8 \cdot 7 = 56 =$ common denominator

$$\frac{5}{8} \times \frac{7}{7} = \frac{35}{56} \qquad \frac{4}{7} \times \frac{8}{8} = \frac{32}{56}$$

Since $32 < 35$,

$$\frac{32}{56} < \frac{35}{56} \text{ and } \frac{4}{7} < \frac{5}{8}$$

Reducing to Lowest Terms

The principle that

$$\frac{m \times a}{m \times b} = \frac{a}{b}$$

can be particularly useful in reducing fractions to lowest terms. Fractions are expressed in *lowest terms* when the numerator and denominator have no common factor except 1. One way to reduce a fraction to an equivalent fraction in lowest terms is to express the numerator and denominator as products of their prime factors. Each time a prime appears in the numerator over the same prime in the denominator, $\frac{p}{p}$, substitute its equal value, 1.

Example

Reduce $\dfrac{30}{42}$ to an equivalent fraction in lowest terms:

$$\frac{30}{42} = \frac{2 \cdot 3 \cdot 5}{2 \cdot 3 \cdot 7} = 1 \cdot 1 \cdot \frac{5}{7} = \frac{5}{7}$$

In practice, this can be done even more quickly by dividing the numerator and the denominator by any number, prime or not, which will divide both evenly. Repeat this process until there is no prime factor remaining that is common to both numerator and denominator:

$$\frac{30}{42} = \frac{15}{21} = \frac{5}{7}$$

PROPER FRACTIONS, IMPROPER FRACTIONS, AND MIXED NUMBERS

Definitions

A *proper fraction* is a fraction whose numerator is smaller than its denominator. Proper fractions always have a value less than 1:

$$\frac{3}{4} \qquad \frac{5}{8} \qquad \frac{121}{132} \qquad \frac{0}{1}$$

An *improper fraction* is a fraction whose numerator is equal to or greater than the denominator. Improper fractions always have a value equal to or greater than 1:

$$\frac{3}{2} \qquad \frac{17}{17} \qquad \frac{9}{1} \qquad \frac{15}{14}$$

A *mixed number* is a number composed of a whole number and a proper fraction. It is always greater than 1 in value:

$$3\frac{7}{8} \qquad 5\frac{1}{4} \qquad 11\frac{3}{14}$$

To Change a Mixed Number into an Improper Fraction

Multiply the denominator by the whole number and add this product to the numerator. Use the sum so obtained as the new numerator, and keep the original denominator.

Example

Write $9\dfrac{4}{11}$ as an improper fraction:

$$9\frac{4}{11} = \frac{(11 \times 9) + 4}{11} = \frac{99 + 4}{11} = \frac{103}{11}$$

To Change an Improper Fraction into a Mixed Number

Divide the numerator by the denominator. The result is the whole-number part of the mixed number. If there is a remainder in the division process because the division does not come out evenly, put the remainder over the denominator (divisor). This gives the fractional part of the mixed number:

$$\frac{20}{3} = 3\overline{)20} \quad\quad = 6\frac{2}{3}$$
$$\quad\quad\quad \frac{18}{2} \text{ remainder}$$

Multiplication

Proper and Improper Fractions

Multiply the two numerators and then multiply the two denominators. If the numerator obtained is larger than the denominator, divide the numerator of the resulting fraction by its denominator:

$$\frac{3}{8} \times \frac{15}{11} = \frac{45}{88} \quad\quad \frac{3}{8} \times \frac{22}{7} = \frac{66}{56} = 1\frac{10}{56}$$

The product in the multiplication of fractions is usually expressed in lowest terms.

Canceling

In multiplying fractions, if any of the numerators and denominators have a common divisor (factor), divide each of them by this common factor, and the value of the fraction remains the same. This process is called *canceling* or *cancellation*.

Example

$$\frac{27}{18} \times \frac{90}{300} = \frac{27}{18} \times \frac{9}{30} \quad\quad \text{Divide second fraction by } \frac{10}{10}$$

$$= \frac{\overset{9}{\cancel{27}}}{\underset{2}{\cancel{18}}} \times \frac{\overset{1}{\cancel{9}}}{\underset{10}{\cancel{30}}} \quad\quad \text{Cancel: 18 and 9 each divisible by 9;}$$
$$\text{27 and 30 each divisible by 3}$$

$$= \frac{9 \times 1}{2 \times 10} = \frac{9}{20} \quad \text{Multiply numerators; multiply denominators}$$

Note: Canceling can take place only between a numerator and a denominator, in the same or a different fraction, never between two numerators or between two denominators.

Mixed Numbers

Mixed numbers should be changed to improper fractions before multiplying. Then multiply as described above.

Example

To multiply

$$\frac{4}{7} \times 3\frac{5}{8}$$

change $3\frac{5}{8}$ to an improper fraction:

$$3\frac{5}{8} = \frac{(8 \times 3) + 5}{8} = \frac{24 + 5}{8} = \frac{29}{8}$$

Multiply

$$\overset{1}{\cancel{\frac{4}{7}}} \times \frac{29}{\underset{2}{\cancel{8}}} = \frac{29}{14}$$

The answer can be left in this form or changed to a mixed number: $2\frac{1}{14}$

Fractions with Whole Numbers

Write the whole number as a fraction with a denominator of 1 and then multiply:

$$\frac{3}{4} \times 7 = \frac{3}{4} \times \frac{7}{1} = \frac{21}{4} = 5\frac{1}{4}$$

Division

Reciprocals

Division of fractions involves reciprocals. One fraction is the *reciprocal* of another if the product of the fractions is 1.

Example

$\frac{3}{4}$ and $\frac{4}{3}$ are reciprocals since

$$\overset{1}{\underset{1}{\cancel{\frac{3}{4}}}} \times \overset{1}{\underset{1}{\cancel{\frac{4}{3}}}} = \frac{1 \times 1}{1 \times 1} = 1$$

Example

$\frac{1}{3}$ and 3 are reciprocals since

$$\frac{1}{\cancel{3}} \times \frac{\cancel{3}}{1} = 1$$

To find the reciprocal of a fraction, interchange the numerator and denominator—that is, invert the fraction, or turn it upside down.

Proper and Improper Fractions

Multiply the first fraction (dividend) by the reciprocal of the second fraction (divisor). Reduce by cancellation if possible. If you wish to, change the answer to a mixed number when possible:

Example

$$\frac{9}{2} \div \frac{4}{7} = \frac{9}{2} \times \frac{7}{4} \quad \text{The reciprocal of } \frac{4}{7} \text{ is } \frac{7}{4} \text{ because } \frac{4}{7} \times \frac{7}{4} = 1$$

$$= \frac{63}{8}$$

$$= 7\frac{7}{8}$$

Mixed Numbers and/or Whole Numbers

Both mixed numbers and whole numbers must first be changed to equivalent improper fractions. Then proceed as described above.

Addition

Fractions can be added only if their denominators are the same (called the *common denominator*). Add the numerators; the denominator remains the same. Reduce the sum to the lowest terms:

$$\frac{3}{8} + \frac{2}{8} + \frac{1}{8} = \frac{3 + 2 + 1}{8} = \frac{6}{8} = \frac{3}{4}$$

When the fractions have different denominators, you must find a common denominator. One way of doing this is to find the product of the different denominators.

Example

$$\frac{5}{6} + \frac{1}{4} = ?$$

A common denominator is $6 \cdot 4 = 24$.

$$\frac{5}{6} \times \frac{4}{4} = \frac{20}{24} \quad \text{and} \quad \frac{1}{4} \times \frac{6}{6} = \frac{6}{24}$$

$$\frac{5}{6} + \frac{1}{4} = \frac{20}{24} + \frac{6}{24} = \frac{26}{24} = \frac{13}{12} = 1\frac{1}{12}$$

Sometimes, a denominator can often be found that is smaller than the product of the different denominators. If the denominator of each fraction will divide into such a number evenly and it is the *smallest* such number, it is called the *least* (or *lowest*) *common denominator,* abbreviated as LCD. Finding a least-common denominator may make it unnecessary to reduce the answer and enables one to work with smaller numbers.

Addition of Mixed Numbers
Change any mixed numbers to fractions. If the fractions have the same denominator, add the numerators. If the fractions have different denominators, find the LCD of the several denominators and then add numerators. Reduce the answer if possible. Write the answer as a mixed number if you wish.

Example

$$5\frac{1}{2} + 1\frac{2}{9} = ?$$

$$5\frac{1}{2} + 1\frac{2}{9} = \frac{11}{2} + \frac{11}{9} = \frac{99}{18} + \frac{22}{18} = \frac{121}{18} = 6\frac{13}{18}$$

Subtraction

Fractions can be subtracted only if the denominators are the same. If the denominators are the same, find the difference between the numerators. The denominator remains unchanged.

When fractions have different denominators, find equivalent fractions with a common denominator, and then subtract numerators.

Example

$$\frac{7}{8} - \frac{3}{4} = ?$$

$$\frac{7}{8} - \frac{3}{4} = \frac{7}{8} - \frac{6}{8} = \frac{1}{8}$$

Mixed Numbers

To subtract mixed numbers, change each mixed number to a fraction. Find the LCD for the fractions. Write each fraction as an equivalent fraction whose denominator is the common denominator. Find the difference between the numerators.

Fraction Problems

Perform the indicated operations and reduce your answers to lowest terms.

1. $\frac{3}{5} + \frac{2}{7} =$

2. $\frac{5}{7} - \frac{1}{2} =$

3. $\frac{2}{3} \times \frac{12}{8} =$

4. $\frac{3}{4} \div \frac{7}{8} =$

5. $1\frac{4}{5} \times 2\frac{2}{3} =$

6. $16\frac{4}{7} - 5\frac{6}{7} =$

NOW CHECK YOUR ANSWERS

Answers to Whole Number Problems

1. 9, 18, 27, 36, 45, 54, 63

2. $176 = 2 \times 88 = 2 \times 2 \times 44 = 2 \times 2 \times 2 \times 22 = 2 \times 2 \times 2 \times 2 \times 11$

3. The divisors of 60 are 1, 2, 3, 4, 6, 10, 15, 20, 30, 60.

4. The Associative Property of Multiplication

5. The Commutative Property of Addition

Answers to Fraction Problems

1. $\dfrac{3}{5} + \dfrac{2}{7} = \dfrac{21}{35} + \dfrac{10}{35} = \dfrac{31}{35}$

2. $\dfrac{5}{7} - \dfrac{1}{2} = \dfrac{10}{14} - \dfrac{7}{14} = \dfrac{3}{14}$

3. $\dfrac{2}{3} \times \dfrac{12}{8} = \dfrac{\cancel{2}^{1}}{\cancel{3}_{1}} \times \dfrac{\cancel{12}^{4}}{\cancel{8}_{4}} = \dfrac{1}{1} \times \dfrac{4}{4} = 1$

4. $\dfrac{3}{4} \div \dfrac{7}{8} = \dfrac{3}{4} \times \dfrac{8}{7} = \dfrac{3}{\cancel{4}_{1}} \times \dfrac{\cancel{8}^{2}}{7} = \dfrac{6}{7}$

5. $1\dfrac{4}{5} \times 2\dfrac{2}{3} = \dfrac{9}{5} \times \dfrac{8}{3} = \dfrac{\cancel{9}^{3}}{5} \times \dfrac{8}{\cancel{3}_{1}} = \dfrac{24}{5} = 4\dfrac{4}{5}$

6. $16\dfrac{4}{7} - 5\dfrac{6}{7} = \dfrac{116}{7} - \dfrac{41}{7} = \dfrac{75}{7} = 10\dfrac{5}{7}$

MATHEMATICS AND ENGLISH GRAMMAR REVIEW

MATHEMATICS REVIEW

Decimals

The system of whole numbers can be extended to fractions by using a period called a *decimal point.* The digits after a decimal point form a *decimal fraction.* Decimal fractions are smaller than 1—for example, .3, .37, .372, and .105. The first position to the right of the decimal point is called the *tenths' place* since the digit in that position tells how many tenths there are. The second digit to the right of the decimal point is in the *hundredths' place.* The third digit to the right of the decimal point is in the *thousandths' place,* and so on.

Examples

.3 is read "three tenths"

.37 is read "thirty-seven hundredths"

Rounding Off

To round off a decimal, identify the place to be rounded off. If the digit to the right of it is 0, 1, 2, 3, or 4, the round-off place digit remains the same. If the digit to the right is 5, 6, 7, 8, or 9, add 1 to the round-off place digit.

Examples

.6386 rounded to the nearest thousandth is .639.

1.624 rounded to the nearest whole number is 2.

Decimals and Fractions

Changing a Decimal to a Fraction

Place the digits to the right of the decimal point over the value of the place in which the last digit appears and reduce if possible. The whole number remains the same.

Example

Change 2.14 to a fraction or mixed number. Observe that 4 is the last digit and is in the hundredths' place.

$$.14 = \frac{14}{100} = \frac{7}{50} \qquad \text{so,} \qquad 2.14 = 2\frac{7}{50}$$

Changing a Fraction to a Decimal

Divide the numerator of the fraction by the denominator. Add and divide until there is no remainder, or round to the desired place.

Example

Change $\frac{3}{8}$ to a decimal.

Divide: $3 \div 8 = .375$

Addition

Addition of decimals is both commutative and associative. Decimals are simpler to add than fractions. Place the decimals in a column with the decimal points aligned under each other. Add in the usual way. The decimal point of the answer is also aligned under the other decimal points.

Example

$43 + 2.73 + .9 + 3.01 = ?$

$$\begin{array}{r} 43. \\ 2.73 \\ .9 \\ 3.01 \\ \hline 49.64 \end{array}$$

Subtraction

For subtraction, the decimal points must be aligned under each other. Add zeros to the right of the decimal point if desired. Subtract as with whole numbers.

Examples

$$\begin{array}{r} 21.567 \\ -9.4 \\ \hline 12.167 \end{array} \qquad \begin{array}{r} 21.567 \\ -9.48 \\ \hline 12.087 \end{array} \qquad \begin{array}{r} 39.00 \\ -17.48 \\ \hline 21.52 \end{array}$$

Multiplication

Multiply the decimals as if they were whole numbers. The total number of decimal places in the product is the sum of the number of places (to the right of the decimal point) in all of the numbers multiplied.

Example

$8.64 \times .003 = ?$

$$\begin{array}{r} 8.64 \\ \times .003 \\ \hline .02592 \end{array} \qquad \begin{array}{r} 2 \\ +3 \\ \hline 5 \end{array} \quad \begin{array}{l} \text{places to right of decimal point} \\ \text{places to right of decimal point} \\ \text{places to right of decimal point} \end{array}$$

A zero had to be added to the left of the product before writing the decimal point to ensure that there would be five decimal places in the product.

64

Note: To multiply a decimal by 10, simply move the decimal point one place to the right; to multiply by 100, move the decimal point two places to the right.

Division

To divide one decimal (the dividend) by another (the divisor), move the decimal point in the divisor as many places as necessary to the right to make the divisor a whole number. Then move the decimal point in the dividend (expressed or understood) a corresponding number of places, adding zeros if necessary. Then divide as with whole numbers. The decimal point in the quotient is placed above the decimal point in the dividend after the decimal point has been moved.

Example

Divide 7.6 by .32.

$$
.32\overline{)7.60} = 32\overline{)760.00}
$$

$$
\begin{array}{r}
23.75 \\
32\overline{)760.00} \\
\underline{64} \\
120 \\
\underline{96} \\
240 \\
\underline{224} \\
160 \\
\underline{160} \\
\end{array}
$$

Decimal Problems

1. Change the following fractions into decimals.

   a. ⅝
   b. ⅚

2. Change the following fractions into decimals and reduce.

   a. 13.56
   b. 21.002

3. 5.746 + 354.34

4. 3.261 − 2.59

5. 9.2 × 0.03

6. $\dfrac{0.033}{0.11}$

Percents

Percents, like fractions and decimals, are ways of expressing parts of whole numbers, as 93%, 50%, and 22.4%. Percents are expressions of hundredths—that is, of fractions whose denominator is 100. The symbol for percent is "%."

Example

$$25\% = \text{twenty-five hundredths} = \frac{25}{100} = \frac{1}{4}$$

The word *percent* means *per hundred.* Its main use is in comparing fractions with equal denominators of 100.

Changing a Percent into a Decimal

Divide the percent by 100 and drop the symbol for percent. Add zeros to the left when necessary:

$$30\% = .30 \qquad 1\% = .01$$

Remember that the short method of dividing by 100 is to move the decimal point two places to the left.

Changing a Decimal into a Percent

Multiply the decimal by 100 by moving the decimal point two places to the right, and add the symbol for percent:

$$.375 = 37.5\% \qquad .001 = .1\%$$

To change a percent to a fraction, first change it to a decimal.

It is also a good idea to memorize the equivalent fractions for certain percents. This will save you time, as they will typically come up several times on the ACT Assessment.

$$\frac{1}{2} = .50 = 50\% \qquad \frac{3}{5} = .60 = 60\% \qquad \frac{7}{8} = .87\frac{1}{2} = 87\frac{1}{2}\%$$

$$\frac{1}{4} = .25 = 25\% \qquad \frac{4}{5} = .80 = 80\% \qquad \frac{1}{10} = .10 = 10\%$$

$$\frac{3}{4} = .75 = 75\% \qquad \frac{1}{6} = .16\frac{2}{3} = 16\frac{2}{3}\% \qquad \frac{3}{10} = .30 = 30\%$$

$$\frac{1}{3} = .33\frac{1}{3} = 33\frac{1}{3}\% \qquad \frac{5}{6} = .83\frac{1}{3} = 83\frac{1}{3}\% \qquad \frac{7}{10} = .70 = 70\%$$

$$\frac{2}{3} = .66\frac{2}{3} = 66\frac{2}{3}\% \qquad \frac{1}{8} = .12\frac{1}{2} = 12\frac{1}{2}\% \qquad \frac{9}{10} = .90 = 90\%$$

$$\frac{1}{5} = .20 = 20\% \qquad \frac{3}{8} = .37\frac{1}{2} = 37\frac{1}{2}\% \qquad 1 = 100\%$$

$$\frac{2}{5} = .40 = 40\% \qquad \frac{5}{8} = .62\frac{1}{2} = 62\frac{1}{2}\%$$

Percent Problems

1. Change the following decimals into percents:

    a.   0.875
    b.   12.34

2. Change the following percents into decimals:

    a.   8.75%
    b.   0.07%

3. Change the following percents into fractions:

    a.   37.5%
    b.   80%

4. Change the following fractions into percents:

    a.   ⅗
    b.   ⅛

Word Problems

When doing percent problems, it is usually easier to change the percent to a decimal or a fraction before computing. When we take a percent of a certain number, that number is called the *whole,* the percent we take is called the *percent,* and the result is called the *part.* If we let W represent the whole, % the percent, and P the part, the relationship between these quantities is expressed by the following formula:

$$P = \% \times W$$

All percent problems can be done with the help of this formula.

Example

In a class of 24 students, 25% received an A. How many students received an A? The number of students (24) is the whole, and 25% is the percent. Change the percent to a fraction for ease of handling and apply the formula.

$$25\% = \frac{25}{100} = \frac{1}{4}$$

$$P = \% \times W$$

$$= \frac{1}{\cancel{4}} \times \frac{\overset{6}{\cancel{24}}}{1}$$

$$= 6 \text{ students}$$

Example

What percent of a 40-hour week is a 16-hour schedule?

40 hours is the whole and 16 hours is the part.

$$P = \% \times W$$

$$16 = \% \times 40$$

$$16 \div 40 = 0.4 = 40\%$$

16 hours is 40% of 40 hours.

Percent of Increase or Decrease

This kind of problem is not really new but follows immediately from the previous problems. First calculate the amount of increase or decrease. This amount is the P (part) from the formula $P = \% \times W$. The whole, W, is the original amount, regardless of whether there was a loss or gain.

Example

By what percent does Mary's salary increase if her present salary is $20,000 and she accepts a new job at a salary of $28,000?

Amount of increase is:

$$\$28,000 - \$20,000 = \$8,000$$

$$P = \% \times W$$

$$\$8,000 = \% \times \$20,000$$

Divide each side of the equation by $20,000. Then:

$$\frac{\overset{40}{\cancel{8000}}}{\underset{100}{\cancel{20,000}}} = \frac{40}{100} = \% = 40\% \text{ increase}$$

Discount and Interest

These special kinds of percent problems require no new methods of attack.

Discount

The amount of discount is the difference between the original price and the sale, or discount, price. The rate of discount is usually given as a fraction or as a percent. Use the formula of the percent problems $P = \% \times W$, but now P stands for the part or discount, % is the percent of discount, and W, the whole, is the original price.

Example

A table listed at $160 is marked 20% off. What is the sale price?

$$P = \% \times W$$
$$= .20 \times \$160 = \$32$$

This is the amount of discount or how much must be subtracted from the original price. Then:

$160 - \$32 = \$128$ sale price

Successive Discounting

When an item is discounted more than once, it is called successive discounting.

Example

In one store, a dress tagged at $40 was discounted 15%. When it did not sell at the lower price, it was discounted an additional 10%. What was the final selling price?

Discount = % × original price

First discount = .15 × $40 = $6

$40 − $6 = $34 selling price after first discount

Second discount = .10 × $34 = $3.40

$34 − $3.40 = $30.60 final selling price

Notice that successive discounts of 15% and 10% are not equal to a onetime discount of 25%.

25% of $40 = $10, leaving a selling price of $30.

Interest

Interest problems are similar to discount and percent problems. If money is left in the bank for a year and the interest is calculated at the end of the year, the usual formula $P = \% \cdot W$ can be used, where P is the *interest*, % is the *rate*, and W is the *principal* (original amount of money borrowed or loaned).

Example

A certain bank pays interest on savings accounts at the rate of 4% per year. If a man has $6,700 on deposit, find the interest earned after 1 year.

$$P = \% \times W$$

Interest = rate $\times$ principal

$$P = .04 \times \$6,700 = \$268 \text{ interest}$$

Interest problems frequently involve more or less time than 1 year. Then the formula becomes

Interest = rate $\times$ principal $\times$ time

Example

If the money is left in the bank for 3 years at simple interest (the kind we are discussing), the interest is

$$3 \times \$268 = \$804$$

Example

Suppose $6,700 is deposited in the bank at 4% interest for 3 months. How much interest is earned?

Interest = rate $\times$ principal $\times$ time

Here the 4% rate is for 1 year. Since 3 months is $\dfrac{3}{12} = \dfrac{1}{4}$

Interest = $.04 \times \$6,700 \times \dfrac{1}{4} = \$67$

Percent Word Problems

1. After having lunch, Ian leaves a tip of $4.32. If this amount represents 18 percent of the lunch bill, how much was the bill?

2. Before beginning her diet, Janet weighed 125 pounds. After completing the diet, she weighed 110 pounds. What percent of her weight did she lose?

3. If a $12,000 car loses 10 percent of its value every year, what is it worth after three years?

4. The population of Tonawanda is 224,000, which represents an increase of 12 percent over the population the previous year. What was the population the previous year?

5. Peter invests $5,000 at 4 percent simple annual interest. How much is his investment worth after two months?

NOW CHECK YOUR ANSWERS

Answers to Decimal Problems

1. a. $5/8 = 5 \div 8 = 0.625$
    b. $5/6 = 5 \div 6 = 0.8333\ldots$

2. a. $13.56 = 13\dfrac{56}{100} = 13\dfrac{28}{50} = 13\dfrac{14}{25}$

    b. $21.002 = 21\dfrac{2}{1000} = 21\dfrac{1}{500}$

3. $\begin{array}{r} 5.746 \\ +354.34 \\ \hline 360.086 \end{array}$

4. $\begin{array}{r} 3.261 \\ -2.59 \\ \hline 0.671 \end{array}$

5. $9.2 \times 0.03 = 0.276$

6. $\dfrac{0.033}{0.11} = \dfrac{3.3}{11} = 0.3$

Answers to Percent Problems

1. a. $0.875 = 87.5\%$
    b. $12.34 = 1234\%$

2. a. $8.75\% = 0.0875$
    b. $0.07\% = 0.0007$

3. a. $37.5\% = 0.375 = \dfrac{375}{1000} = \dfrac{15}{40} = \dfrac{3}{8}$

    b. $80\% = 0.80 = \dfrac{80}{100} = \dfrac{4}{5}$

4. a. $3/5 = 0.6 = 60\%$
    b. $1/8 = 0.125 = 12.5\%$ or $12\dfrac{1}{2}\%$

Answers to Percent Word Problems

1. Amount of bill $= \dfrac{\text{Amount of tip}}{\text{Percent of tip}} = \dfrac{4.32}{0.18} = \$24.00$

2. Amount of weight lost $= 125 - 110 = 15$ lb.

    Percent of weight lost $= \dfrac{\text{Amount of weight lost}}{\text{Original weight}} = \dfrac{15}{125} = 12$ percent

3. Value of car after one year   = $12,000 × 0.90 = $10,800
   Value of car after two years   = $10,800 × 0.90 = $9,720
   Value of car after three years = $9,720 × 0.90 = $8,748

4. Previous population $= \dfrac{\text{Current population}}{100\% + \text{Percent of increase}}$

   $= \dfrac{224,000}{100\% + 12\%} = \dfrac{224,000}{112\%} = 200,000$

5. Value of investment = Principal × Rate × Time
   $= 5,000 × 0.04 × ⅙ = \$33.33$

ENGLISH GRAMMAR REVIEW

On Day 1, you reviewed the strategies for answering the questions on the English Test. In order to do well on this test, you will need a basic knowledge of grammar. This section will give you an overview of these basics. Take your time reading through this section, make notes if you don't understand the material, and go back and review again, if necessary.

USAGE REVIEW

NOUNS

A NOUN is the name of a person, place, or thing.

actor,   *city,*   *lamp*

There are three kinds of nouns, according to the type of person, place, or thing the noun names.

(1) A *common* noun refers to a general type: girl, park, army.

(2) A *proper* noun refers to a particular person, place, or thing and always begins with a capital letter: Mary, Central Park, U.S. Army.

(3) A *collective* noun signifies a number of individuals organized into one group: team, crowd, Congress.

Singular/Plural

Every noun has a number. That means every noun is either singular or plural. Singular means only one; plural means more than one. There are four ways to form the plurals of nouns:

(1) by adding *s* to the singular (horses, kites, rivers)

(2) by adding *-es* to the singular (buses, churches, dishes, boxes, buzzes)

(3) by changing the singular (*man* becomes *men*, *woman* becomes *women*, *child* becomes *children*, *baby* becomes *babies*, *alumnus* becomes *alumni*)

(4) by leaving the singular as it is (moose, deer, and sheep are all plural as well as singular)

Possessive Nouns

A noun is said to be possessive when it shows ownership. The correct use of the possessive case is often tested on the exam. The following rules will help you answer such questions correctly.

A.   The possessive case of most nouns is formed by adding an apostrophe and *s* to the singular.

> The *boy's* book
> *Emile's* coat

B.   If the singular ends in *s* add an apostrophe, or apostrophe *s*.

> The *bus's* wheels.
>   or
> The *bus'* wheels.
> *Charles'* books.
>   or
> *Charles's* books.

C.   The possessive case of plural nouns ending in *s* is formed by adding just an apostrophe.

> The *dogs'* bones.

Note: If *dog* was singular, the possessive case would be *dog's*.

D.   If the plural noun does not end in *s* then add an apostrophe and *s*.

> The *children's* toys.
> The *men's* boots.

E.   The possessive case of compound nouns is formed by adding an apostrophe and *s* to the last word if it is singular, or by adding an *s* and an apostrophe if the word is plural.

> My *brother-in-law's* house.
> My *two brothers'* house.

F.   To show individual ownership, add an apostrophe and *s* to each owner.

> *Joe's* and *Jim's* boats. (They each own their own boat.)

G.   To show joint ownership, add an apostrophe and *s* to the last name.

> Joe and *Jim's* boat. (They both own the same boat.)

PRACTICE PROBLEMS IN PLURALS AND POSSESSIVES

In September 1991, eight researchers set foot in a 3-acre world called

Biosphere 2, where they were scheduled to remain, having no physical

contact with the outside world, for two years. Inside the complex were

living quarter's, three greenhouses, and a wilderness area. The goal of the
<u>_____</u>
             1

inhabitants was to effect complete isolation in their sealed habitat in order to

study the Earths ecosystems; but the experiment failed, providing fodder
<u>_____</u>
             2

for television's many late-night comedians. Now, under the direction of
<u>_____</u>
             3

Columbia University, Biosphere 2 is opening <u>museum and research facilitys.</u>
                                                              4

The living areas have been sealed off to contain hands-on exhibits. The

agricultural bays have likewise been sealed and will be used to study the

effects of rapidly rising greenhouse gases. In addition to their learning

important information about the environment, Columbia <u>scientists hope to</u>
                                                                       5

<u>raise the publics interest</u> in environmental science.
          5

1. (A) NO CHANGE
   (B) living quarters, three greenhouses,
   (C) living quarters', three greenhouses,
   (D) living quarter's, three greenhouse's,

2. (F) NO CHANGE
   (G) study the Earthes ecosystems
   (H) study the Earths' ecosystems
   (J) study the Earth's ecosystems

3. (A) NO CHANGE
   (B) for televisions' many late-night comedians
   (C) for televisions many late-night comedians
   (D) for television many late-night comedians

4. (F) NO CHANGE
   (G) museums and research facilitys.
   (H) museum and research facilities.
   (J) museum and researcher's facilitys.

5. (A) NO CHANGE
   (B) scientists hope to raise the publics interests
   (C) scientists hope to raise the publics' interest
   (D) scientists hope to raise the public's interest

PRONOUNS

A pronoun is used in place of a noun. The noun for which a pronoun is used is called the *antecedent*. The use of pronouns, particularly the relationship between a pronoun and its antecedent, is one of the most common items found on the test. Always make sure a pronoun has a clear antecedent.

John had a candy bar and a cookie. He ate *it* quickly. (Ambiguous) (What is the antecedent of *it—candy bar* or *cookie?*)

The boy rode his bike through the hedge, *which* was very large. (Ambiguous) (What was very large—the *bike* or the *hedge?*)

The captain was very popular. *They* all liked him. (Ambiguous) (Who liked him? *They* has no antecedent.)

There are ten kinds of pronouns:

(1) Expletive pronoun. The words *it* and *there* followed by the subject of the sentence are expletive pronouns.

> *There* were only a few tickets left.

> *It* was a long list of chores.

When using an expletive, the verb agrees with the subject.

> There *remains* one *child* on the bus.

> There *remain* many *children* on the bus.

(2) Intensive pronoun. This is a pronoun, ending in *self* or *selves*, which follows its antecedent and emphasizes it.

> He *himself* will go.

> The package was delivered to the boys *themselves*.

(3) A reflexive pronoun. This is a pronoun, ending in *self* or *selves*, which is usually the object of a verb or preposition, or the complement of a verb.

> I hate *myself*.
>
> They always laugh at *themselves*.

Myself, yourself, himself, herself, and *itself* are all singular. *Ourselves, yourselves*, and *themselves* are all plural. There is no such pronoun as hisself or theirselves. Do not use *myself* instead of *I* or *me*.

(4) Demonstrative pronoun. This is used in place of a noun and points out the noun. Common demonstrative pronouns are *this, that, these, those*.

> I want *those*.

(5) Indefinite pronoun. This pronoun refers to any number of persons or objects. Following is a list of some singular and plural indefinite pronouns.

> SINGULAR
>
> anybody, anyone, each, everybody, everyone, no one, nobody, none, somebody, someone
>
> PLURAL
>
> all, any, many, several, some

If the singular form is used as a subject, the verb must be singular.

> *Everyone* of *them* sings. (One person sings.)

If the singular form is used as an antecedent, its pronoun must be singular.

> Did *anybody* on any of the teams lose *his* sneakers? (One person lost *his* sneakers.)

(6) Interrogative pronoun. This pronoun is used in asking a question. Such pronouns are *who, whose, whom, what*, and *which. Whose* shows possession. *Whom* is in the objective case. *Whom* is used only when an object pronoun is needed.

(7) Reciprocal pronoun. This pronoun is used when referring to mutual relations. The reciprocal pronouns are *each other* and *one another*.

> They love *one another*.
>
> They often visit *each other's* houses.

Note that the possessive is formed by an *'s* after the word *other*.

(8) Possessive pronoun. This pronoun refers to a noun that owns something. The possessive pronouns are as follows:

SINGULAR

mine (my), yours, his, hers, its

PLURAL

ours, yours, theirs

Notice that possessive pronouns do not use an *'s*. *It's* is a contraction meaning *it is*; *its* denotes possession.

(9) Personal pronouns

	Singular	*Plural*
NOMINATIVE CASE		
First person	I	we
Second person	you	you
Third person	he, she, it	they
OBJECTIVE CASE		
First person	me	us
Second person	you	you
Third person	him, her, it	them
POSSESSIVE CASE		
First person	mine (my)	ours (our)
Second person	yours (your)	yours (your)
Third person	his, hers, its	theirs (their)
	(his, her, its)	

Personal pronouns denote what is called *person*. First-person pronouns show the person or thing that is speaking.

I am going. (First person speaking)

Second-person pronouns show the person or thing being spoken to.

You are my friend. (Second person spoken to)

Third-person pronouns show the person or thing being spoken about.

Bea did not see *her*. (Third person spoken about)

(10) Relative pronoun.

> Nominative case—who, that, which
>
> Objective case—whom, that, which
>
> Possessive case—whose

A relative pronoun used as the *subject* of a dependent clause is in the nominative case.

> I know *who* stole the car.
>
> Give the prize to *whoever* won it.

A relative pronoun used as the *object* of a dependent clause is in the objective case.

> He is the thief *whom* I know. (Object of verb *know*)

Note that the difficulty always comes between choosing *who* or *whom*. Remember that *who* is in the nominative case and is used for the appropriate situations discussed under nominative case in the section on nouns. *Whom* is in the objective case and is used for the appropriate situations discussed under objective case in the section on nouns.

> *Who* is coming? (*Who* is the subject.)
>
> *Whom* are you going with? (*Whom* is the object of the preposition *with*.)

The relative pronoun in the possessive case is *whose*. Notice there is no apostrophe in this word. The contraction *who's* means *who is*.

Important for Exam

Pronouns must agree with their antecedents in person, number, and gender.

1. *Who* refers to persons only.

2. *Which* refers to animals or objects.

3. *That* refers to persons, animals, or objects.

> I don't know *who* the actor is. (Person)
>
> They missed their dog, *which* died. (Animal)
>
> I finished the book *which* (or *that*) you recommended. (Object)
>
> They are the people *who* started the fight. (Person)
>
> That is the tiger *that* ran loose. (Animal)
>
> The light *that* failed was broken. (Object)

Note that the singular indefinite antecedents always take a singular pronoun.

> *Everyone* of the girls lost *her* hat.
>
> *None* of the boys lost *his*.
>
> *Someone* left *his* bike outside.

Note that collective singular nouns take singular pronouns; collective plural nouns take plural pronouns.

> The choir sang *its* part beautifully.
>
> The choirs sang *their* parts beautifully.

Note that two or more antecedents joined by *and* take a plural pronoun.

> Dave *and* Steve lost *their* way.

Note that two or more singular antecedents joined by *or* or *nor* take a singular pronoun.

> Tanya or Charita may use *her* ball.
>
> Neither Tanya nor Charita may use *her* ball.

If two antecedents are joined by *or* or *nor*, and if one is plural and the other is singular, the pronoun agrees in number with the nearer antecedent.

> Neither the *ball* nor the *rackets* were in *their* place.

Case

Remember that pronouns must also be in the correct case.

(1) A pronoun must be in the nominative case when it is the subject of a sentence.

> James and *I* went to the airport.
>
> *We* freshmen helped the seniors.
>
> Peter calls her more than *I* do.
>
> Peter calls her more than *I*. (Here, the verb *do* is understood, and *I* is the subject of the understood verb *do*.)

(2) A pronoun is in the objective case when it is a direct object of the verb.

> Leaving James and *me*, they ran away.
>
> John hit *them*.
>
> The freshmen helped *us* seniors.

A pronoun is in the objective case when it is the indirect object of a verb.

> Give *us* the ball.

(3) A pronoun is in the objective case when it is an object of a preposition.

> To Ben and *me*
>
> With Sheila and *her*
>
> Between you and *them*

(4) A pronoun is in the possessive case when it shows ownership.

> *Her* car broke down.
>
> *Theirs* did also.

A pronoun is in the possessive case when it appears before a gerund (see verbals).

> *His* going was a sad event.

For a more detailed analysis of the three cases, see the section on cases of nouns.

ADJECTIVES

An adjective describes or modifies a noun or a pronoun. An adjective usually answers the question *which one?* Or *what kind?* Or *how many?* You need to pay attention to the use of articles.

(1) Articles (a, an, the)

An article must agree in number with the noun or pronoun it modifies.

If the noun or pronoun begins with a consonant, use *a*. If the noun or pronoun begins with a vowel, use *an*.

> *A* pear
>
> *An* orange
>
> *The* girls

Important for Exam

An adjective is used as a predicate adjective after a linking verb. If the modifier is describing the verb (a nonlinking verb) we must use an adverb.

> The boy is *happy*. (Adjective)
> Joe appeared *angry*. (Adjective)
> The soup tasted *spicy*. (Adjective)
> Joe looked *angrily* at the dog. (Adverb—*angrily* modifies *looked*)

Positive, Comparative, and Superlative Adjectives

(1) The positive degree states the quality of an object.

(2) The comparative degree compares two things. It is formed by using *less* or *more* or adding *-er* to the positive.

(3) The superlative degree compares three or more things. It is formed by using *least* or *most* or adding *-est* to the positive.

Positive	Comparative	Superlative
Easy	easier; more easy; less easy	easiest; most easy; least easy
Pretty	prettier; more pretty; less pretty	prettiest; least pretty; most pretty

Do Not Use Two Forms Together

> She is the most prettiest. (Incorrect)
> She is the prettiest. (Correct)
> She is the most pretty. (Correct)

PRACTICE PROBLEMS IN PRONOUN AND ADJECTIVE USAGE

Museums collect quilts not only because of their beauty, but also

because of its history. When I see a quilt, I imagine it's history. In the bits and
$\overline{1}$ $\overline{2}$

blocks, the fabrics, and the even and not so even stitches, I hear the story of

a circle of friends. They talk as they stitch about their days and disappoint-

ments, their children and husbands, and <u>the dreams you dare</u> to dream. The
3

<u>quilt tells me their most deepest secrets.</u>
4

Once <u>my friends and myself</u> made a quilt for a friend's baby. The quilt
5

preserved memories for everyone, even for the <u>mother who we made the</u>
6

quilt for. Even now, when I see the quilt, I hear our voices and remember the
6

history of this <u>brief moment in their lives.</u>
7

1. (A) NO CHANGE
   (B) because of it's history
   (C) because of their history
   (D) because of there history

2. (F) NO CHANGE
   (G) I imagine its history
   (H) we imagine it's history
   (J) you imagine it's history

3. (A) NO CHANGE
   (B) the dreams I dare
   (C) the dreams we dare
   (D) the dreams they dare

4. (F) NO CHANGE
   (G) tells myself their most deepest secrets
   (H) tells me their deepest secrets
   (J) tells me they're most deepest secrets

5. (A) NO CHANGE
   (B) my friends and I made
   (C) my friends and me made
   (D) my friends and us made

6. (F) NO CHANGE
   (G) mother for who we made the quilt.
   (H) mother to who we made the quilt for.
   (J) mother for whom we made the quilt.

7. (A) NO CHANGE
   (B) brief moment in your life
   (C) brief moment in our lives
   (D) brief, moment in their lives

NOW CHECK YOUR ANSWERS

Answers for Practice Problems in Plurals and Possessives

1. **The correct answer is (B).** The word *quarters* should be plural, but not possessive.

2. **The correct answer is (J).** The singular *Earth* is made possessive by adding *'s*.

3. **The correct answer is (A).** In this construction, the possessive is needed to show ownership.

4. **The correct answer is (H).** To make plural a noun ending in *y*, drop the *y* and add *-ies*.

5. **The correct answer is (D).** *Public* is a singular noun made possessive by adding *'s*.

Answers for Practice Problems in Pronoun and Adjective Usage

1. **The correct answer is (C).** To be consistent with the phrase *their beauty*, the possessive plural pronoun *their* is needed.

2. **The correct answer is (G).** The contraction *it's* means *it is* and is not a pronoun. The possessive pronoun *its* is correct. Remember, there are no apostrophes in possessive pronouns.

3. **The correct answer is (D).** To be consistent with the rest of the sentence, the plural pronoun *they* is needed.

4. **The correct answer is (H).** The *-est* ending is used to form the superlative form of the adjective *deep*. The use of *most* is incorrect. Do not show degree of comparison using two forms at once.

5. **The correct answer is (B).** Use a nominative pronoun as the subject of a clause or sentence.

6. **The correct answer is (J).** *For whom* is a prepositional phrase, which requires an objective case pronoun.

7. **The correct answer is (C).** The possessive pronoun *our* agrees with the voice of the second paragraph.

MATHEMATICS REVIEW

SIGNED NUMBERS

The set of *integers* is the set of all *signed* whole numbers and zero. It is the set {..., −4, −3, −2, −1, 0, 1, 2, 3, 4, ...}.

The first three dots symbolize the fact that the negative integers go on indefinitely, just as the positive integers do. Integers preceded by a minus sign (called *negative integers*) appear to the left of 0 on a number line.

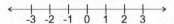

Decimals, fractions, and mixed numbers can also have negative signs. Together with positive fractions and decimals, they appear on the number line in this fashion:

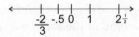

All numbers to the right of 0 are called *positive numbers.* They have the sign +, whether it is actually written or not. Business gains or losses, feet above or below sea level, and temperature above and below zero can all be expressed by means of signed numbers.

Addition

If the numbers to be added have the same sign, add the numbers (integers, fractions, decimals) as usual and use their common sign in the answer:

$$+9 + (+8) + (+2) = +19 \text{ or } 19$$
$$-4 + (-11) + (-7) + (-1) = -23$$

If the numbers to be added have different signs, add the positive numbers and then the negative numbers. Ignore the signs and subtract the smaller total from the larger total. If the larger total is positive, the answer will be positive; if the larger total is negative, the answer will be negative. The answer may be zero.

Example

$$+3 + (-5) + (-8) + (+2) = ?$$
$$+3 + (+2) = +5$$
$$-5 + (-8) = -13$$
$$13 - 5 = 8$$

Since the larger total (13) has a negative sign, the answer is -8.

Subtraction

The second number in a subtraction problem is called the *subtrahend*. In order to subtract, change the sign of the subtrahend and then continue as if you were *adding* signed numbers. If there is no sign in front of the subtrahend, it is assumed to be positive.

Examples

Subtract the subtrahend (bottom number) from the top number.

15	5	-35	-35	42
5	15	-42	42	35
10	-10	7	-77	7

Multiplication

If two and only two signed numbers are to be multiplied, multiply the numbers as you would if they were not signed. Then, if the two numbers have the *same sign,* the product is *positive.* If the two numbers have *different signs,* the product is *negative.* If more than two numbers are being multiplied, proceed two at a time in the same way as before, finding the signed product of the first two numbers, then multiplying that product by the next number, and so on. The product has a positive sign if all the factors are positive or there is an even number of negative factors. The product has a negative sign if there is an odd number of negative factors.

Example

$$-3 \cdot (+5) \cdot (-11) \cdot (-2) = -330$$

The answer is negative because there is an odd number (three) of negative factors.

The product of a signed number and zero is zero. The product of a signed number and 1 is the original number. The product of a signed number and -1 is the original number with its sign changed.

Examples

$$-5 \times 0 = 0$$
$$-5 \times 1 = -5$$
$$-5 \times (-1) = +5$$

Division

If the divisor and the dividend have the same sign, the answer is positive. Divide the numbers as you normally would. If the divisor and the dividend have different signs, the answer is negative. Divide the numbers as you normally would.

Examples

$$-3 \div (-2) = \frac{3}{2} = 1\frac{1}{2}$$

$$8 \div (-.2) = -40$$

If zero is divided by a signed number, the answer is zero. If a signed number is divided by zero, the answer does not exist. If a signed number is divided by 1, the number remains the same. If a signed number is divided by -1, the quotient is the original number with its sign changed.

Examples

$$0 \div (-2) = 0$$

$$-\frac{4}{3} \div 0 \quad \text{not defined}$$

$$\frac{2}{3} \div 1 = \frac{2}{3}$$

$$4 \div -1 = -4$$

Signed Numbers Problems

Perform the indicated operations:

1. $+7 + (-2) + (-8) + (+3)$

2. $-3 - (-7) - (+4) + (-2)$

3. $-6 \times (+2) \times (-1) \times (-7)$

4. $\dfrac{+12 \times (-2)}{-4}$

EXPONENTS

The product $10 \cdot 10 \cdot 10$ can be written 10^3. We say 10 is raised to the *third power*. In general, $a \times a \times a \dots a$ n times is written a^n. The *base* a is raised to the nth power, and n is called the *exponent*.

Examples

$3^2 = 3 \cdot 3$ read "3 squared"

$2^3 = 2 \cdot 2 \cdot 2$ read "2 cubed"

$5^4 = 5 \cdot 5 \cdot 5 \cdot 5$ read "5 to the fourth power"

If the exponent is 1, it is usually understood and not written; thus, $a^1 = a$.

Since

$$a^2 = a \times a \qquad \text{and} \qquad a^3 = a \times a \times a$$

then

$$a^2 \times a^3 = (a \times a)(a \times a \times a) = a^5$$

There are three rules for exponents. In general, if k, m, and n are any counting numbers or zero, and a and b are any number,

Rule 1: $a^k \times a^m = a^{k+m}$

Rule 2: $a^m \times b^m = (ab)^m$

Rule 3: $(a^k)^n = a^{kn}$

Examples

Rule 1: $2^2 \cdot 2^3 = 4 \times 8 = 32$
and $2^2 \times 2^3 = 2^5 = 32$

Rule 2: $3^2 \times 4^2 = 9 \times 16 = 144$
and $3^2 \times 4^2 = (3 \times 4)^2 = 12^2 = 144$

Rule 3: $(3^2)^3 = 9^3 = 729$
and $(3^2)^3 = 3^6 = 729$

ROOTS

The definition of roots is based on exponents. If $a^n = c$, where a is the base and n the exponent, a is called the nth *root* of c. This is written $a = \sqrt[n]{c}$. The symbol $\sqrt{\ }$ is called a *radical sign*. Since $5^4 = 625$, $\sqrt[4]{625} = 5$, and 5 is the fourth root of 625. The most frequently used roots are the second (called the square) root and the third (called the cube) root. The square root is written $\sqrt{\ }$ and the cube root is written $\sqrt[3]{\ }$.

Square Roots

If c is a positive number, there are two values, one negative and one positive, which when multiplied together will produce c.

Example

$+4 \cdot (+4) = 16 \quad \text{and} \quad -4 \cdot (-4) = 16$

The positive square root of a positive number c is called the *principal* square root of c (briefly, the *square root* of c) and is denoted by $\sqrt{c}$:

$$\sqrt{144} = 12$$

If $c = 0$, there is only one square root, 0. If c is a negative number, there is no real number that is the square root of c:

$\sqrt{-4}$ is not a real number

Cube Roots

Both positive and negative numbers have real cube roots. The cube root of 0 is 0. The cube root of a positive number is positive; that of a negative number is negative.

Examples

$2 \cdot 2 \cdot 2 = 8$ Therefore $\sqrt[3]{8} = 2$

$-3 \cdot (-3) \cdot (-3) = -27$ Therefore $\sqrt[3]{-27} = -3$

Each number has only one real cube root.

FRACTIONAL EXPONENTS

The values of k, m, and n from the three exponent rules can be expanded to include positive and negative fractions. In particular, roots can be expressed as fractional exponents. In Rule 3, $(a^k)^n = a^{kn}$. Let $k = \dfrac{1}{n}$. Then $(a^{\frac{1}{n}})^n = a^1 = a$ and $a^{\frac{1}{n}}$ is the nth root of a. Rule 2, $a^m \times b^m = (a \times b)^m$, which is true when a and b are any numbers and m is an integer, can be extended to include the case in which the exponent is a fraction. Suppose $m = \dfrac{1}{k}$. Then:

$$a^{\frac{1}{k}} \times b^{\frac{1}{k}} = (a \times b)^{\frac{1}{k}}$$

$$\text{or } \sqrt[k]{a \times b} = \sqrt[k]{a} \times \sqrt[k]{b}$$

This last formulation justifies the simplification of square roots. If the number under the radical sign is a square number, the process will terminate in a number without the radical sign. If the number is not square, the process should terminate when the number remaining under the radical sign no longer contains a square.

Example

Simplify $\sqrt{98}$

$\sqrt{98} = \sqrt{2 \times 49}$

$\quad = \sqrt{2} \times \sqrt{49}$ where 49 is a square number

$$= \sqrt{2 \times 7}$$

Therefore, $\sqrt{98} = 7\sqrt{2}$ and the process terminates because there is no whole number whose square is 2. $7\sqrt{2}$ is called a radical expression or simply a *radical*.

Note: Numbers such as $\sqrt{2}$ and $\sqrt{3}$ are called *irrational* numbers to distinguish them from *rational* numbers, which include the integers and the fractions. Irrational numbers also have places on the number line. They may have positive or negative signs. The combination of rational and irrational numbers, all the numbers we have used so far, make up the *real* numbers. Arithmetic, algebra, and geometry deal with real numbers. The number π, the ratio of the circumference of a circle to its diameter, is also a real number; it is irrational, although it is approximated by 3.14159. . . . Instructions for taking the ACT say that the numbers used are real numbers. This means that answers may be expressed as fractions, decimals, radicals, or integers, whatever is required.

Radicals can be added and subtracted only if they have the same number under the radical sign. Otherwise, they must be reduced to expressions having the same number under the radical sign.

Example

Add $2\sqrt{18} + 4\sqrt{8} - \sqrt{2}$.

$\sqrt{18} = \sqrt{9 \times 2} = \sqrt{9} \times \sqrt{2} = 3\sqrt{2}$

therefore $2\sqrt{18} = 2(3\sqrt{2}) = 6\sqrt{2}$

and $\sqrt{8} = \sqrt{4 \times 2} = \sqrt{4} \times \sqrt{2} = 2\sqrt{2}$

therefore $4\sqrt{8} = 4(2\sqrt{2}) = 8\sqrt{2}$

giving $2\sqrt{18} + 4\sqrt{8} - \sqrt{2} = 6\sqrt{2} + 8\sqrt{2} - \sqrt{2} = 13\sqrt{2}$

Radicals are multiplied using the rule that

$$\sqrt[k]{a \times b} = \sqrt[k]{a} \times \sqrt[k]{b}$$

Example

$$\sqrt{2}\left(\sqrt{2} - 5\sqrt{3}\right) = \sqrt{4} - 5\sqrt{6} = 2 - 5\sqrt{6}$$

A quotient rule for radicals similar to the product rule is:

$$\sqrt[k]{\frac{a}{b}} = \frac{\sqrt[k]{a}}{\sqrt[k]{b}}$$

Example

$$\sqrt{\frac{9}{4}} = \frac{\sqrt{9}}{\sqrt{4}} = \frac{3}{2}$$

Exponents and Roots Problems

1. Simplify $\sqrt{192}$

2. Find the sum of $\sqrt{45} + \sqrt{125}$

3. Combine $\sqrt{12} - 6\sqrt{3} + 2\sqrt{48}$

4. Simplify $(3\sqrt{32})(7\sqrt{2})$

5. Simplify $\dfrac{20\sqrt{96}}{5\sqrt{4}}$

6. Evaluate $-3^2 + (3^2)^3$

NOW CHECK YOUR ANSWERS

Answers to Signed Numbers Problems

1. $+7 + (-2) = +7 - 2 = +5$
$+5 + (-8) = +5 - 8 = -3$
$-3 + (+3) = 0$

2. $-3 - (-7) = -3 + 7 = +4$
$+4 - (+4) = +4 - 4 = 0$
$0 + (-2) = -2$

3. $-6 \times (+2) = -12$
$-12 \times (-1) = +12$
$+12 \times (-7) = -84$

4. $+12 \times -2 = -24$
$$\frac{-24}{-4} = +6$$

Answers to Exponents and Roots Problems

1. $\sqrt{192} = \sqrt{2 \times 2 \times 2 \times 2 \times 2 \times 2 \times 3} = 8\sqrt{3}$

2. $\sqrt{45} + \sqrt{125} = 3\sqrt{5} + 5\sqrt{5} = 8\sqrt{5}$

3. $\sqrt{12} - 6\sqrt{3} + 2\sqrt{48} = 2\sqrt{3} - 6\sqrt{3} + 8\sqrt{3} = 4\sqrt{3}$

4. $(3\sqrt{32})(7\sqrt{2}) = 21(\sqrt{64}) = 21(8) = 168$

5. $\dfrac{20\sqrt{96}}{5\sqrt{4}} = \left(\dfrac{20}{5}\right)\left(\sqrt{\dfrac{96}{4}}\right) = 4\sqrt{24} = 8\sqrt{6}$

6. $-3^2 + (3^2)^3 = -9 + 3^6 = -9 + 729 = 720$

ENGLISH GRAMMAR REVIEW

VERBS

A verb either denotes action or a state of being. There are four major types of verbs: transitive, intransitive, linking, and auxiliary.

(1) Transitive verbs are action words that must take a direct object. The direct object, which receives the action of the verb, is in the objective case.

> Joe *hit* the ball. (*Ball* is the direct object of *hit*.)
>
> Joe *killed* Bill. (*Bill* is the direct object of *killed*.)

(2) Intransitive verbs denote action but do not take a direct object.

> The glass *broke*.
>
> The boy *fell*.

Important for Exam

Set, lay, and *raise* are always transitive and take an object. *Sit, lie*, and *rise* are always intransitive and do not take a direct object.

> *Set* the book down, *lay* the pencil down, and *raise* your hands. (*Book, pencil*, and *hands* are direct objects of *set, lay*, and *raise*.)
>
> *Sit* in the chair.
>
> She *lies* in bed all day.
>
> The sun also *rises*.

The same verb can be transitive or intransitive, depending on the sentence.

> The pitcher *threw* wildly. (Intransitive)
>
> The pitcher *threw* the ball wildly. (Transitive)

(3) Linking verbs have no action. They denote a state of being. Linking verbs mean "equal." Here are some examples: *is, are, was, were, be, been, am* (any form of the verb *to be*), *smell, taste, feel, look, seem, become, appear*.

Sometimes, these verbs are confusing because they can be linking verbs in one sentence and action verbs in another. You can tell if the verb is a linking verb if it means equal in the sentence.

> He felt nervous. (*He* equals *nervous*.)
>
> He felt nervously for the door bell. (*He* does not equal *door bell*.)

Linking verbs take a predicate nominative or predicate adjective. (See sections on nouns, pronouns, and adjectives.)

> It *is I.*
> It *is she.*

(4) Auxiliary verbs are sometimes called "helping" verbs. These verbs are used with an infinitive verb (*to* plus the verb) or a participle to form a verb phrase.

The common auxiliary verbs are:

> All forms of *to be, to have, to do, to keep.*
>
> The verbs *can, may, must, ought to, shall, will, would, should.*
>
> > He *has to go.* (Auxiliary *has* plus the infinitive *to go*)
> >
> > He *was going.* (Auxiliary *was* plus the present participle *going*)
> >
> > He *has gone.* (Auxiliary *has* plus the past participle *gone*)

There is no such form as *had ought.* Use *ought to have* or *should have.*

> He *ought to have gone.*
>
> He *should have gone.*

Every verb can change its form according to five categories. Each category adds meaning to the verb. The five categories are: *tense, mood, voice, number,* and *person.*

Tense: This indicates the *time,* or *when* the verb occurs. There are six tenses. They are:

present	past	future
present perfect	past perfect	future perfect

Three principal parts of the verb—the present, the past, and the past participle—are used to form all the tenses.

The *present tense* shows that the action is taking place in the present.

> The dog *sees* the car and *jumps* out of the way.

The present tense of a regular verb looks like this:

	SINGULAR	PLURAL
First person	I jump	We jump
Second person	You jump	You jump
Third person	He, she, it jumps	They jump

Notice that an *s* is added to the third-person singular.

The *past tense* shows that the action took place in the past.

The dog *saw* the car and *jumped* out of the way.

The past tense of a regular verb looks like this:

	SINGULAR	PLURAL
First person	I jumped	We jumped
Second person	You jumped	You jumped
Third person	He, she, it jumped	They jumped

Notice that *ed* is added to the verb. Sometimes just *d* is added, as in the verb *used*, for example. In regular verbs the past participle has the same form as the past tense, but it is used with an auxiliary verb.

The dog *had jumped*.

The *future tense* shows that the action is going to take place in the future. The future tense needs the auxiliary verbs *will* or *shall*.

The dog *will see* the car and *will jump* out of the way.

The future tense of a regular verb looks like this:

	SINGULAR	PLURAL
First person	I shall jump	We shall jump
Second person	You will jump	You will jump
Third person	He, she, it will jump	They will jump

Notice that *shall* is used in the first person of the future tense.

To form the *three perfect tenses,* the verb *to have* and the past participle are used.

- The present tense of *to have* is used to form the *present perfect*.

  The dog *has seen* the car and *has jumped* out of the way.

- The present perfect tense shows that the action has started in the past and is continuing or has just been implemented in the present.

- The past tense of *to have* is used to form the *past perfect*.

  The dog *had seen* the car and *jumped* out of the way.

- The past perfect tense shows that the action had been completed in the past.

- The future tense of *to have* is used to form the *future perfect*.

  The dog *will have seen* the car and *will have jumped* out of the way.

- The future perfect tense shows that an action will have been completed before a definite time in the future.

Following is a table that shows the present, past, and future tenses of *to have*.

PRESENT TENSE		
	SINGULAR	PLURAL
First person	I have	We have
Second person	You have	You have
Third person	He, she, it has	They have

PAST TENSE		
	SINGULAR	PLURAL
First person	I had	We had
Second person	You had	You had
Third person	He, she, it had	They had

FUTURE TENSE		
	SINGULAR	PLURAL
First person	I shall have	We shall have
Second person	You will have	You shall have
Third person	He, she, it will have	They shall have

The perfect tenses all use the past participle. Therefore, you must know the past participle of all the verbs. As we said, the past participle usually is formed by adding *d* or *-ed* to the verb. However, there are many irregular verbs. Following is a table of the principal parts of some irregular verbs.

PRESENT	PAST	PAST PARTICIPLE
arise	arose	arisen
be	was	been
become	became	become
begin	began	begun
bind	bound	bound

PRESENT	PAST	PAST PARTICIPLE
bite	bit	bitten
bleed	bled	bled
blow	blew	blown
break	broke	broken
bring	brought	brought
build	built	built
burn	burned	burned, burnt
buy	bought	bought
catch	caught	caught
choose	chose	chosen
come	came	come
cost	cost	cost
dive	dived, dove	dived
do	did	done
draw	drew	drawn
drink	drank	drunk
drive	drove	driven
eat	ate	eaten
fall	fell	fallen
fight	fought	fought
fly	flew	flown
forget	forgot	forgotten, forgot
freeze	froze	frozen
get	got	gotten, got
give	gave	given
go	went	gone
grow	grew	grown
hide	hid	hidden
hold	held	held
know	knew	known
lay	laid	laid
lead	led	led
lie (recline)	lay	lain
lie (untruth)	lied	lied
light	lit	lit
pay	paid	paid
raise (take up)	raised	raised
read	read	read
ride	rode	ridden

PRESENT	PAST	PAST PARTICIPLE
ring	rang	rung
rise (go up)	rose	risen
run	ran	run
say	said	said
see	saw	seen
shake	shook	shaken
shine (light)	shone	shone
show	showed	shown, showed
shrink	shrank	shrunk, shrunken
sing	sang	sung
sit	sat	sat
speak	spoke	spoken
spend	spent	spent
spring	sprang	sprung
stand	stood	stood
steal	stole	stolen
swear	swore	sworn
swim	swam	swum
take	took	taken
teach	taught	taught
tear	tore	torn
throw	threw	thrown
wear	wore	worn
weave	wove, weaved	woven, weaved
weep	wept	wept
win	won	won
write	wrote	written

Another aspect of tense that appears on the test is the *correct sequence* or *order of tenses. Be sure if you change tense you know why you are doing so. These rules will help you.*

- The present participle (verb + *ing*) is used when its action occurs at the same time as the action of the main verb.

  John, *answering* the bell, *knocked* over the plant. (*Answering* and *knocked* occur at the same time.)

- The past participle is used when its action occurs before the main verb.

  The elves, *dressed* in costumes, will *march* proudly to the shoe-maker. (The elves dressed *before* they will march.)

Mood

The mood or mode of a verb shows the manner of the action. There are three moods.

1. The *indicative mood* shows the sentence is factual. Most of what we say is in the indicative mode.

2. The *subjunctive mood* is used for conditions contrary to fact or for strong desires. The use of the subjunctive mood for the verb *to be* is a test item.

    Following is the conjugation (list of forms) of the verb *to be* in the subjunctive mood:

PRESENT TENSE

	SINGULAR	PLURAL
First person	I be	We be
Second person	You be	You be
Third person	He, she, it be	They be

PAST TENSE

	SINGULAR	PLURAL
First person	I were	We were
Second person	You were	You were
Third person	He, she, it were	They were

If I *be* wrong, then punish me.

If he *were* king, he would pardon me.

Also, *shall* and *should* are used for the subjunctive mood.
If he *shall* fail, he will cry.
If you *should* win, don't forget us.

3. The *imperative mood* is used for commands.

    Go at once!

    If strong feelings are expressed, the command ends with an exclamation point. In commands, the subject *you* is not stated but is understood.

Voice

There are two voices of verbs. The active voice shows that the subject is acting upon something or doing something *to* something else. The active voice has a direct object.

> subject   object
> The *car* hit the *boy*.

The passive voice shows that the subject is acted upon *by* something. Something was done *to* the subject. The direct object becomes the subject. The verb *to be* plus the past participle is used in the passive voice.

> subject
> The *boy* was hit by the car.

Within a sentence or paragraph, the voice should be consistent.

Number

This, as before, means singular or plural. A verb must agree with its subject in number.

> The *list was* long. (Singular)
> The *lists were* long. (Plural)

Nouns appearing between subject and verb do not change subject/verb agreement.

> The *list* of chores *was* long. (Singular)
> The *lists* of chores *were* long. (Plural)

Subjects joined by *and* are singular if the subject is one person or unit.

> My *friend and colleague has* decided to leave. (Singular)
> *Five and five is* ten. (Singular)
> *Tea and milk is* my favorite drink. (Singular)

Singular subjects joined by *or, either-or,* and *neither-nor* take singular verbs.

> Either Alvin or Lynette *goes* to the movies.

If one subject is singular and one is plural, the verb agrees with the nearer subject.

> Either Alvin or the girls *go* to the movies.

The use of the expletive pronouns *there* and *it* do not change subject/verb agreement.

> There *is no one* here.
> There *are snakes* in the grass.

> Think: No one is there; snakes are in the grass.

A relative pronoun takes a verb that agrees in number with the pronoun's antecedent.

It is the *electrician who suggests* new wiring. (Singular)
It is the *electricians who suggest* new wiring. (Plural)

Singular indefinite pronouns take singular verbs.

Everybody *buys* tickets.

It is hard to tell if some nouns are singular. Following is a list of tricky nouns that take singular verbs.

Collective nouns—*army, class, committee, team*

Singular nouns in plural form—*news, economics, mathematics, measles, mumps, news, politics*

Titles, although plural in form, refer to a single work—*The New York Times*, Henry James's *The Ambassadors*.

The *army is* coming.
News travels fast.
Jaws is a good movie.

Don't (do not) is incorrect for third-person singular. *Doesn't (does not)* is correct.

He *doesn't* agree.

PRACTICE PROBLEMS IN VERB USAGE

According to a recent study, female soccer players is twice as likely to
_____
                                1
be injured as their male counterparts. Female basketball players report injury
_____
   1
rates four times higher than males. Why was there a difference? Some theories
                                     _____   _____
                                             2   3
suggests extrinsic factors such as body movement, muscle strength, and
_____
   3
coordination. Others points to the physiological differences between males
              _____
                    4
and females. Overall, girls will have greater flexibility and ligament laxity than
                      _____
                                      5
boys, which some researchers suggest contribute to greater occurrences of
      _____
                            6
sprains and other injuries to joints.

1. (A) NO CHANGE
   (B) female soccer players had been twice as likely to be injured
   (C) female soccer players was twice as likely to be injured
   (D) female soccer players are twice as likely to be injured

2. (F) NO CHANGE
   (G) Why is there a difference?
   (H) Why are there a difference?
   (J) Why were there a difference?

3. (A) NO CHANGE
   (B) Some theorys suggests
   (C) Some theories will suggest
   (D) Some theories suggest

4. (F) NO CHANGE
   (G) Other points
   (H) Others point
   (J) Others pointed

5. (A) NO CHANGE
   (B) girls have greater flexibility
   (C) girls have had greater flexibility
   (D) girls has greater flexibility

6. (F) NO CHANGE
   (G) which some researchers suggests contribute to
   (H) which some researchers suggest contributes to
   (J) which some researchers suggested contribute to

NOW CHECK YOUR ANSWERS

Answers to Practice Problems in Verb Usage

1. **The correct answer is (D).** The plural subject *players* requires a plural verb form. The use of had been is not consistent with use of the word *recent,* which suggests present tense.

2. **The correct answer is (G).** The tense of the passage is present tense. A singular verb is needed to agree with the singular subject difference.

3. **The correct answer is (D).** The plural verb *suggest* agrees with the plural subject *theories.*

4. **The correct answer is (H).** The plural verb *point* agrees with the plural subject *others.*

5. **The correct answer is (B).** The best choice is B because it continues the tense of the passage.

6. **The correct answer is (H).** *Contributes* agrees in number with *which.* In this sentence *which* refers to the singular fact stated in the beginning clause of the sentence.

MATHEMATICS REVIEW

ALGEBRA

Algebra is a generalization of arithmetic. It provides methods for solving problems that cannot be done by arithmetic alone or that can be done by arithmetic only after long computations. Expressions such as wl and $2(w + l)$ are called *algebraic expressions*. An *equation* is a statement that two algebraic expressions are equal. A *formula* is a special type of equation.

Evaluating Formulas

If we are given an expression and numerical values to be assigned to each letter, the expression can be evaluated.

Example

Evaluate $2x + 3y - 7$ if $x = 2$ and $y = -4$.

Substitute given values.

$2(2) + 3(-4) - 7 = ?$

Multiply numbers using rules for signed numbers.

$4 + -12 - 7 = ?$

Combine numbers.

$4 - 19 = -15$

We have already evaluated formulas in arithmetic when solving percent, discount, and interest problems.

Example

The formula for temperature conversion is:

$$F = \frac{9}{5}C + 32$$

where C stands for the temperature in degrees Celsius and F for degrees Fahrenheit. Find the Fahrenheit temperature that is equivalent to 20°C.

$$F = \frac{9}{5}(20°C) + 32 = 36 + 32 = 68°F$$

Algebraic Expressions

Formulation

A more difficult problem than evaluating an expression or formula is to translate from a verbal expression to an algebraic one:

Verbal	Algebraic
Thirteen more than x	$x + 13$
Six less than twice x	$2x - 6$
The square of the sum of x and 5	$(x + 5)^2$
The sum of the square of x and the square of 5	$x^2 + 5^2$
The distance traveled by a car going	
50 miles an hour for x hours	$50x$
The average of 70, 80, 85, and x	$\dfrac{70 + 80 + 85 + x}{4}$

Simplification

After algebraic expressions have been formulated, they can usually be simplified by means of the laws of exponents and the common operations of addition, subtraction, multiplication, and division. Algebraic expressions and equations frequently contain parentheses, which are removed in the process of simplifying. If an expression contains more than one set of parentheses, remove the inner set first and then the outer set. Parentheses are used to indicate multiplication. Thus, $3(x + y)$ means that 3 is to be multiplied by the sum of x and y. The *distributive law* is used to accomplish this:

$a(b + c) = ab + ac$

The expression in front of the parentheses is multiplied by each term inside. Rules for signed numbers apply.

If there is a (+) before the parentheses, the signs of the terms inside the parentheses remain the same when the parentheses are removed. If there is a (−) before the parentheses, the sign of each term inside the parentheses changes when the parentheses are removed.

Once parentheses have been removed, the order of operations is multiplication and division, then addition and subtraction from left to right.

Example

$(-15 + 17) \cdot 3 - [(4 \cdot 9) \div 6] = ?$

Work inside the parentheses first:

$(2) \cdot 3 - [36 \div 6] = ?$

Then work inside the brackets:

$2 \cdot 3 - [6] = ?$

Multiply first, then subtract, proceeding from left to right:

$6 - 6 = 0$

Operations

When letter symbols and numbers are combined with the operations of arithmetic ($+$, $-$, $\cdot$, $\div$) and with certain other mathematical operations, we have an *algebraic expression*. Algebraic expressions are made up of several parts connected by a plus or a minus sign; each part is called a *term*. Terms with the same letter part are called *like terms*. Since algebraic expressions represent numbers, they can be added, subtracted, multiplied, and divided.

When we defined the commutative law of addition in arithmetic by writing $a + b = b + a$, we meant that a and b could represent any number. The expression $a + b = b + a$ is an *identity* because it is true for all numbers. The expression $n + 5 = 14$ is not an identity because it is not true for all numbers; it becomes true only when the number 9 is substituted for n. Letters used to represent numbers are called *variables*. If a number stands alone (the 5 or 14 in $n + 5 = 14$), it is called a *constant* because its value is constant or unchanging. If a number appears in front of a variable, it is called a *coefficient*. Because the letter x is frequently used to represent a variable, or *unknown*, the times sign $\times$, which can be confused with it in handwriting, is rarely used to express multiplication in algebra. Other expressions used for multiplication are a dot, parentheses, or simply writing a number and letter together:

$5 \cdot 4$ or $5(4)$ or $5a$

Of course, 54 still means fifty-four.

Addition and Subtraction

Only like terms can be combined. Add or subtract the coefficients of like terms, using the rules for signed numbers.

Example

Add $x + 2y - 2x + 3y$.

$x - 2x + 2y + 3y = -x + 5y$

Example

Perform the subtraction:

$$-30a - 15b + 4c$$
$$- (-5a + 3b - c + d)$$

Change the sign of each term in the subtrahend and then add, using the rules for signed numbers:

$$
\begin{array}{r}
-30a - 15b + 4c \\
5a - 3b + c - d \\
\hline
-25a - 18b + 5c - d
\end{array}
$$

Multiplication

Multiplication is accomplished by using the *distributive property*. If the multiplier has only one term, then

$$a(b + c) = ab + ac$$

Example

$$9x(5m + 9q) = (9x)(5m) + (9x)(9q)$$
$$= 45mx + 81qx$$

When the multiplier contains more than one term and you are multiplying two expressions, multiply each term of the first expression by each term of the second and then add like terms. Follow the rules for signed numbers and exponents at all times.

Example

$$(3x + 8)(4x^2 + 2x + 1)$$
$$= 3x(4x^2 + 2x + 1) + 8(4x^2 + 2x + 1)$$
$$= 12x^3 + 6x^2 + 3x + 32x^2 + 16x + 8$$
$$= 12x^3 + 38x^2 + 19x + 8$$

If more than two expressions are to be multiplied, multiply the first two, then multiply the product by the third factor, and so on, until all factors have been used.

Algebraic expressions can be multiplied by themselves (squared) or raised to any power.

Example

$$(a + b)^2 = (a + b)(a + b)$$
$$= a(a + b) + b(a + b)$$
$$= a^2 + ab + ba + b^2$$
$$= a^2 + 2ab + b^2$$

since $ab = ba$ by the commutative law

Example

$$(a + b)(a - b) = a(a - b) + b(a - b)$$
$$= a^2 - ab + ba - b^2$$
$$= a^2 - b^2$$

Factoring

When two or more algebraic expressions are multiplied, each is called a factor and the result is the *product*. The reverse process of finding the factors when given the product is called *factoring*. A product can often be factored in more than one way. Factoring is useful in multiplication, division, and solving equations.

One way to factor an expression is to remove any single-term factor that is common to each of the terms and write it outside the parentheses. It is the distributive law that permits this.

Example

$$3x^3 + 6x^2 + 9x = 3x(x^2 + 2x + 3)$$

The result can be checked by multiplication.

Expressions containing squares can sometimes be factored into expressions containing letters raised to the first power only, called *linear factors.* We have seen that

$$(a + b)(a - b) = a^2 - b^2$$

Therefore, if we have an expression in the form of a difference of two squares, it can be factored as:

$$a^2 - b^2 = (a + b)(a - b)$$

Example

Factor $4x^2 - 9$.

$$4x^2 - 9 = (2x)^2 - (3)^2 = (2x + 3)(2x - 3)$$

Again, the result can be checked by multiplication.

A third type of expression that can be factored is one containing three terms, such as $x^2 + 5x + 6$. Since

$$
\begin{aligned}
(x + a)(x + b) &= x(x + b) + a(x + b) \\
&= x^2 + xb + ax + ab \\
&= x^2 + (a + b)x + ab
\end{aligned}
$$

an expression in the form $x^2 + (a + b)x + ab$ can be factored into two factors of the form $(x + a)$ and $(x + b)$. We must find two numbers whose product is the constant in the given expression and whose sum is the coefficient of the term containing x.

Example

Find factors of $x^2 + 5x + 6$.

First find two numbers which, when multiplied, have $+6$ as a product. Possibilities are 2 and 3, -2 and -3, 1 and 6, and -1 and -6. From these select the one pair whose sum is 5. The pair 2 and 3 is the only possible selection, and so:

$$x^2 + 5x + 6 = (x + 2)(x + 3) \quad \text{written in either order}$$

Example

Factor $x^2 - 5x - 6$.

Possible factors of -6 are -1 and 6, 1 and -6, 2 and -3, and -2 and 3. We must select the pair whose sum is -5. The only pair whose sum is -5 is $+1$ and -6, and so

$$x^2 - 5x - 6 = (x + 1)(x - 6)$$

In factoring expressions of this type, notice that if the last sign is plus, both a and b have the same sign and it is the same as the sign of the middle term. If the last sign is minus, the numbers have opposite signs.

Many expressions cannot be factored.

Division

Write a division example as a fraction. If numerator and denominator each contain one term, divide the numbers using laws of signed numbers and use the laws of exponents to simplify the letter part of the problem.

Example

Method 1: Law of Exponents

$$\frac{36mx^2}{9m^2x} = 4m^1x^2m^{-2}x^{-1}$$

$$= 4m^{-1}x^1 = \frac{4x}{m}$$

Method 2: Cancellation

$$\frac{36mx^2}{9m^2x} = \frac{\overset{4}{\cancel{36mxx}}}{\underset{1}{\cancel{9mmx}}} = \frac{4x}{m}$$

These methods cannot be followed if there are two terms or more in the denominator since

$$\frac{a}{b + c} \neq \frac{a}{b} + \frac{a}{c}$$

In this case, write the example as a fraction. Factor the numerator and denominator if possible. Then use laws of exponents or cancel.

Example

Divide $x^3 - 9x$ by $x^3 + 6x^2 + 9x$.

Write as:

$$\frac{x^3 - 9x}{x^3 + 6x^2 + 9x}$$

Both numerator and denominator can be factored to give:

$$\frac{x(x^2 - 9)}{x(x^2 + 6x + 9)} = \frac{\cancel{x}\cancel{(x + 3)}(x - 3)}{\cancel{x}\cancel{(x + 3)}(x + 3)} = \frac{x - 3}{x + 3}$$

Algebra Problems

1. Simplify: $(5x^2 - 3x + 2) - (3x^2 + 5x - 1) + (6x^2 - 2)$

2. Multiply: $(a + 1)^2 (a + 2)$

3. Multiply: $(2x + 1)(3x^2 - x + 6)$

4. Factor completely: $12x^2 + 14x + 4$

5. Factor completely: $6x^4 - 150x^2$

6. Divide: $\dfrac{2x - 10}{x - 3} \div \dfrac{8x - 40}{x^2 - 9}$

NOW CHECK YOUR ANSWERS

Answers to Algebra Problems

1. $(5x^2 - 3x + 2) - (3x^2 + 5x - 1) + (6x^2 - 2)$
    $= 5x^2 - 3x + 2 - 3x^2 - 5x + 1 + 6x^2 - 2 = 8x^2 - 8x + 1$

2. $(a + 1)^2 (a + 2) = (a + 1)(a + 1)(a + 2) = (a^2 + 2a + 1)(a + 2)$
    $= a^3 + 2a^2 + 2a^2 + 4a + a + 2 = a^3 + 4a^2 + 5a + 2$

3. $(2x + 1)(3x^2 - x + 6) = 2x(3x^2 - x + 6) + 1(3x^2 - x + 6)$
    $= 6x^3 - 2x^2 + 12x + 3x^2 - x + 6 = 6x^3 + x^2 + 11x + 6$

4. $12x^2 + 14x + 4 = 2(6x^2 + 7x + 2) = 2(3x + 2)(2x + 1)$

5. $6x^4 - 150x^2 = 6x^2 (x^2 - 25) = 6x^2 (x - 5)(x + 5)$

6. $\dfrac{2x - 10}{x - 3} \div \dfrac{8x - 40}{x^2 - 9} = \dfrac{2x - 10}{x - 3} \times \dfrac{x^2 - 9}{8x - 40}$

    $$= \dfrac{2\overset{1}{\cancel{(x - 5)}}}{\cancel{x - 3}} \times \dfrac{\cancel{(x - 3)}(x + 3)}{8\underset{1}{\cancel{(x - 5)}}} = \dfrac{2(x + 3)}{8} = \dfrac{x + 3}{4}$$

ENGLISH GRAMMAR REVIEW

ADVERBS

An adverb describes or modifies a verb, an adjective, or another adverb. Adverbs usually answer the questions *why? where? when? how? to what degree?* Many adverbs end in *-ly*. There are two types of adverbs similar in use to the same type of adjective.

- *Interrogative adverbs* ask questions.

    Where are you going?
    When will you be home?

- *Relative adverbs* join two clauses and modify some word in the dependent clause.

    No liquor is sold *where* I live.

As with adjectives, there are three degrees of comparison for adverbs and a corresponding form for each.

1. The positive degree is often formed by adding *-ly* to the adjective.

    She was *angry*. (Adjective)
    She screamed *angrily*. (Adverb)

2. The *comparative* is formed by using *more* or *less* or adding *-er* to the positive.

3. The *superlative* is formed by using *most* or *least* or adding *-est* to the positive.

    Here are two typical adverbs:

POSITIVE DEGREE	COMPARATIVE DEGREE	SUPERLATIVE DEGREE
easily	easier, more easily, less easily	easiest, most easily, least easily
happily	happier, more happily, less happily	happiest, most happily, least happily

CONJUNCTIONS

Conjunctions connect words, phrases, or clauses. Conjunctions can connect equal parts of speech.

> and
> but
> for
> or
> so
> yet

Some conjunctions are used in pairs:

> either . . . or
> neither . . . nor
> not only . . . but also

Here are some phrases and clauses using conjunctions:

John *or* Mary (Nouns are connected.)
On the wall *and* in the window (Phrases are connected.)
Mark had gone *but* I had not. (Clauses are connected)
Either you go *or* I will. (Clauses are connected.)

If the conjunction connects two long clauses, a comma is used after the first clause.

Julio had gone to the game in the afternoon, but Pedro had not.

When other words are used to connect two clauses, a semicolon is needed.

Mike found his wallet; however, he still left the auction.

PREPOSITIONS

A preposition shows the relationship between a noun or pronoun and some other word in the sentence.

The following are all prepositions:

about	for	through
above	in	to
across	inside	under
around	into	up
behind	of	upon
beneath	off	within
during	over	without

Sometimes groups of words are treated as single prepositions. Here are some examples:

according to
ahead of
in front of
in between

The preposition together with the noun or pronoun it introduces is called a prepositional phrase.

Under the table
In front of the oil painting
Behind the glass jar
Along the waterfront
Beside the canal

Very often on the test, idiomatic expressions are given that depend upon prepositions to be correct. Following is a list of idioms showing the correct preposition to use:

Abhorrence of: He showed an *abhorrence of* violence.

Abound in (or *with*): The lake *abounded with* fish.

Accompanied by (a person): He was *accompanied by* his friend.

Accompanied with: He *accompanied* his visit *with* a house gift.

Accused by, of: He was *accused by* a person *of* a crime.

Adept in: He is *adept in* jogging.

Agree to (an offer): I *agree to* the terms of the contract.

Agree with (a person): I *agree with* my son.

Agree upon (or *on*) (a plan): I *agree upon* that approach to the problem.

Angry at (a situation): I was *angry at* the delay.

Available for (a purpose): I am *available for* tutoring.

Available to (a person): Those machines are *available to* the tenants.

Burden with: I won't *burden* you *with* my problems.

Centered on (or *in*): His efforts *centered on* winning.

Compare to (shows similarity): An orange can be *compared to* a grapefruit.

Compare with (shows difference): An orange can't be *compared with* a desk.

Conform to (or *with*): He does not *conform to* the rules.

Differ with (an opinion): I *differ with* his judgment.

Differ from (a thing): The boss's car *differs from* the worker's car.

Different from: His book is *different from* mine. (Use *different than* with a clause.)

Employed at (salary): He is *employed at* $25 a day.

Employed in (work): He is *employed in* building houses.

Envious of: She is *envious of* her sister.

Fearful of: She is *fearful of* thunder.

Free of: She will soon be *free of* her burden.

Hatred of: He has a *hatred of* violence.

Hint at: They *hinted at* a surprise.

Identical with: Your dress is *identical with* mine.

Independent of: I am *independent of* my parents.

In search of: He went in *search of* truth.

Interest in: He was not *interested in* his friends.

Jealous of: He was *jealous of* them.

Negligent of: He was *negligent of* his responsibilities.

Object to: I *object to* waiting so long.

Privilege of: He had the *privilege of* being born a millionaire.

Proficient in: You will be *proficient in* grammar.

Wait for: We will *wait for* them.

Wait on (service): The maid *waited on* them.

Like is used as a preposition. He wanted his dog to act *like* Lassie.

DAY 6

PRACTICE PROBLEMS IN ADVERB, CONJUNCTION, AND PREPOSITION USAGE

The year was 1961. It was a time <u>where athletes were still heroes, and the best team</u> in baseball wore the pinstripes of the New York Yankees.
¹

<u>Always in the public eye was the team captain Mickey Mantle whose</u> combi-
²

nation of speed and power, despite crippling injuries, made him the obvious fan favorite. Because of his speed, most fans did not realize the extent of the damage to his legs and knees, which included osteomyelitis in his left leg. Mantle finished the regular season with a career-high 54 home runs. But as great as Mickey's accomplishments were, another Yankee stepped into the limelight. Roger Maris, was less appreciated <u>by the fans but he went on to</u>
³

make baseball history. In 1961 Maris hit 61 home runs to better Babe Ruth's season high by one. <u>Maris angry endured</u> intense pressure from the fans and
⁴

<u>media that year; in fact, he was</u> sometimes booed by those who believed
⁵

Ruth's record should never be broken. Plagued by injuries, Maris was only one season away from the end of <u>his career yet in 1961, the baseball world</u>
⁶

belonged to Maris and Mantle, the M&M boys.

1. (A) NO CHANGE
   (B) where athletes were still heroes and the best team
   (C) where athletes were still heroes; and the best team
   (D) when athletes were still heroes, and the best team

2. (F) NO CHANGE
   (G) Always in the public eye, was the team captain Mickey Mantle whose
   (H) Always in the public eye was the team captain, Mickey Mantle whose
   (J) Always, in the public eye was the team captain Mickey Mantle whose

3. (A) NO CHANGE
 (B) by the fans, but he went on
 (C) by the fans, nevertheless, he went on
 (D) by the fans; but he went on

4. (F) NO CHANGE
 (G) Maris was angry endured
 (H) Maris angrily endured
 (J) Maris angrier endured

5. (A) NO CHANGE
 (B) that year, in fact, he was
 (C) that year in fact, he was
 (D) that year in fact he was

6. (F) NO CHANGE
 (G) his career yet in 1961; the baseball world
 (H) his career, yet in 1961, the baseball world
 (J) his career; yet in 1961, the baseball world

Peterson's ■ Panic Plan for
the ACT Assessment
117
www.petersons.com

NOW CHECK YOUR ANSWERS

Answers to Practice Problems in Adverb, Conjunction, and Preposition Usage

1. **The correct answer is (D).** The relative adverb *when* logically modifies the noun *time.*

2. **The correct answer is (F).** *Always in the public eye* is a modifying phrase that precedes the verb. It is part of the main clause and should not be separated from the verb *was.*

3. **The correct answer is (B).** If a conjunction connects two long independent clauses, a comma is used after the first independent clause. When two independent clauses are connected with a transitional word, such as nevertheless, the first clause is followed by a semicolon, and the transitional word is followed by a comma.

4. **The correct answer is (H).** The adverb *angrily* is needed to modify the verb *endured.* The other choices use adjectives illogically.

5. **The correct answer is (A).** *In fact* is a transitional phrase connecting two independent clauses. It must be preceded by a semicolon and followed by a comma.

6. **The correct answer is (H).** The conjunction *yet* connects two independent clauses and must be preceded by a comma.

MATHEMATICS AND ENGLISH GRAMMAR REVIEW

MATHEMATICS REVIEW

EQUATIONS

Solving equations is one of the major objectives in algebra. If a variable x in an equation is replaced by a value or expression that makes the equation a true statement, the value or expression is called a *solution* of the equation. (Remember that an equation is a mathematical statement that one algebraic expression is equal to another.)

An equation may contain one or more variables. We begin with one variable. Certain rules apply to equations whether there are one or more variables. The following rules are applied to give equivalent equations that are simpler than the original:

Addition: If $s = t$, then $s + c = t + c$.
Subtraction: If $s + c = t + c$, then $s = t$.
Multiplication: If $s = t$, then $cs = ct$.
Division: If $cs = ct$ and $c \neq 0$, then $s = t$.

Example

Solve $4x = 8$.

Write $\dfrac{4x}{4} = \dfrac{8}{4}$

$x = 2$

Example

Solve $2x - (x - 4) = 5(x + 2)$ for x.

$2x - (x - 4) = 5(x + 2)$	
$2x - x + 4 = 5x + 10$	Remove parentheses by distributive law.
$x + 4 = 5x + 10$	Combine like terms.
$x = 5x + 6$	Subtract 4 from each side.
$-4x = 6$	Subtract $5x$ from each side.
$x = \dfrac{6}{-4}$	Divide each side by -4.
$= -\dfrac{3}{2}$	Reduce fraction to lowest terms.

Negative sign now applies to the entire fraction.

Check the solution for accuracy by substituting in the original equation:

$$2\left(-\frac{3}{2}\right) - \left(-\frac{3}{2} - 4\right) \overset{?}{=} 5\left(-\frac{3}{2} + 2\right)$$

$$-3 - \left(-\frac{11}{2}\right) \overset{?}{=} 5\left(\frac{1}{2}\right)$$

$$-3 + \frac{11}{2} \overset{?}{=} \frac{5}{2}$$

$$-\frac{6}{2} + \frac{11}{2} \overset{?}{=} \frac{5}{2} \quad \text{check}$$

Equation Problems

Solve the following equations for x:

1. $-5x + 3 = x + 2$

2. $x + 3(2x + 5) = -20$

3. $4(x + 2) - (2x + 1) = x + 5$

4. $3(2x + 5) = 10x + 7 + 2(x - 8)$

Word Problems Involving One Unknown

In many cases, if you read a word problem carefully, assign a letter to the quantity to be found, and understand the relationships between known and unknown quantities, you can formulate an equation in one unknown.

Number Problems

In a number problem, the relationship between numbers is given. Often, a total is given. Age problems are similar to number problems.

Example

One number is 3 times another, and their sum is 48. Find the two numbers.

Let x = second number. Then the first is $3x$. Since their sum is 48,

$$3x + x = 48$$
$$4x = 48$$
$$x = 12$$

Therefore, the first number is $3x = 36$.

$36 + 12 = 48$ check

Distance Problems

The basic concept is:

Distance = rate · time

Example

In a mileage test, a man drives a truck at a fixed rate of speed for 1 hour. Then he increases the speed by 20 miles per hour and drives at that rate for 2 hours. He then reduces that speed by 5 miles per hour and drives at that rate for 3 hours. If the distance traveled was 295 miles, what are the rates of speed over each part of the test?

Let x be the first speed, $x + 20$ the second, and $x + (20 - 5) = x + 15$ the third. Because distance = rate · time, multiply these rates by the time and formulate the equation by separating the two equal expressions for distance by an equal sign:

$$1x + 2(x + 20) + 3(x + 15) = 295$$
$$x + 2x + 3x + 40 + 45 = 295$$
$$6x = 210$$
$$x = 35$$

The speeds are 35, 55, and 50 miles per hour.

Consecutive Number Problems

This type usually involves only one unknown. Two numbers are consecutive if one is the successor of the other. Three consecutive numbers are of the form x, $x + 1$, and $x + 2$. Since an even number is divisible by 2, consecutive even numbers are of the form $2x$, $2x + 2$, and $2x + 4$. An odd number is of the form $2x + 1$.

Example

Find three consecutive whole numbers whose sum is 75.

Let the first number be x, the second $x + 1$, and the third $x + 2$. Then:

$$x + (x + 1) + (x + 2) = 75$$
$$3x + 3 = 75$$
$$3x = 72$$
$$x = 24$$

The numbers whose sum is 75 are 24, 25, and 26.

Work Problems

These problems concern the speed with which work can be accomplished and the time necessary to perform a task if the size of the work force is changed.

Example

If Joe can type a chapter alone in 6 days and Ann can type the same chapter in 8 days, how long will it take them to type the chapter if they both work on it?

We let x = number of days required if they work together, and then put our information into tabular form:

	Joe	Ann	Together
Days to type chapter	6	8	x
Part typed in 1 day	$\dfrac{1}{6}$	$\dfrac{1}{8}$	$\dfrac{1}{x}$

Since the part done by Joe in 1 day plus the part done by Ann in 1 day equals the part done by both in 1 day, we have

$$\frac{1}{6} + \frac{1}{8} = \frac{1}{x}$$

Next we multiply each side of the equation by $24x$ to clear the fractions, giving:

$$4x + 3x = 24$$
$$7x = 24$$
$$x = 3\frac{3}{7} \text{ days}$$

Word Problems Involving One Unknown

1. If 6 times a number is decreased by 4, the result is the same as when 3 times the number is increased by 2. What is the number?

2. The smaller of two numbers is 31 less than three times the larger. If the numbers differ by 7, what is the smaller number?

3. At the Nichols School Christmas program, student tickets cost $3, and adult tickets cost twice as much. If a total of 200 tickets were sold, and $900 was collected, how many student tickets were sold?

4. Find the largest of three consecutive even integers such that 5 times the first minus twice the second is equal to the third.

5. Mike is 3 years older than Al. In 9 years the sum of their ages will be 47. How old is Mike now?

6. Working together, Brian, Peter, and Jared can shovel the driveway in 12 minutes. If Brian alone can shovel the driveway in 21 minutes, and Peter alone can shovel the driveway in 84 minutes, how long would it take Jared to shovel the driveway alone?

Literal Equations

An equation may have other letters in it besides the variable (or variables). Such an equation is called a *literal equation.* An illustration is $x + b = a$, with x the variable. The solution of such an equation will not be a specific number but will involve letter symbols. Literal equations are solved by exactly the same methods as those involving numbers, but we must know which of the letters in the equation is to be considered the variable. Then the other letters are treated as constants.

Example

Solve $ax - 2bc = d$ for x.

$$ax = d + 2bc$$

$$x = \frac{d + 2bc}{a} \text{ if } a \neq 0$$

Example

Solve $ay - by = a^2 - b^2$ for y.

$y(a - b) = a^2 - b^2$	Factor out common term.
$y(a - b) = (a + b)(a - b)$	Factor expression on right side.
$y = a + b$	Divide each side by $a - b$ if $a \neq b$.

Quadratic Equations

An equation containing the square of an unknown quantity is called a *quadratic equation.* One way of solving such an equation is by factoring. If the product of two expressions is zero, at least one of the expressions must be zero.

Example

Solve $y^2 + 2y = 0$.

$y(y + 2) = 0$	Remove common factor
$y = 0$ or $y + 2 = 0$	Since product is 0, at least one of factors must be 0.
$y = 0$ or $y = -2$	

Check by substituting both values in the original equation:

$$(0)^2 + 2(0) = 0$$

$$(-2)^2 + 2(-2) = 4 - 4 = 0$$

In this case there are two solutions.

Example

Solve $x^2 + 7x + 10 = 0$.

$x^2 + 7x + 10 = (x + 5)(x + 2) = 0$

$$x + 5 = 0 \quad \text{or } x + 2 = 0$$

$$x = -5 \quad \text{or} \quad x = -2$$

Check:

$$(-5)^2 + 7(-5) + 10 = 25 - 35 + 10 = 0$$

$$(-2)^2 + 7(-2) + 10 = \ 4 - 14 + 10 = 0$$

Not all quadratic equations can be factored using only integers, but solutions can usually be found by means of a formula. A quadratic equation may have two solutions, one solution, or occasionally no real solutions. If the quadratic equation is in the form $Ax^2 + Bx + C = 0$, x can be found from the following formula:

$$x = \frac{-B \pm \sqrt{B^2 - 4AC}}{2A}$$

Example

Solve $2y^2 + 5y + 2 = 0$ by formula.

Assume $A = 2$, $B = 5$, and $C = 2$.

$$x = \frac{-5 \pm \sqrt{5^2 - 4(2)(2)}}{2(2)}$$

$$= \frac{-5 \pm \sqrt{25 - 16}}{4}$$

$$= \frac{-5 \pm \sqrt{9}}{4}$$

$$= \frac{-5 \pm 3}{4}$$

This yields two solutions:

$$x = \frac{-5 + 3}{4} = \frac{-2}{4} = \frac{-1}{2} \text{ and}$$

$$x = \frac{-5 - 3}{4} = \frac{-8}{4} = -2$$

It is also possible for a quadratic equation to have no real solution at all.

Example

If we attempt to solve $x^2 + x + 1 = 0$, by formula, we get:

$$x = \frac{-1 \pm \sqrt{1 - 4(1)(1)}}{2} = \frac{-1 \pm \sqrt{-3}}{2}$$

Since $\sqrt{-3}$ is not defined, this quadratic has no real answer.

Rewriting Equations

Some equations containing a radical sign can be converted into a quadratic equation. The solution of this type of problem depends on the principle that

$$\text{If } A = B \quad \text{then} \quad A^2 = B^2$$
$$\text{and If } A^2 = B^2 \quad \text{then} \quad A = B \quad \text{or} \quad A = -B$$

Example

Solve $y = \sqrt{3y + 4}$

$$y = \sqrt{3y + 4}$$
$$y^2 = 3y + 4$$
$$y^2 - 3y - 4 = 0$$
$$(y - 4)(y + 1) = 0$$
$$y = 4 \text{ or } y = -1$$

Check by substituting values into the original equation:

$$4 \overset{?}{=} \sqrt{3(4) + 4} \text{ and } -1 \overset{?}{=} \sqrt{3(-1) + 4}$$
$$4 \overset{?}{=} \sqrt{16} \qquad\qquad -1 \overset{?}{=} \sqrt{1}$$
$$4 = 4 \qquad -1 \neq 1$$

The single solution is $y = 4$: the false root $y = -1$ was introduced when the original equation was squared.

Equation Solving Problems

Solve the following equations for the variable indicated:

1. Solve for b_2: $2A = (b_1 + b_2)h$

2. Solve for d: $\dfrac{a}{b} = \dfrac{c}{d}$

3. Solve for x: $3x^2 - 12 = x(1 + 2x)$

4. Solve for x: $5x^2 = 36 + x^2$

5. Solve for x: $\sqrt{3x - 12} + 2 = 5$

NOW CHECK YOUR ANSWERS

Answers for Equation Problems

1.
$$-5x + 3 = x + 2$$
$$\underline{+5x \qquad +5x}$$
$$3 = 6x + 2$$
$$\underline{-2 \qquad -2}$$
$$1 = 6x$$
$$1/6 = x$$

2.
$$x + 3(2x + 5) = -20$$
$$x + 6x + 15 = -20$$
$$7x + 15 = -20$$
$$7x = -35$$
$$x = -5$$

3.
$$4(x + 2) - (2x + 1) = x + 5$$
$$4x + 8 - 2x - 1 = x + 5$$
$$2x + 7 = x + 5$$
$$x = -2$$

4.
$$3(2x + 5) = 10x + 7 + 2(x - 8)$$
$$6x + 15 = 10x + 7 + 2x - 16$$
$$6x + 15 = 12x - 9$$
$$24 = 6x$$
$$x = 3$$

Answers to Word Problems Involving One Unknown

1. Let x = the number. Then,

$6x - 4 = 3x + 2$	Thus,
$3x = 6$	And
$x = 2$	The number is 2.

2. Let S = the smaller number. Then, the larger number = $S + 7$, and

   $$S + 31 = 3(S + 7)$$
   $$S + 31 = 3S + 21$$
   $$2S = 10$$
   $$S = 5 \qquad \text{The smaller number is 5.}$$

3. Let S = the number of student tickets sold. Then,

$200 - S$ = the number of adult tickets sold.

Thus, the money from student tickets is $3S$, and the money received from adult tickets is $6(200 - S)$. Since a total of \$900 was collected,

$$3S + 6(200 - S) = 900$$
$$3S + 1{,}200 - 6S = 900$$
$$3S = 300$$
$$S = 100$$

Therefore, 100 student tickets were sold.

4. Let x = the smallest integer

$$x + 2 = \text{the next integer}$$
$$x + 4 = \text{the largest integer}$$

$$5x - 2(x + 2) = x + 4$$
$$5x - 2x - 4 = x + 4$$
$$3x - 4 = x + 4$$
$$2x = 8$$
$$x = 4$$

Thus, the smallest integer is 4, the next one is 6, and the largest is 8.

5. Let M = Mike's age now. Then,

$M - 3$ = Al's age. In 9 years, Mike will be $M + 9$, and Al will be $M + 6$. Therefore,

$$M + 9 + M + 6 = 47$$
$$2M + 15 = 47$$
$$2M = 32$$
$$M = 16 \qquad \text{Thus, Mike is 16 now.}$$

6. Let J = the time Jared needs to shovel the driveway alone.

In 12 minutes, Brian can shovel $\dfrac{12}{21}$ of the driveway.

In 12 minutes, Peter can shovel $\dfrac{12}{84}$ of the driveway.

In 12 minutes, Jared can shovel $\dfrac{12}{J}$ of the driveway. Therefore,

$$\frac{12}{21} + \frac{12}{84} + \frac{12}{J} = 1 \qquad \text{Multiply both sides by 84J}$$

$$48J + 12J + 1{,}008 = 84J$$
$$1{,}008 = 24J$$
$$42 = J \qquad \text{Jared can shovel the driveway in 42 minutes.}$$

Answers for Equation Solving Problems

1. $2A = (b_1 + b_2)h$

$2A = b_1h + b_2h$

$2A - b_1h = b_2h$

$(2A - b_1h)/h = b_2$

2. $\dfrac{a}{b} = \dfrac{c}{d}$

$ad = bc$

$d = \dfrac{bc}{a}$

3. $3x^2 - 12 = x(1 + 2x)$

$3x^2 - 12 = x + 2x^2$

$x^2 - x - 12 = 0$

$(x + 3)(x - 4) = 0$ Thus, $x = -3$ or 4

4. $5x^2 = 36 + x^2$

$4x^2 - 36 = 0$

$4(x^2 - 9) = 0$

$4(x + 3)(x - 3) = 0$ Thus, $x = \pm 3$

5. $\sqrt{3x - 12} + 2 = 5$

$\sqrt{3x - 12} = 3$ Square both sides

$3x - 12 = 9$

$3x = 21$

$x = 7$

ENGLISH GRAMMAR REVIEW

Sentence Elements

VERBALS

Sometimes verbs can change their form and be used as nouns, adverbs, or adjectives. These forms are called verbals.

1. The infinitive is formed by adding *to* in front of the verb. The infinitive may act as a noun, adjective, or adverb.

   > I love *to sing*. (Noun)
   >
   > Music *to sing* is my favorite kind. (Adjective)
   > He went *to sing* in the choir. (Adverb)

2. The participle can be either present or past. The present participle is usually formed by adding *-ing* to a verb. The past participle is usually formed by adding *-ed* to a verb. The past participle form of irregular verbs can be formed in different ways. The participle is used as an adjective.

   > The *swaying* crane struck the *fallen* boy.
   >
   > (*Swaying* is a present participle; *fallen* is a past participle.)

   A participle phrase is used as an adjective.

   > *Blowing the crane fiercely*, the wind caused much danger.

Important for Exam

Beware of dangling participle phrases. They should be placed near the words they modify.

> *Blowing the crane fiercely*, the crowd ran.
>
> (The wind is blowing the crane, not the crowd.)

3. The gerund is formed by adding *-ing* to a verb. Although the gerund may look like a present participle, it is used only as a noun.

   > *Seeing* clearly is important for good *driving*.
   >
   > (*Seeing* is the subject; *driving* is the object of the preposition *for*.)
   >
   > A participle phrase is used as a noun.
   >
   > *Seeing traffic signals* is important for good driving.

PHRASES

A prepositional phrase begins with a preposition.

"Over the hill" was the slogan of the geriatric club.

The top *of the statue* was broken.

The owl sat *in the nest*.

Important for Exam

A dangling or misplaced modifier is a word or phrase acting as a modifier that does not refer clearly to the word or phrase it modifies.

A bright light blinded his eyes *over the door*. (Misplaced modifier—his eyes were not over the door.)

The following sentence shows correct placement of the modifying phrase.

A bright light over the door blinded his eyes.

CLAUSES

Clauses are groups of words that contain a subject and a predicate (verb part of the sentence). There are two main kinds of clauses. One kind is the *independent clause*, which makes sense when it stands alone. Independent clauses are joined by a coordinating conjunction preceded by a comma. They can also be joined using a semicolon and a transtional word or phrase.

I know how to clean silver, *but* I never learned how to clean copper.

I know how to clean silver; however, I never learned how to clean copper.

The other kind of clause is a *dependent* or *subordinate clause*. Although this type of clause has a subject and a predicate, it cannot stand alone. A dependent clause begins with a subordinating conjunction.

When I learn to clean copper, I will keep my pots sparkling.

When I learn to clean copper cannot stand alone. It is a dependent clause begun by the subordinating conjunction *when*.

I noticed *that he was very pale*.

That he was very pale is a clause—the object of the verb *noticed*. *That* is the subordinating conjunction.

She lost the belt *when she dropped the bag*.

When she dropped the bag is an adverbial clause answering the question *when* about the predicate. *When* is the subordinating conjunction.

Clauses should refer clearly and logically to the part of the sentence they modify.

We bought a dress at Bloomingdale's *which was expensive*.

(Misplaced adjective clause. Did the writer mean Bloomingdale's was expensive?)

Correct: We bought a dress *which was expensive* at Bloomingdale's.

SENTENCES

A sentence is a group of words that express a complete thought. An independent clause can stand by itself and may or may not be a complete sentence.

Beth and Terry rode the Ferris wheel; they enjoyed the ride. (Two independent clauses connected by a semicolon)

Beth and Terry rode the Ferris wheel. They enjoyed the ride. (Two independent clauses—each is a sentence)

1. A simple sentence has one independent clause. A dependent clause is never a sentence by itself. Here are some simple sentences:

   John and Fred played.

   John laughed and sang.

   John and Fred ate hot dogs and drank beer.

2. A compound sentence has at least two independent clauses.

   Darryl bought the meat, and *Laverne bought the potatoes*.

3. A complex sentence has one independent clause and at least one dependent clause.

   Because she left early, she missed the end.

   (*Because she left early* is the dependent clause. *She missed the end* is an independent clause.)

4. A compound-complex sentence has two independent clauses and one or more dependent clauses.

   You prefer math and I prefer music, although I am the math major.

   (*You prefer math* and *I prefer music* are the independent clauses. The dependent clause is *although I am a math major*.)

COMMON SENTENCE ERRORS

Sentence Fragments

These are parts of sentences that are incorrectly written with the capitals and punctuation of a sentence.

> Around the corner.
> Because she left early.
> Going to the movies.
> A terrible tragedy.

Remember that sentences must have at least a subject and a verb.

Run-on Sentences

These clauses are linked incorrectly.

> The rain was heavy, lightning was crackling he could not row the boat. (Incorrect)

> Because the rain was heavy and lightning was crackling, he could not row the boat. (Correct)

> The rain was heavy. Lightning was crackling. He could not row the boat. (Correct)

Faulty Parallelism

Elements of equal importance within a sentence should have parallel structure or similar form.

> To sing, *dancing*, and to laugh make life happy. (Incorrect)

> To sing, to dance, and to laugh make life happy. (Correct)

> He wants health, wealth, and *to be happy*. (Incorrect)

> He wants health, wealth, and happiness. (Correct)

Practice Problems in Sentence Elements and Common Errors

The finding of an undisturbed dinosaur egg site is particularly exciting to paleontologists because of the increased possibility of finding an intact and identifiable embryo. <u>Studying embryos, more can be learned</u> about the
$$\overline{}$$
$$1$$
relationship between dinosaurs and their descendants, the birds. Embryos may also help scientists establish whether dinosaurs were warm-blooded. The

remnants of a dinosaur embryo are usually nothing more than a jumble of

bones at the <u>bottom of the egg, nearly intact specimens</u> have been found. To
2

gather information from the <u>embryo, a paleontological technician drills</u> tiny
3

holes in the shell of the egg to determine whether the embryo is present.

Then <u>the egg places in a dilute solution</u> of acetic acid. As bones are exposed
4

by the acid <u>the technician</u> saturates them in liquid plastic. Once the fossil is
5

prepared for further analysis, criteria such as size, shape, <u>texture, and whether</u>
6

<u>the airholes form patterns</u> are used to assign a name to the egg species.
6

1. (A) NO CHANGE
   (B) Studying embryos,
        scientists can learn more
   (C) Studying embryos more
        can be learned
   (D) Studying embryos, more
        will be learned

2. (F) NO CHANGE
   (G) bottom of the egg nearly
        intact specimens
   (H) bottom of the egg, but
        nearly intact specimens
   (J) bottom of the egg, and
        nearly intact specimens

3. (A) NO CHANGE
   (B) embryo a paleontological
        technician drills
   (C) embryo, there are
   (D) embryo. A paleontological
        technician drills

4. (F) NO CHANGE
   (G) the egg is placed in a
        dilute solution
   (H) the egg places itself in a
        dilute solution
   (J) the egg will place in a
        dilute solution

5. (A) NO CHANGE
   (B) the acid. The technician
   (C) the acid, and the techni-
        cian
   (D) the acid, the technician

6. (F) NO CHANGE
   (G) texture and whether the
        airholes form patterns
   (H) texture, and patterns of
        airholes
   (J) texture; whether the
        airholes form patterns

NOW CHECK YOUR ANSWERS

Answers to Practice Problems in Sentence Elements and Common Errors

1. **The correct answer is (B).** This is a dangling participle. The subject *more* does not study the egg. The sentence must be rewritten to provide an appropriate subject.

2. **The correct answer is (H).** A conjunction is needed to connect the two independent clauses. Since the second clause contradicts the meaning of the first, the conjunction *but* makes sense.

3. **The correct answer is (A).** The subject *technician* is correctly placed near the infinitive phrase modifier.

4. **The correct answer is (G).** As written, the sentence does not make sense. The egg cannot perform the action of the sentence. The verb phrase *is placed* shows that the action happens to the egg.

5. **The correct answer is (D).** An introductory dependent clause must be followed by a comma.

6. **The correct answer is (H).** The series, which joins three nouns and a dependent clause, lacks parallel construction. The clause must be rewritten so that the information is expressed as a noun. The prepositional phrase that modifies the noun *patterns* preserves the meaning of the original clause.

MATHEMATICS AND ENGLISH GRAMMAR REVIEW

MATHEMATICS REVIEW

LINEAR INEQUALITIES

An *algebraic inequality* is a statement that one algebraic expression is greater than (or less than) another algebraic expression.

There are three rules for producing equivalent inequalities:

1. The same quantity can be added or subtracted from each side of an inequality.

2. Each side of an inequality can be multiplied or divided by the same *positive* quantity.

3. If each side of an inequality is multiplied or divided by the same *negative* quantity, the sign of the inequality must be reversed so that the new inequality is equivalent to the first.

Example

Solve $5x - 5 > -9 + 3x$.

$5x > -4 + 3x$	Add 5 to each side.
$2x > -4$	Subtract $3x$ from each side.
$x > -2$	Divide by $+2$.

Any number greater than -2 is a solution to this inequality.

Example

Solve $2x - 12 < 5x - 3$.

$2x < 5x + 9$	Add 12 to each side.
$-3x < 9$	Subtract $5x$ from each side.
$x > -3$	Divide each side by -3, changing sign of inequality.

Any number greater than -3—for example, $-2\frac{1}{2}$, 0, 1, or 4—is a solution to this inequality.

Linear Equations in Two Unknowns

Graphing Equations

The number line is useful in picturing the values of one variable. When two variables are involved, a coordinate system is effective. The Cartesian coordinate system is constructed by placing a vertical number line and a horizontal number line on a plane so that the lines intersect at their zero points. This meeting place is called the *origin*. The horizontal number line is called the *x*-axis, and the vertical number line (with positive numbers above the *x*-axis) is called the *y*-axis. Points in the plane correspond to ordered pairs of real numbers.

Example

The points in this example are:

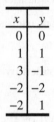

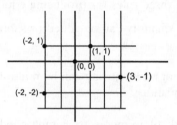

x	y
0	0
1	1
3	−1
−2	−2
−2	1

A first-degree equation in two variables is an equation that can be written in the form $ax + by = c$, where a, b, and c are constants. *First-degree* means that x and y appear to the first power. *Linear* refers to the graph of the solutions (x, y) of the equation, which is a straight line. We have already discussed linear equations of one variable.

Example

Graph the line $y = 2x - 4$.

First make a table and select small integral values of x. Find the value of each corresponding y and write it in the table:

x	y
0	−4
1	−2
2	0
3	2

If $x = 1$, for example, $y = 2(1) - 4 = -2$. Then plot the four points on a coordinate system. It is not necessary to have four points; two would do since two points determine a line, but plotting three or more points reduces the possibility of error.

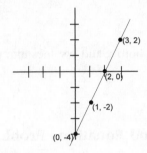

After the points have been plotted (placed on the graph), draw a line through the points and extend it in both directions. This line represents the equation $y = 2x - 4$.

Solving Simultaneous Linear Equations

Two linear equations can be solved together (simultaneously) to yield an answer (x, y) if it exists. On the coordinate system, this amounts to drawing the graphs of two lines and finding their point of intersection. If the lines are parallel and therefore never meet, no solution exists.

Simultaneous linear equations can be solved in the following manner without drawing graphs. From the first equation find the value of one variable in terms of the other; substitute this value in the second equation. The second equation is now a linear equation in one variable and can be solved. After the numerical value of the one variable has been found, substitute that value into the first equation to find the value of the second variable. Check the results by putting both values into the second equation.

Example

Solve the system:

$2x + y = 3$

$4x - y = 0$

From the first equation, $y = 3 - 2x$. Substitute this value of y into the second equation to get

$4x - (3 - 2x) = 0$

$4x - 3 + 2x = 0$

$6x = 3$

$x = \dfrac{1}{2}$

Substitute $x = \dfrac{1}{2}$ in the first of the original equations:

$$2\left(\dfrac{1}{2}\right) + y = 3$$
$$1 + y = 3$$
$$y = 2$$

Check by substituting both x and y values into the second equation:

$$4\left(\dfrac{1}{2}\right) - 2 = 0$$
$$2 - 2 = 0$$

Linear Inequalities and Equations Problems

1. Solve for x: $12 - 2x > 4$
2. Solve for x: $\left(\dfrac{x}{6}\right) - \left(\dfrac{x}{2}\right) < 1$

3. Solve for a common solution:
   $$5x + 3y = 28$$
   $$7x - 2y = 2$$

4. A piece of wood that is 36 inches long is cut into two pieces such that twice the longer piece is 2 inches more than 3 times the shorter piece. How many inches is the shorter piece?

5. Brian is now 3 times as old as Carl. Six years from now, Brian will be twice as old as Carl will be then. How old is Brian now?

Ratio and Proportion

Many problems in arithmetic and algebra can be solved using the concept of *ratio* to compare numbers. The ratio of a to b is the fraction $\dfrac{a}{b}$. If the two ratios $\dfrac{a}{b}$ and $\dfrac{c}{d}$ represent the same comparison, we write:

$$\dfrac{a}{b} = \dfrac{c}{d}$$

This equation (statement of equality) is called a *proportion*. A proportion states the equivalence of two different expressions for the same ratio.

Example

In a class of 39 students, 17 are men. Find the ratio of men to women.

39 students – 17 men = 22 women

Ratio of men to women is 17/22, also written 17:22.

Example

A fertilizer contains 3 parts nitrogen, 2 parts potash, and 2 parts phosphate by weight. How many pounds of fertilizer will contain 60 pounds of nitrogen?

The ratio of pounds of nitrogen to pounds of fertilizer is 3 to 3 + 2 + 2 = 3/7. Let x be the number of pounds of mixture. Then:

$$\frac{3}{7} = \frac{60}{x}$$

Multiply both sides of the equation by $7x$ to get:

$3x = 420$

$x = 140$ pounds

Computing Averages and Medians

Mean

Several statistical measures are used frequently. One of them is the *average* or *arithmetic mean*. To find the average of N numbers, add the numbers and divide their sum by N.

Example

Seven students attained test scores of 62, 80, 60, 30, 50, 90, and 20. What was the average test score for the group?

$62 + 80 + 60 + 30 + 50 + 90 + 20 = 392$

Since there are 7 scores, the average score is

$$\frac{392}{7} = 56$$

Median

If a set of numbers is arranged in order, the number in the middle is called the *median*.

Example

Find the median test score of 62, 80, 60, 30, 50, 90, and 20.

Arrange the numbers in increasing (or decreasing) order

20, 30, 50, 60, 62, 80, 90

Since 60 is the number in the middle, it is the median. It is not the same as the arithmetic mean, which is 56.

If the number of scores is an even number, the median is the arithmetic mean of the middle two scores.

Ratio, Proportion, Average, and Median Problems

1. The Smiths purchased a home for $130,000, and the annual property tax was $1,625. If they make improvements so that the home is valued at $150,000, how much will they pay in property taxes annually?

2. A technician can run diagnostic tests on 4 computer systems in 6 hours. How many systems can she test in a 40-hour work week?

3. Stuart had scores of 82, 96, 88, and 84 on four tests. Hiba had scores of 90, 91, 84, and 87 on the same tests. Who had the higher average score?

4. Find the average (to the nearest tenth) and median of the following set of data: 100, 94, 92, 98, 62, 85, 55

NOW CHECK YOUR ANSWERS

Answers for Linear Inequalities and Equations Problems

1. $12 - 2x > 4$

   $\quad -2x > -8$ Divide by -2, flip inequality sign

   $\quad\quad x < 4$

2. $\dfrac{x}{6} - \dfrac{x}{2} < 1$ Multiply both sides by 6

   $x - 3x < 6$

   $\quad -2x < 6$ Divide by -2, flip the inequality sign

   $\quad\quad x > -3$

3. $5x + 3y = 28$

   $7x - 2y = 2$ Multiply first equation by 2, second equation by 3

   $2(5x + 3y) = 2(28)$

   $3(7x - 2y) = 3(2)$ Thus,

   $\begin{aligned}
   10x + 6y &= 56 \\
   \underline{21x - 6y} &= \underline{\ \ 6} \\
   31x \quad\quad &= 62
   \end{aligned}$

   $\quad\quad\quad x = 2$ Now, solve for y by plugging $x = 2$ into (say) the second equation

   $7(2) - 2y = 2$

   $\quad 14 - 2y = 2$

   $\quad\quad -2y = -12$

   $\quad\quad\quad y = 6$ Thus, the common solution is $(2, 6)$

4. Let $x =$ the number of inches in the shorter piece. Then,

   $36 - x =$ the number of inches in the longer piece. Therefore,

   $2(36 - x) = 2 + 3x$ so that

   $72 - 2x = 2 + 3x$

   $\quad\quad 5x = 70$ and

   $\quad\quad\ x = 14$ Thus, the shorter piece is 14 inches long

5. Let C = Carl's age. Then,

   $3C$ = Brian's age

   Then, in six years, Carl will be $C + 6$, and Brian will be $3C + 6$, and

   $2(C + 6) = 3C + 6$ or

   $2C + 12 = 3C + 6$

   $C = 6$

   Thus, Carl is now 6. Therefore, Brian is now 18.

Answers for Ratio, Proportion, Average, and Median Problems

1. $$\frac{130,000}{1,625} = \frac{150,000}{x}$$

    $130,000x = 1,625(150,000)$

    $130,000x = 243,750,000$

    $x = 1,875$

2. $$\frac{4}{6} = \frac{x}{40}$$

    $4(40) = 6x$

    $160 = 6x$

    $26.67 \approx x$

3. Stuart: $82 + 96 + 88 + 84 = 350$ $\dfrac{350}{4} = 87.5$

    Hiba: $90 + 91 + 84 + 87 = 352$ $\dfrac{352}{4} = 88$

4. Average:

    $100 + 94 + 92 + 98 + 62 + 85 + 55 = 586$ $\dfrac{586}{7} = 83.7$

    Median:

    Arrange in order and find the middle number: 100, 98, 94, <u>92</u>, 85, 62, 55

ENGLISH GRAMMAR REVIEW

Study these rules of capitalization and punctuation. Then answer the practice
questions that follow.

CAPITALIZATION

1. Capitalize all proper nouns.

    Capitalize names of specific people, places, things, peoples, and their
    languages: Americans, America, Spanish. Note: Henry takes Spanish three
    times a week. Henry takes math three times a week.

2. Capitalize religions and holy books: Islam, Koran, Bible.

3. Capitalize calendar words: Monday, April.

4. Capitalize historic periods and events but not the names of decades or
    centuries. Renaissance, Civil War, twentieth century.

5. Always capitalize the first word in a sentence: It is Henry.

6. Capitalize the first word in a letter salutation: Dear John, Dear Sir.

7. Capitalize the first word of a letter closing: Very truly yours,

8. Capitalize the first word in a direct quote: He said, "Go away."

9. Capitalize the first, last, and important words in titles: *The Man Without
    a Country.*

    Note: *A, an, and, the* are usually not capitalized unless they are the first
    word.

    Note also that conjunctions and prepositions with less than five letters
    are usually not capitalized in a title.

10. Capitalize words used as part of a proper noun: Hudson Street, Uncle Fritz.

11. Capitalize specific regions: I want to move to the South.

12. Capitalize abbreviations of capitalized words: D. B. Edelson.

13. Capitalize acronyms formed from capitalized words: NASA, NATO.

14. Capitalize the pronoun *I*:

    I wish I had a better car.

    Note that capitals are not used for seasons (summer, winter).

    Note that capitals are not used for compass directions (east, northeast).

    Note that capitals are not used for the second part of a quote: "I see,"
    she said, "how smart Henry is."

PUNCTUATION

The Period

1. Use the period to end full sentences.

   Harry loves candy.

   Although John knew the course was difficult, he did not expect to fail.

2. Use the period with abbreviations:

   Mr.   Ph.D.   C.I.A.

The Question Mark

Use the question mark to end a direct question:

Are you going to the store?

Note that indirect questions end with a period:

He asked how Sue knew the right answer.

The Exclamation Point

Use the exclamation point to denote strong feeling:

Act now!

The Colon

1. The colon can introduce a series or an explanation, but it must always follow an independent clause.

   The following sciences are commonly taught in college: biology, chemistry, and physics. (Correct)

   The sciences are: biology, chemistry, and physics. (Incorrect)

   The sciences are is not an independent clause.

2. The colon is used after the salutation in a business letter.

   Dear Sir:

3. The colon is used to express the time:

   It is 1:45.

The Semicolon

1. The semicolon is used to link related independent clauses not linked by *and, but, or, nor, for, so,* or *yet*:

   No person is born prejudiced; prejudice must be taught.

2. The semicolon is used before transitional words and phrases placed between independent clauses:

   No person is born prejudiced; however, he has been taught well.

   No person is born prejudiced; nevertheless, he has always appeared bigoted.

3. The semicolon is used to separate a series that already contains commas:

   The team had John, the pitcher; Paul, the catcher; and Peter, the short stop.

The Comma

1. The comma is used before long independent clauses linked by *and, but, or, nor, for, so,* or *yet*:

   No person is born prejudiced, but some people learn quickly.

2. The comma is used following clauses, phrases, or expressions that introduce a sentence:

   As I was eating, the waiter cleared the table.

   In a great country like ours, people enjoy traveling.

3. The comma is used with nonrestrictive, or parenthetical, expressions (not essential to the meaning of the main clause).

   He pulled the ice cream sundae, topped with whipped cream, toward him.

   John is afraid of all women who carry hand grenades. *Notice there is no comma.* John is not afraid of all women. He is afraid of all women who carry hand grenades (restrictive clause).

4. Use commas between items in a series:

   Beth loves cake, candy, cookies, and ice cream.

5. Use the comma in direct address:

   Pearl, come here.

6. Use the comma before and after terms in apposition:

   Give it to Pearl, our good friend.

7. Use the comma in dates or addresses:

   June 3, 1996

   Freeport, Long Island

8. Use the comma after the salutation in a friendly letter:

   Dear Henry,

9. Use the comma after the closing in letters:

   Sincerely yours,

10. Use a comma between a direct quotation and the rest of the sentence:

    "Our fudge," the cook bragged, "is the best in town."

11. Be sure to use two commas when needed to set off a sentence element:

    A good dancer, generally speaking, loves to dance.

12. Do not separate subjects and verbs with a comma:

    Students and teachers, receive rewards. (Incorrect)

13. Do not separate verbs and their objects with a comma:

    He scolded and punished, the boys. (Incorrect)

The Apostrophe

1. Use the apostrophe to denote possession (see nouns).

   John's friend

2. Use the apostrophe in contractions:

   Didn't (did not)

   There's (there is)

3. Do not use an apostrophe with his, hers, ours, yours, theirs, or whose. Use an apostrophe with *its* if *its* is a contraction:

   The dog chewed *its* bone; *it's* hard for a little dog to chew such a big bone. (*It's* means it is; *its* is a pronoun that denotes possession.)

Quotation Marks

1. Use quotation marks in direct quotes:

   "Get up," she said.

2. Use single quotes for a quote within a quote:

   Mark said, "Denise keeps saying 'I love you' to Ralph."

Parentheses

Use parentheses to set off nonrestrictive or unnecessary parts of a sentence:

   This book (an excellent review tool) will help students.

The Dash

1. Use the dash instead of parentheses:

   This book—an excellent review—will help students.

2. Use the dash to show interruption in thought:

   There are eight—remember, eight—parts of speech.

Practice Problems in Capitalization and Punctuation Review

Mapping the Earth has always been <u>problematical because the Earths</u>

<u>surface</u> cannot be cut and displayed on a flat <u>surface without wrinkling,</u>

1   2

<u>stretching and tearing.</u> As a result, the land masses shown on early maps were

2

extremely distorted, which caused navigation to be markedly difficult and

dangerous. The first successful attempt to create an optimal projection of the

Earth was made by Gerardus <u>Mercator in the 16th century.</u> Mercator realized

3

that if he placed the Earth inside a cylinder with <u>a north-south axis; he would</u>

4

<u>be able</u> to change meridians from lines that converged at the poles to parallel

4

vertical lines. This presentation also stretched the <u>latitudes (east-west lines—</u>

5

<u>which had</u> the effect of distorting the size of land masses near the poles.

5

For example, <u>Greenland appeared</u> to be extremely large on Mercator's map.

6

However, Mercator's great concern was that the angle between two lines on

the Earth be preserved on the map. <u>As he hoped his new</u> projection allowed

7

navigators to measure <u>angles directly on the map, and set their courses</u>

8

accurately to cross the seas.

1. (A) NO CHANGE
  (B) problematical because the earths surface
  (C) problematical because the Earth's surface
  (D) problematical; because the Earths surface

2. (F) NO CHANGE
  (G) surface without wrinkling, stretching, and tearing.
  (H) surface without wrinkling, stretching, and, tearing.
  (J) surface, without wrinkling, stretching and tearing.

3. (A) NO CHANGE
  (B) Mercator in the 16th Century
  (C) Mercator, in the 16th century
  (D) Mercator—in the 16th century

4. (F) NO CHANGE
  (G) a North-South axis; he would be able
  (H) a north-south axis, he would be able
  (J) a north-south axis, and he would be able

5. (A) NO CHANGE
   (B) latitudes, east-west lines which had
   (C) latitudes, east-west lines—which had
   (D) latitudes (east-west lines) which had

6. (F) NO CHANGE
   (G) For example Greenland appeared
   (H) For example Greenland, appeared
   (J) For example, Greenland, appeared

7. (A) NO CHANGE
   (B) As he hoped; however, his new
   (C) As he hoped, and his new
   (D) As he hoped, his new

8. (F) NO CHANGE
   (G) angles directly on the map and set
   (H) angles directly, on the map, and set
   (J) angles, directly on the map, and set

NOW CHECK YOUR ANSWERS

1. **The correct answer is (C).** The apostrophe is needed before the *s* to show possession.

2. **The correct answer is (G).** Set off the items in a series with commas. Do not put a comma after the conjunction used to connect the items in the series, but do put one after the last item before the conjunction.

3. **The correct answer is (A).** Do not capitalize decades or centuries. Also, do not set off a prepositional phrase with commas when the phrase is needed to add meaning to the sentence.

4. **The correct answer is (H).** The clause that is begun by the word *that* is a dependent clause followed by an independent clause. A comma is needed to separate the dependent clause from the independent clause. Do not use a semicolon to join clauses unless both thoughts are complete and related.

5. **The correct answer is (D).** Commas, dashes, and parentheses are used in pairs to set off nonessential information from the rest of the sentence. In this case, east-west lines explains the meaning of latitudes but is not necessary for the reader's understanding of the sentence.

6. **The correct answer is (F).** The introductory phrase is correctly followed by a comma. Do not use a comma to separate the subject from the verb.

7. **The correct answer is (D).** An introductory dependent clause should always be followed by a comma.

8. **The correct answer is (G).** The verbs *measured* and *set* are joined by the conjunction *and*. As part of an infinitive phrase, they should not be separated by punctuation.

MATHEMATICS REVIEW

COORDINATE GEOMETRY

You have already seen that a coordinate system is an effective way to picture relationships involving two variables. In this section, you will learn more about the study of geometry using coordinate methods.

Lines

Recall that the general equation of a line has the following form:

$Ax + By + C = 0,$

where A and B are constants and are not both 0. This means that if you were to find all of the points (x, y) that satisfy the above equation, they would all lie on the same line as graphed on a coordinate axis.

If the value of B is not 0, a little algebra can be used to rewrite the equation in the form

$y = mx + b,$

where m and b are two constants. Since the two numbers m and b determine this line, let's see what their geometric meaning is. First of all, note that the point $(0, b)$ satisfies the above equation. This means that the point $(0, b)$ is one of the points on the line; in other words, the line crosses the y-axis at the point b. For this reason, the number b is called the *y-intercept* of the line.

To interpret the meaning of m, choose any two points on the line. Let us call these points (x_1, y_1) and (x_2, y_2). Both of these points must satisfy the equation of the line above, and so:

$y_1 = mx_1 + b$ and $y_2 = mx_2 + b.$

If we subtract the first equation from the second we obtain

$y_2 - y_1 = m(x_2 - x_1),$

and solving for m, we find

$m = (y_2 - y_1)/(x_2 - x_1).$

The above equation tells us that the number *m* in the equation $y = mx + b$ is the ratio of the difference of the *y*-coordinates to the difference of the *x*-coordinates. This number is called the *slope* of the line. Therefore, the ratio $m = (y_2 - y_1)/(x_2 - x_1)$ is a measure of the number of units the line rises (or falls) in the *y* direction for each unit moved in the *x* direction. Another way to say this is that the slope of a line is a measure of the rate at which the line rises (or falls). Intuitively, a line with a positive slope rises from left to right; one with a negative slope falls from left to right.

Because the equation $y = mx + b$ contains both the slope and the *y*-intercept, it is called the *slope-intercept* form of the equation of the line. This, however, is not the only form in which the equation of the line can be written.

If the line contains the point (x_1, y_1), its equation can also be written as:

$$y - y_1 = m(x - x_1).$$

This form of the equation of a line is called the *point-slope* form of the equation of a line, since it contains the slope and the coordinates of one of the points on the line.

Two lines are parallel if and only if they have the same slope. Two lines are perpendicular if and only if their slopes are negative inverses of each other. This means that if a line has a slope *m*, any line perpendicular to this line must have a slope of $-1/m$. Also note that a horizontal line has a slope of 0. For such a line, the slope-intercept form of the equation reduces to $y = b$.

Finally, note that if $B = 0$ in the equation $Ax + By + C = 0$, the equation simplifies to

$$Ax + C = 0,$$

and represents a vertical line (a line parallel to the *y*-axis) that crosses the *x*-axis at $-C/A$. Such a line is said to have no slope.

Example

Find the slope and the *y*-intercept of the following lines.

    a. $y = 5x - 7$

        $y = 5x - 7$ is already in slope-intercept form. The slope is 5, and the *y*-intercept is −7.

    b. $3x + 4y = 5$

        Write $3x + 4y = 5$ in slope-intercept form:

            $4y = -3x + 5$

              $y = (-3/4)x + (5/4)$

The slope is $-3/4$, and the y-intercept is $5/4$. This means that the line crosses the y-axis at the point $5/4$, and for every 3 units moved in the x-direction, the line falls 4 units in the y-direction.

Example

Find the equation of the following line:

the line containing the points (4, 5) and (7, 11)

First, we need to determine the slope of the line.

$m = (11 - 5)/(7 - 4) = 6/3 = 2$.

Now, using the point-slope form:

$y - 5 = 2(x - 4)$. If desired, you can change this to the slope-intercept form: $y = 2x - 3$.

Circles

From a geometric point of view, a circle is the set of points in the plane, each of whose members is the same distance from a particular point called the center of the circle. We can determine the equation of a circle by manipulating the distance formula.

Suppose that we have a circle whose radius is a given positive number r, and whose center lies at the point (b, k). If (x, y) is a point on the circle, then its distance from the center of the circle would be

$$\sqrt{(x - b)^2 + (y - k)^2},$$

and since this distance is r, we can say

$$\sqrt{(x - b)^2 + (y - k)^2} = r.$$

Squaring both sides, we get the following result: the equation of a circle whose center is at (b, k) and whose radius is r is given by:

$$(x - b)^2 + (y - k)^2 = r^2$$

Example

Find the equation of the circle with radius 7 and center at (0, −5).

Substituting into the formula above, we obtain $x^2 + (y + 5)^2 = 49$.

Coordinate Geometry Problems

1. Find the slope of the line containing the points $(-2, -4)$ and $(2, 4)$.

2. Find the slope of the line given by the equation $4x + 5y = 7$.

3. Find the equation of the line with y-intercept 4 and x-intercept 7.

4. Find the equation of the line through the point (7, 2) and having the same slope as the line through (2, 4) and (3, −1).

5. Find the equation of the line through (−2, 3) and perpendicular to the line $2x - 3y = 4$.

6. What is the center and the radius of the circle given by the equation $(x - 3)^2 + (y + 7)^2 = 81$?

PLANE GEOMETRY

Lines and Angles

Angles

A line in geometry is always a straight line. When two straight lines meet at a point, they form an *angle*. The lines are called *sides* or *rays* of the angle, and the point is called the *vertex*. The symbol for angle is ∠. When no other angle shares the same vertex, the name of the angle is the name given to the vertex, as in angle *A:*

An angle may be named with three letters. Following, for example, *B* is a point on one side and *C* is a point on the other. In this case the name of the vertex must be the middle letter, and we have angle *BAC.*

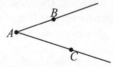

Occasionally an angle is named by a number or small letter placed in the angle.

Angle 2

Angle *y*

Angles are usually measured in degrees. An angle of 30 degrees, written 30°, is an angle whose measure is 30 degrees.

Vertical Angles

When two lines intersect, four angles are formed. The angles opposite each other are called *vertical angles* and are equal to each other.

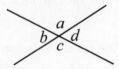

a and *c* are vertical angles.
$$\angle a = \angle c$$
b and *d* are vertical angles.
$$\angle b = \angle d$$

Straight Angle

A *straight angle* has its sides lying along a straight line. It is always equal to 180°.

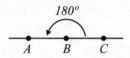

$$\angle ABC = \angle B = 180°$$
∠B is a straight angle.

Adjacent Angles

Two angles are *adjacent* if they share the same vertex and a common side but no angle is inside another angle. ∠*ABC* and ∠*CBD* are adjacent angles. Even though they share a common vertex *B* and a common side *AB*, ∠*ABD* and ∠*ABC* are not adjacent angles because one angle is inside the other.

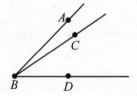

Supplementary Angles

If the sum of two angles is a straight angle (180°), the two angles are *supplementary* and each angle is the supplement of the other.

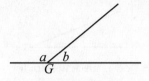

$\angle G$ is a straight angle = 180°.
$\angle a + \angle b = 180°$
$\angle a$ and $\angle b$ are supplementary angles.

Right Angles

If two supplementary angles are equal, they are both *right* angles. A *right* angle is one-half a straight angle. Its measure is 90°. A right angle is symbolized by ⌐.

$\angle G$ is a straight angle.
$\angle b + \angle a = \angle G$, and $\angle a = \angle b$.
$\angle a$ and $\angle b$ are right angles.

Complementary Angles

Complementary angles are two angles whose sum is a right angle (90°).

$\angle Y$ is a right angle.
$\angle a + \angle b = \angle Y = 90°$.
$\angle a$ and $\angle b$ are complementary angles.

Acute Angles

Acute angles are angles whose measure is less than 90°. Two acute angles can be complementary angles.

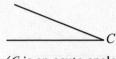

∠C is an acute angle.

Obtuse Angles

Obtuse angles are angles that are greater than 90° and less than 180°.

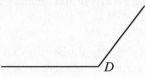

∠D is an obtuse angle.

Example

In the figure, what is the value of x?

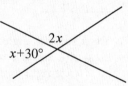

Since the two labeled angles are supplementary angles, their sum is 180°.

$$(x + 30°) + 2x = 180°$$
$$3x = 150°$$
$$x = 50°$$

Example

If angle Y is a right angle and angle b measures 30°, what does angle a measure?

Since angle Y is a right angle, angles a and b are complementary angles and their sum is 90°.

$$\angle a + \angle b = 90°$$
$$\angle a + 30° = 90°$$
$$\angle a = 60°$$

Lines

A *line* in geometry is always assumed to be a straight line. It extends infinitely far in both directions. It is determined if two of its points are known. It can be expressed in terms of the two points, which are written as capital letters. The following line is called AB.

Or, a line may be given one name with a small letter. The following line is called line k.

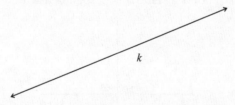

A *line segment* is a part of a line between two *endpoints*. It is named by its endpoints, for example, A and B.

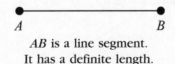

AB is a line segment.
It has a definite length.

If point P is on the line and is the same distance from A as from B, then P is the *midpoint* of segment AB. When we say $AP = PB$, we mean that the two line segments have the same length.

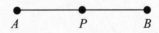

A part of a line with one endpoint is called a *ray. AC* is a ray of which *A* is an endpoint. The ray extends infinitely far in the direction away from the endpoint.

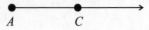

Parallel Lines

Two lines in the same plane that never meet no matter how far they are extended are said to be *parallel,* for which the symbol is ‖. In the following diagram *a* ‖ *b.*

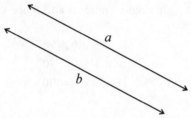

If two lines in the same plane are parallel to a third line, they are parallel to each other. Since *a* ‖ *b* and *b* ‖ *c,* we know that *a* ‖ *c.*

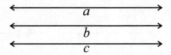

Two lines that meet each other at right angles are said to be *perpendicular,* for which the symbol is ⊥. Line *a* is perpendicular to line *b.*

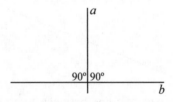

A line intersecting two other lines is called a *transversal.* Line *c* is a transversal intersecting lines *a* and *b.*

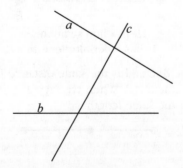

The transversal and the two given lines form eight angles. The four angles between the given lines are called *interior angles;* the four angles outside the given lines are called *exterior angles.* If two angles are on opposite sides of the transversal, they are called *alternate angles.*

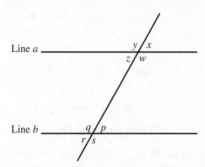

$\angle z$, $\angle w$, $\angle q$, and $\angle p$ are interior angles.

$\angle y$, $\angle x$, $\angle s$, and $\angle r$ are exterior angles.

$\angle z$ and $\angle p$ are alternate interior angles; so are $\angle w$ and $\angle q$.

$\angle y$ and $\angle s$ are alternate exterior angles; so are $\angle x$ and $\angle r$.

Pairs of *corresponding* angles are $\angle y$ and $\angle q$; $\angle z$ and $\angle r$; $\angle x$ and $\angle p$; $\angle w$ and $\angle s$. Corresponding angles are sometimes called exterior-interior angles.

When the two given lines cut by a transversal are parallel lines:

1. the corresponding angles are equal.
2. the alternate interior angles are equal.
3. the alternate exterior angles are equal.
4. interior angles on the same side of the transversal are supplementary.

If line *a* is parallel to line *b:*

1. $\angle y = \angle q$, $\angle z = \angle r$, $\angle x = \angle p$, and $\angle w = \angle s$.
2. $\angle z = \angle p$ and $\angle w = \angle q$.
3. $\angle y = \angle s$ and $\angle x = \angle r$.
4. $\angle z + \angle q = 180°$, and $\angle p + \angle w = 180°$

Polygons

A *polygon* is a closed plane figure composed of line segments joined together at points called *vertices* (singular, *vertex*). A polygon is usually named by giving its vertices in order.

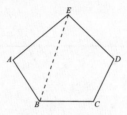

Polygon *ABCDE*

In the figure, points *A, B, C, D,* and *E* are the vertices, and the sides are *AB, BC, CD, DE,* and *EA. AB* and *BC* are *adjacent* sides, and *A* and *B* are adjacent vertices. A *diagonal* of a polygon is a line segment joining any two nonadjacent vertices. *EB* is a diagonal.

Polygons are named according to the number of sides or angles. A *triangle* is a polygon with three sides, a *quadrilateral* a polygon with four sides, a *pentagon* a polygon with five sides, and a *hexagon* a polygon with six sides. The number of sides is always equal to the number of angles.

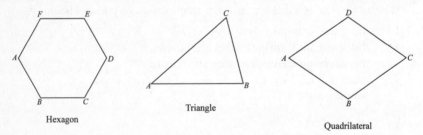

Hexagon

Triangle

Quadrilateral

The *perimeter* of a polygon is the sum of the lengths of its sides. If the polygon is *regular* (all sides equal and all angles equal), the perimeter is the product of the length of *one* side and the number of sides.

Congruent and Similar Polygons

If two polygons have equal corresponding angles and equal corresponding sides, they are said to be *congruent*. Congruent polygons have the same size and shape. The symbol for congruence is ≅.

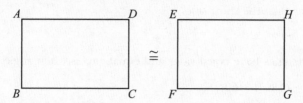

When two sides of congruent or different polygons are equal, we indicate the fact by drawing the same number of short lines through the equal sides.

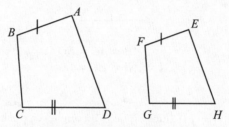

This indicates that $AB = EF$ and $CD = GH$.

Two polygons with equal corresponding angles and corresponding sides in proportion are said to be *similar*. The symbol for similar is ∼.

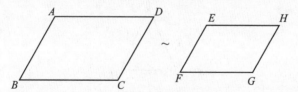

Similar figures have the same shape but not necessarily the same size.

Triangles

A *triangle* is a polygon of three sides. Triangles are classified by measuring their sides and angles. The sum of the angles of a plane triangle is always 180°. The symbol for a triangle is Δ. The sum of any two sides of a triangle is always greater than the third side.

Equilateral

Equilateral triangles have equal sides and equal angles. Each angle measures 60° because $\frac{1}{3}(180°) = 60°$.

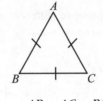

$$AB = AC = BC.$$
$$\angle A = \angle B = \angle C = 60°.$$

Isosceles

Isosceles triangles have two sides equal. The angles opposite the equal sides are equal. The two equal angles are sometimes called the *base* angles and the third angle is called the *vertex* angle. Note that an equilateral triangle is isosceles.

$$FG = FH.$$
$$FG \neq GH.$$
$$\angle G = \angle H.$$
$\angle F$ is vertex angle.
$\angle G$ and $\angle H$ are base angles.

Scalene

Scalene triangles have all three sides of different length and all angles of different measure. In scalene triangles, the shortest side is opposite the angle of smallest measure, and the longest side is opposite the angle of greatest measure.

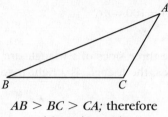

$AB > BC > CA$; therefore
$\angle C > \angle A > \angle B$.

Right

Right triangles contain one right angle. Since the right angle is 90°, the other two angles are complementary. They may or may not be equal to each other. The side of a right triangle opposite the right angle is called the *hypotenuse*. The other two sides are called *legs*. The *Pythagorean theorem* states that the square of the length of the hypotenuse is equal to the sum of the squares of the lengths of the legs.

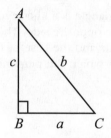

AC is the hypotenuse.
AB and BC are legs.
$\angle B = 90°$.
$\angle A + \angle C = 90°$.
$a^2 + c^2 = b^2$.

Example

If *ABC* is a right triangle with right angle at *B,* and if *AB* = 6 and *BC* = 8, what is the length of *AC?*

$$AB^2 + BC^2 = AC^2$$
$$6^2 + 8^2 = 36 + 64 = 100 = AC^2$$
$$AC = 10$$

If the lengths of the three sides of a triangle are *a, b,* and *c* and the relation $a^2 + b^2 = c^2$ holds, the triangle is a right triangle and side *c* is the hypotenuse.

Example

Show that a triangle of sides 5, 12, and 13 is a right triangle.

The triangle will be a right triangle if $a^2 + b^2 = c^2$.

$$5^2 + 12^2 = 13^2$$
$$25 + 144 = 169$$

Therefore, the triangle is a right triangle and 13 is the length of the hypotenuse.

Area of a Triangle

An *altitude* (or height) of a triangle is a line segment dropped as a perpendicular from any vertex to the opposite side. The area of a triangle is the product of one-half the altitude and the base of the triangle. (The base is the side opposite the vertex from which the perpendicular was drawn.)

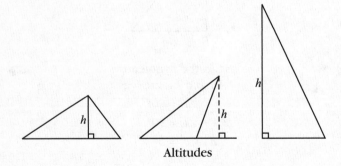

Altitudes

Example

Find the area A of the following isosceles triangle.

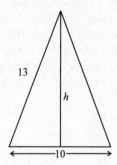

In an isosceles triangle the altitude from the vertex angle bisects the base (cuts it in half).

The first step is to find the altitude. By the Pythagorean theorem,

$$a^2 + b^2 = c^2; \ c = 13, \ a = b, \text{ and } b = \frac{1}{2}(10) = 5.$$

$$b^2 + 5^2 = 13^2$$

$$b^2 + 25 = 169$$

$$b^2 = 144$$

$$b = 12$$

$$A = \frac{1}{2} \cdot \text{base} \cdot \text{height}$$

$$= \frac{1}{2} \cdot 10 \cdot 12$$

$$= 60$$

Similarity

Two triangles are *similar* if all three pairs of corresponding angles are equal. The sum of the three angles of a triangle is 180°; therefore, if two angles of triangle I equal two corresponding angles of triangle II, the third angle of triangle I must be equal to the third angle of triangle II and the triangles are similar. The lengths of the sides of similar triangles are in proportion to each other. A line drawn parallel to one side of a triangle divides the triangle into two portions, one of which is a triangle. The new triangle is similar to the original triangle.

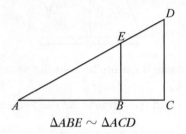

$$\triangle ABE \sim \triangle ACD$$

Example

In the following figure, if $AC = 28$ feet, $AB = 35$ feet, $BC = 21$ feet, and $EC = 12$ feet, find the length of DC if $DE \parallel AB$.

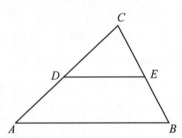

Because $DE \parallel AB$, $\triangle CDE \sim \triangle CAB$. Since the triangles are similar, their sides are in proportion:

$$\frac{DC}{AC} = \frac{EC}{BC}$$

$$\frac{DC}{28} = \frac{12}{21}$$

$$DC = \frac{12 \cdot 28}{21} = 16 \text{ feet}$$

Plane Geometry Problems

1. A chair is 5 feet from one wall of a room and 7 feet from the wall at a right angle to it. How far is the chair from the intersection of the two walls?

2. In triangle XYZ, $XZ = YZ$. If angle Z has a°, how many degrees are there in angle Y?

3. The perimeter of scalene triangle EFG is 95 mm. If $FG = 20$ mm and $EF = 45$ mm, what is the measure of EG?

4. In the figure, two parallel lines are cut by a transversal. Find the measure of angle y.

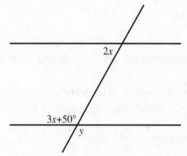

5. In the following figure, MN and PQ are parallel. Find the length of MN.

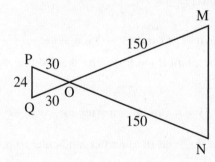

NOW CHECK YOUR ANSWERS

Answers to Coordinate Geometry Problems

1. If (x_1, y_1) and (x_2, y_2) are two points on a line, the slope is given by
    slope $= \dfrac{y_2 - y_1}{x_2 - x_1}$. For the two given points, $(-2, -4)$ and $(2, 4)$, the slope
    is slope $= \dfrac{y_2 - y_1}{x_2 - x_1} = \dfrac{4 - (-4)}{2 - (-2)} = \dfrac{4 + 4}{2 + 2} = \dfrac{8}{4} = 2$

2. The easiest way to find the slope of the line is to rewrite the equation in
    the slope-intercept form.

    $4x + 5y = 7$ Subtract $4x$

    $ 5y = -4x + 7$ Divide by 5

    $$y = \left(-\frac{4}{5}\right)x + \frac{7}{5}$$

    The slope of the line is the coefficient of x, that is, $-\dfrac{4}{5}$.

3. The line has y-intercept 4, which means it passes through $(0, 4)$; it also
    has x-intercept 7, which means it passes through $(7, 0)$.

    By the formula, slope $= \dfrac{y_2 - y_1}{x_2 - x_1} = \dfrac{4 - 0}{0 - 7} = -\dfrac{4}{7}$. Since we know the slope
    and the y-intercept, we can simply plug into the slope-intercept form,
    $y = mx + b$, and get $y = \left(-\dfrac{4}{7}\right)x + 4$.

4. The line through $(2, 4)$ and $(3, -1)$ has slope $\dfrac{4 - (-1)}{2 - 3} = \dfrac{5}{-1} = -5$.
    Then, using the point-slope form, the desired line can be written as
    $y - 2 = -5(x - 7)$.

5. The line $2x - 3y = 4$ can be rewritten as $-3y = -2x + 4$, or $y = \dfrac{2}{3}x - \dfrac{4}{3}$.
    Thus, its slope is $\dfrac{2}{3}$, and the line perpendicular to it would have slope
    $-\dfrac{3}{2}$. Then, using the point-slope form, the requested line can be written
    as $y - 3 = -\dfrac{3}{2}(x + 2)$.

6. The general form for the equation of a circle is $(x - h)^2 + (y - k)^2 = r^2$,
    where (h, k) is the center, and r is the radius. In this case, the given
    equation can be written as $(x - 3)^2 + (y - (-7))^2 = 9^2$. Thus, the center
    is $(3, -7)$ and the radius is 9.

Answers to Plane Geometry Problems

1. As the drawing below shows, you need to find the length of the hypotenuse of a right triangle with legs of 5 and 7. The formula tells you that $5^2 + 7^2 = x^2$, or $74 = x^2$. Thus, $x = \sqrt{74}$.

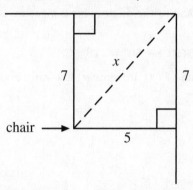

2. The diagram below shows that triangle XYZ is isosceles, and thus angle X and angle Y are the same. If you call the measure of these angles $x°$, you have $x° + x° + a° = 180°$, or $2x° + a° = 180°$. From this, you have $2x° = 180° - a°$ or $x° = \dfrac{180° - a}{2}$.

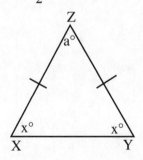

3. $20 + 45 + x = 95$
    $65 + x = 95$
    $x = 30$ mm.

4. The two labeled angles are supplementary.

$$2x + (3x + 50°) = 180°$$
$$5x = 130°$$
$$x = 26°$$

Since $\angle y$ is vertical to the angle whose measure is $3x + 50°$, it has the same measure.

$$y = 3x + 50° = 3(26°) + 50° = 128°$$

5. Triangles *MNO* and *PQO* are similar. Use ratio and proportion to solve.

$$\frac{30}{24} = \frac{150}{x}$$
$$24(150) = 30x$$
$$3,600 = 30x$$
$$120 = x$$

ENGLISH GRAMMAR REVIEW

Use these rules to improve your writing style.

RHETORICAL REVIEW

Style

Good writing is clear and economical.

1. **AVOID AMBIGUOUS PRONOUN REFERENCES**

   Tom killed Jerry. I feel sorry for *him*. (Who is *him*? Tom? Jerry?)

2. **AVOID CLICHÉS**

   Betty is *sharp as a tack*.

   The math exam was *easy as pie*.

3. **AVOID REDUNDANCY**

   Harry is a man who loves to gamble. (Redundant—we know that Harry is a man.)

   Harry loves to gamble. (Correct)

   This July has been particularly hot in terms of weather. (Redundant—*in terms of weather* is not necessary.)

   This July has been particularly hot. (Correct)

4. **AVOID WORDINESS**

   The phrases on the left are wordy. Use the word on the right.

WORDY	PREFERABLE
the reason why is that	because
the question as to whether	whether
in a hasty manner	hastily
be aware of the fact that	know
due to the fact that	because
in light of the fact that	since
regardless of the fact that	although
for the purpose of	to

5. AVOID VAGUE WORDS OR PHRASES

It is always preferable to use specific, concrete language rather than vague words and phrases:

The reality of the situation necessitated action. (Vague)

Bill shot the burglar before the burglar could shoot him. (Specific)

6. BE ARTICULATE—USE THE APPROPRIATE WORD OR PHRASE

The following are words or phrases that are commonly misused:

1. Accept: to receive or agree to (verb)
I *accept* your offer.

Except: preposition that means to leave out
They all left *except* Dave.

2. Adapt: to change (verb)
We must *adapt* to the new ways.

Adopt: to take as one's own, to incorporate (verb)
We will *adopt* a child.

3. Affect: to influence (verb)
Their attitude may well *affect* mine.

Effect: result (noun)
What is the *effect* of their attitude?

4. Allusion: a reference to something (noun)
The teacher made an *allusion* to Milton.

Illusion: a false idea (noun)
He had the *illusion* that he was king.

5. Among: use with more than two items (preposition)
They pushed *among* the soldiers.

Between: use with two items (preposition)
They pushed *between* both soldiers.

6. Amount: cannot be counted (noun)
Sue has a large *amount* of pride.

Number: can be counted (noun)
Sue bought a *number* of apples.

7. Apt: capable (adjective)
She is an *apt* student.

Likely: probably (adjective)
We are *likely* to receive the prize.

8. **Beside:** at the side of (preposition)
He sat *beside* me.

Besides: in addition to (preposition)
There were others there *besides* Joe.

9. **Fewer:** can be counted (adjective)
I have *fewer* pennies than John.

Less: cannot be counted (adjective)
I have *less* pride than John.

10. **Imply:** the speaker or writer is making a hint or suggestion (verb)
He *implied* in his book that women were inferior.

Infer: to draw a conclusion from the speaker or writer (verb)
The audience *inferred* that he was a woman-hater.

11. **Irritate:** to annoy (verb)
His whining *irritated* me.

Aggravate: to make worse (verb)
The soap *aggravated* his rash.

12. **Uninterested:** bored (adjective)
She is *uninterested* in everything.

Disinterested: impartial (adjective)
He wanted a *disinterested* jury at his trial.

Rhetorical Practice

To the Inca, Ampato, the god of the <u>mountain, was divinely sacred.</u>
1

Through his generosity, the life-giving water and good harvests were <u>plentiful</u>
2

<u>so that everyone could have all he needed.</u> However, for these simple
2

blessings, Ampato extracted a great toll. Each year, he claimed the highest

tribute—the sacrifice of one of their own.

The girl's mummy was found on the <u>mountainside between the rocks,</u>
<u>ice, and snow.</u> An avalanche uncovered her <u>body, frozen and cold as ice, and</u>
$\overset{\text{3}}{}$ 4
what was left of her scant earthly possessions. The girl, a young teenager,
must have been ritually sacrificed in the service of Ampato nearly 500 years
ago.

At the time this young girl died, the Inca Empire was one of the most
advanced civilizations to exist in the Western Hemisphere. They are known
today for their engineering feats, for the building of long-lasting roads, and for
their terracing of the land for growing crops. But now, <u>we will also be aware</u>
                                                           5
<u>of their superstitions,</u> and we can only shudder at the price they were willing
      5
to pay for their plentitude.

1. (A) NO CHANGE
   (B) mountain was divinely sacred
   (C) mountain, were
   (D) mountain, was sacred

2. (F) NO CHANGE
   (G) plentiful
   (H) plentiful, so that everyone could have all he needed
   (J) plentiful so that people could have all they needed

3. (A) NO CHANGE
   (B) mountainside, between the rocks, ice, and snow
   (C) mountainside among the rocks, ice, and snow
   (D) mountainside between the rocks, and snow

4. (F) NO CHANGE
   (G) body that was frozen and as cold as ice and
   (H) frozen body and
   (J) body, cold as ice, and

5. (A) NO CHANGE
   (B) we will also know about their superstitions,
   (C) we will be forewarned about their superstitions,
   (D) they will also be known for their superstitions,

NOW CHECK YOUR ANSWERS

1. **The correct answer is (D).** The phrase *divinely sacred* is redundant.

2. **The correct answer is (G).** As written, the sentence is wordy and redundant. The word *plentiful* implies that the people received all that they needed.

3. **The correct answer is (C).** Use *among* when the phrase refers to more than two items.

4. **The correct answer is (H).** The best choice is (H) because it eliminates redundancy and the cliché "as cold as ice."

5. **The correct answer is (D).** The best choice is (D) because it preserves the tone and voice of the paragraph. The sentence before lists several things for which the Incas are known. The use of the word *known* in this sentence echoes the structure sentence, strengthening the impact of the passage.

PLANE GEOMETRY

Quadrilaterals

A quadrilateral is a polygon of four sides. The sum of the angles of a quadrilateral is 360°. If the opposite sides of a quadrilateral are parallel, the quadrilateral is a *parallelogram*. Opposite sides of a parallelogram are equal and so are opposite angles. Any two consecutive angles of a parallelogram are supplementary. A diagonal of a parallelogram divides the parallelogram into congruent triangles. The diagonals of a parallelogram bisect each other.

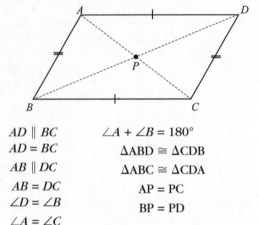

$AD \parallel BC$ $\angle A + \angle B = 180°$

$AD = BC$ $\triangle ABD \cong \triangle CDB$

$AB \parallel DC$ $\triangle ABC \cong \triangle CDA$

$AB = DC$ $AP = PC$

$\angle D = \angle B$ $BP = PD$

$\angle A = \angle C$

Definitions

A *rhombus* is a parallelogram with four equal sides. The diagonals of a rhombus are perpendicular to each other.

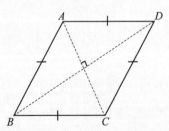

A *rectangle* is a parallelogram with four right angles. The diagonals of a rectangle are equal and can be found using the Pythagorean theorem if the sides of the rectangle are known.

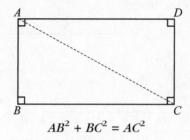

$$AB^2 + BC^2 = AC^2$$

A *square* is a rectangle with four equal sides.

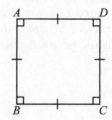

A *trapezoid* is a quadrilateral with only one pair of parallel sides, called *bases*. The nonparallel sides are called *legs*.

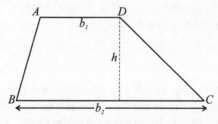

$AD \parallel BC.$
AD and BC are bases.
AB and DC are legs.
h = altitude.

Finding Areas

The area of any *parallelogram* is the product of the base and the height, where the height is the length of an altitude, a line segment drawn from a vertex perpendicular to the base.

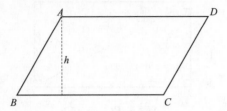

Since rectangles and squares are also parallelograms, their areas follow the same formula. For a *rectangle,* the altitude is one of the sides, and the formula is length times width. Since a *square* is a rectangle for which length and width are the same, the area of a square is the square of its side.

The area of a *trapezoid* is the height times the average of the two bases. The formula is:

$$A = b\frac{b_1 + b_2}{2}$$

The bases are the parallel sides, and the height is the length of an altitude to one of the bases.

If a quadrilateral is not a parallelogram or trapezoid but is irregularly shaped, its area can be found by dividing it into triangles, attempting to find the area of each, and adding the results.

Circles

Definitions

Circles are closed plane curves with all points on the curve equally distant from a fixed point called the *center.* A circle is usually named by its center. A line segment from the center to any point on the circle is called the *radius* (plural, radii). All radii of the same circle are equal.

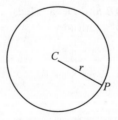

C = center

CP = radius = r

A *chord* is a line segment whose endpoints are on the circle. A *diameter* of a circle is a chord that passes through the center of the circle. A diameter, the longest distance between two points on the circle, is twice the length of the radius. A diameter perpendicular to a chord bisects that chord.

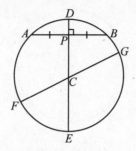

AB is a chord.
C is the center.
DCE is a diameter.
FCG is a diameter.
AB ⊥ DCE so AP = PB.

A *central angle* is an angle whose vertex is the center of a circle and whose sides are radii of the circle. An *inscribed angle* is an angle whose vertex is on the circle and whose sides are chords of the circle.

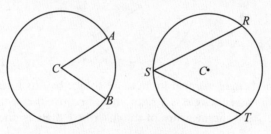

∠ACB is a central angle.
∠RST is an inscribed angle.

An *arc* is a portion of a circle. The symbol ⌒ is used to indicate an arc. Arcs are usually measured in degrees. Since the entire circle is 360°, a semicircle (half a circle) is an arc of 180°, and a quarter of a circle is an arc of 90°.

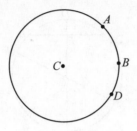

$\overset{\frown}{ABD}$ is an arc.

$\overset{\frown}{AB}$ is an arc.

$\overset{\frown}{BD}$ is an arc.

A central angle is equal in measure to its intercepted arc.

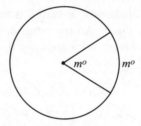

An inscribed angle is equal in measure to one-half its intercepted arc. An angle inscribed in a semicircle is a right angle because the semicircle has a measure of 180°, and the measure of the inscribed angle is one-half of that.

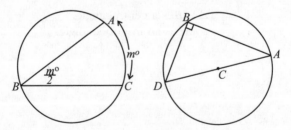

$\overset{\frown}{DA}$ = 180°; therefore,

∠*DBA* = 90°.

Perimeter and Area

The perimeter of a circle is called the *circumference*. The length of the circumference is πd, where d is the diameter, or $2\pi r$, where r is the radius. The number π is irrational and can be approximated by 3.14159..., but in problems dealing with circles it is best to leave π in the answer. There is no fraction exactly equal to π.

Example

If the circumference of a circle is 8π feet, what is the radius?

Since $C = 2\pi r = 8\pi$, $r = 4$ feet.

The length of an arc of a circle can be found if the central angle and radius are known. Then, the length of arc is $\dfrac{n°}{360°}(2\pi r)$, where the central angle of the arc is $n°$. This is true because of the proportion:

$$\frac{\text{Arc}}{\text{Circumference}} = \frac{\text{Central angle}}{360°}$$

Example

If a circle of radius 3 feet has a central angle of $60°$, find the length of the arc intercepted by this central angle.

$$\text{Arc} = \frac{60°}{360°}(2\pi 3) = \pi \text{ feet}$$

The area A of a circle is πr^2, where r is the radius. If the diameter is given instead of the radius,

$$A = \pi\left(\frac{d}{2}\right)^2 = \frac{\pi d^2}{4}.$$

Example

Find the area of a circular ring formed by two concentric circles of radii 6 and 8 inches, respectively. (Concentric circles are circles with the same center.)

The area of the ring will equal the area of the large circle minus the area of the small circle.

$$\begin{aligned}
\text{Area of ring} &= \pi 8^2 - \pi 6^2 \\
&= \pi(64 - 36) \\
&= 28\pi \text{ square inches}
\end{aligned}$$

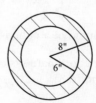

Distance Between Points

In the arithmetic section, we described the Cartesian coordinate system when explaining how to draw graphs representing linear equations. If two points are plotted in the Cartesian coordinate system, it is useful to know how to find the distance between them. If the two points have coordinates (a, b) and (p, q), the distance between them is:

$$d = \sqrt{(a-p)^2 + (b-q)^2}$$

This formula makes use of the Pythagorean theorem.

Example

Find the distance between the two points $(-3, 2)$ and $(1, -1)$.

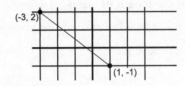

Let $(a, b) = (-3, 2)$ and $(p, q) = (1, -1)$. Then:

$$d = \sqrt{(-3-1)^2 + [2 - (-1)]^2}$$

$$= \sqrt{(-4)^2 + (2+1)^2}$$

$$= \sqrt{(-4)^2 + 3^2}$$

$$= \sqrt{16 + 9} = \sqrt{25} = 5$$

Plane Geometry Problems

1. In a trapezoid of area 20, the two bases measure 4 and 6. What is the height of the trapezoid?

2. A circle is inscribed in a square whose side is 8. What is the area of the circle, in terms of π?

3. PQ is the diameter of a circle whose center is R. If the coordinates of P are $(8, 4)$, and the coordinates of Q are $(4, 8)$, what are the coordinates of R?

4. The volume of a cube is 64 cubic inches. What is its surface area?

5. Using a coordinate system, find the distance between the two points $(2,1)$ and $(6,3)$.

TRIGONOMETRY

Trigonometry enables you to solve problems that involve finding measures of unknown lengths and angles.

The Trigonometric Ratios

Every right triangle contains two acute angles. With respect to each of these angles, it is possible to define six ratios, called the trigonometric ratios, each involving the lengths of two of the sides of the triangle. For example, consider the following triangle *ABC*.

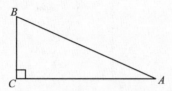

In this triangle, side *AC* is called the side adjacent to angle *A*, and side *BC* is called the side opposite angle *A*. Similarly, side *AC* is called the side opposite angle *B*, and side *BC* is called the side adjacent to angle *B*. Of course, side *AB* is referred to as the hypotenuse with respect to both angles *A* and *B*.

The six trigonometric ratios with respect to angle *A*, along with their standard abbreviations, are given below:

Sine of angle *A* = sin *A* = opposite/hypotenuse = *BC/AB*

Cosine of angle *A* = cos *A* = adjacent/hypotenuse = *AC/AB*

Tangent of angle *A* = tan *A* = opposite/adjacent = *BC/AC*

Cotangent of angle *A* = cot *A* = adjacent/opposite = *AC/AB*

Secant of angle *A* = sec *A* = hypotenuse/adjacent = *AB/AC*

Cosecant of angle *A* = csc *A* = hypotenuse/opposite = *AB/BC*

The last three ratios are actually the reciprocals of the first three, in particular:

cot *A* = 1/tan *A*

sec *A* = 1/cos *A*

csc *A* = 1/sin *A*

Also note that:

sin *A*/cos *A* = tan *A*, and

cos *A*/sin *A* = cot *A*.

In order to remember which of the trigonometric ratios is which, you can memorize the well-known acronym: **SOH–CAH–TOA** ("Sock it to her"). This stands for: **S**ine is **O**pposite over **H**ypotenuse, **C**osine is **A**djacent over **H**ypotenuse, **T**angent is **O**pposite over **A**djacent.

Example

Consider right triangle *DEF* below, whose sides have the lengths indicated. Find sin *D*, cos *D*, tan *D*, sin *E*, cos *E*, and tan *E*.

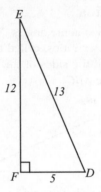

$$\sin D = EF/ED = \frac{12}{13} \qquad \sin E = DF/ED = \frac{5}{13}$$

$$\cos D = DF/ED = \frac{5}{13} \qquad \cos E = EF/ED = \frac{12}{13}$$

$$\tan D = EF/DF = \frac{12}{5} \qquad \tan E = DF/EF = \frac{5}{12}$$

Note that the sine of *D* is equal to the cosine of *E*, and the cosine of *D* is equal to the sine of *E*.

Trigonometric Ratios for Special Angles

The actual values for the trigonometric ratios for most angles are irrational numbers, whose values can most easily be found by looking in a trig table or using a calculator. On the ACT, you will not need to find the values for such trig functions; you can simply leave the answer in terms of the ratio. For example, if the answer to a word problem is 35 tan 37°, the correct answer choice will be, in fact, 35 tan 37°. There are, however, a few angles whose ratios can be obtained exactly. The ratios for 30°, 45°, and 60° can be determined from the properties of the 30-60-90 right triangle and the 45-45-90 right triangle.

Note that the Pythagorean theorem can be used to determine the following side and angle relationships in 30-60-90 and 45-45-90 triangles:

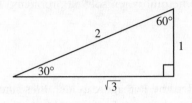
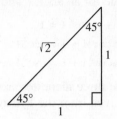

From these diagrams, it is easy to see that:

$\sin 30° = 1/2$, $\cos 30° = \dfrac{\sqrt{3}}{2}$

$\tan 30° = 1/\sqrt{3} = \sqrt{3}/3$

$\sin 60° = \sqrt{3}/2$, $\cos 60° = 1/2$, $\tan 60° = \sqrt{3}$

$\sin 45° = \cos 45° = 1/\sqrt{2} = \sqrt{2}/2$, $\tan 45° = 1$

Example

From a point A, which is directly across from point B on the opposite sides of the banks of a straight river, the measure of angle BAC to a point C, 35 meters upstream from B, is 30. How wide is the river?

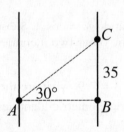

To solve this problem, note that $\tan A = $ opposite/adjacent $= BC/AB = 35/AB$.

Since the measure of angle A is 30°, we have $\tan 30° = 35/AB$. Then:

$AB = 35/\tan 30° = 35/\sqrt{3}/3 = 105/\sqrt{3}$.

Therefore, the width of the river is $\dfrac{105}{\sqrt{3}}$ meters, or approximately 60 meters wide.

The Pythagorean Identities

There are three fundamental relationships involving the trigonometric ratios that are true for all angles, and are helpful when solving problems. They are:

$$\sin^2 A + \cos^2 A = 1$$
$$\tan^2 A + 1 = \sec^2 A$$
$$\cot^2 A + 1 = \csc^2 A$$

These three identities are called the Pythagorean identities since they can be derived from the Pythagorean theorem. For example, in triangle *ABC* below

$$a^2 + b^2 = c^2$$

Dividing by c^2, we obtain,

$$\frac{a^2}{c^2} + \frac{b^2}{c^2} = 1, \ or$$

$$\left(\frac{a}{c}\right)^2 + \left(\frac{b}{c}\right)^2 = 1.$$

Now, note that $a/c = \sin A$ and $b/c = \cos A$. Substituting these values in, we obtain $\sin^2 A + \cos^2 A = 1$. The other two identities are similarly obtained.

Example

If, in triangle *ABC,* $\sin A = 7/9$, what are the values of $\cos A$ and $\tan A$?

Using the first of the trigonometric identities, we obtain:

$$(7/9)^2 + \cos^2 A = 1$$
$$49/81 + \cos^2 A = 1$$
$$\cos^2 A = 1 - 49/81$$
$$\cos A = \sqrt{32/81} = 4\sqrt{2}/9.$$

Then, since $\tan A = \sin A/\cos A$, we have $\tan A = (7/9)/(4\sqrt{2}/9) = 7/4\sqrt{2} = 7\sqrt{2}/8.$

Trigonometry Problems

1. In right triangle PQR, $\cot P = \dfrac{5}{12}$. Find the value of $\tan P$, $\sin A$, and $\sec A$.

2. Find the value of $\cot 45° + \cos 30° + \sin 150°$.

3. If $\sin a = \dfrac{3}{7}$, and $\cos a < 0$, what is the value of $\tan a$?

4. A wire extends from the top of a 50-foot pole to a stake in the ground. If the wire makes an angle of 55° with the ground, find the length of the wire.

5. A road is inclined at an angle of 10° with the horizontal. If John drives 50 feet up the road, how many feet above the horizontal is he?

NOW CHECK YOUR ANSWERS

Answers to Plane Geometry Problems

1. The formula for the area of a trapezoid is $A = \frac{1}{2}h\,(b_1 + b_2)$, where h is the height and b_1 and b_2 are the bases. Plugging in, we have $20 = \frac{1}{2}h\,(4 + 6)$ or $40 = 10h$, so $h = 4$.

2. As the picture below shows, the diameter of the circle is 8 and the radius is 4.

    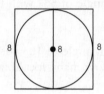

    Since $C = \pi r^2$, we have $C = \pi(4^2) = 16\pi$.

3. The center of the circle is the midpoint of the diameter. The formula for the midpoint of a line segment is $\left(\dfrac{x_1 + x_2}{2}, \dfrac{y_1 + y_2}{2}\right)$. Thus, the center is at $\left(\dfrac{12}{2}, \dfrac{12}{2}\right) = (6, 6)$.

4. Since the volume of a cube is given by $V = s^3$, where s is the side of the square, it can be seen that s is 4 (since $4^3 = 64$). Then, the surface area of one of the sides is $4 \times 4 = 16$, and, since there are six sides in a cube, the surface area is $16 \times 6 = 96$.

5. $2\sqrt{5}$

    Let $(a, b) = (2, 1)$ and $(p, q) = (6, 3)$.

    Then:

    $$
    \begin{aligned}
    \text{distance} &= \sqrt{(2 - 6)^2 + (1 - 3)^2} \\
    &= \sqrt{(-4)^2 + (-2)^2} \\
    &= \sqrt{16 + 4} \\
    &= \sqrt{20} = \sqrt{4} \times \sqrt{5} = 2\sqrt{5}
    \end{aligned}
    $$

Answers to Trigonometry Problems

1.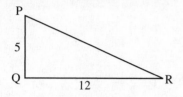

$$\cot P = \frac{5}{12} = \frac{adjacent}{opposite}. \text{ Thus, } \tan P = \frac{12}{5}.$$

From the Pythagorean theorem, we can compute that the hypotenuse of the triangle is 13.

Thus, $\sin P = \dfrac{opposite}{hypotenuse} = \dfrac{12}{13}$, and $\sec P = \dfrac{hypotenuse}{adjacent} = \dfrac{13}{5}$.

2. Note that $\sin 150° = \sin 30°$.

Thus, $\cot 45° + \cos 30° + \sin 150° = 1 + \dfrac{\sqrt{3}}{2} + \dfrac{1}{2} = \dfrac{3}{2} + \dfrac{\sqrt{3}}{2}$

3. Given $\sin a = \dfrac{3}{7}$, and $\cos a < 0$, we can find the value of $\cos a$ using the Pythagorean identity $\sin^2 a + \cos^2 a = 1$.

$$\left(\frac{3}{7}\right)^2 + \cos^2 a = 1$$

$$\frac{9}{49} + \cos^2 a = 1$$

$$\cos^2 a = 1 - \frac{9}{49} = \frac{40}{49}$$

$$\cos a = \frac{\sqrt{40}}{49} = \frac{2\sqrt{10}}{7}$$

Since $\tan a = \dfrac{\sin a}{\cos a}$, we have $\tan a = \dfrac{\left(\dfrac{3}{7}\right)}{\left(\dfrac{2\sqrt{10}}{7}\right)} = \dfrac{3}{(2\sqrt{10})} = \dfrac{3\sqrt{10}}{20}$.

4. Let L = length of the wire

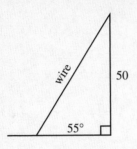

$\sin 55° = \dfrac{50}{L}$, so $L = \dfrac{50}{\sin 55°}$.

5. Let x = the distance above the horizontal.

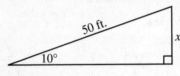

$\sin 10° =$

$\dfrac{x}{50}$. Thus, $x = 50 \sin 10°$

DAY 11

REST DAY

Take the time to relax before attacking the actual ACT Panic Plan Practice Test. Of course, since this is a last-minute study approach, if you need to review additional material, feel free to do so.

ENGLISH TEST—45 MINUTES
75 QUESTIONS

(Answers and Explanations begin on page 237)

DIRECTIONS: In the five passages that follow, certain words and phrases are underlined and numbered. Following the passage, you will find alternatives for each underlined part. You are to choose the one that best expresses the idea, makes the statement appropriate for standard written English, or is worded most consistently with the style and tone of the passage as a whole. If you think the original version is best, choose "NO CHANGE."

Passage 1

Language is possibly mans most powerful possession. How he uses it
<u>effects not only his immediacy,</u> but his past and his future. Language is man's
<u>vehicle of remembrance and projection.</u> Thus, it formulates his legacy and his
hope. Yet, <u>the most greatest characteristic of language</u> is that it <u>enables men</u>
<u>to communicate with his fellowmen</u> as individuals or as masses.

Never before in the history of civilization, has man known such a wealth
of available information. The masses of the world have ready access not only
to their immediate <u>circumstances, but also to the folkways and mores of the</u>
world at large. This transportation of <u>information either for education or</u>
<u>entertainment</u> is referred to as "communication." While the social nature of
man has <u>made him seek and share facts and opinions from the dawn of</u>
<u>history,</u> only in our <u>technological advanced society</u> has this social man

been made to participate in such an adventure with the masses on an
<u>   </u>
            12   13
instantaneous basis.
<u>   </u>
            13

    The mode of sharing can be varied. For either education or entertain-

ment, there are newspapers <u>local, regional, national, or international,</u> maga-
                                                    14
zines, <u>even radio, television, and personal contact.</u>
                    15

1. (A) NO CHANGE
   (B) possibly mens most powerful possession
   (C) possibly men's most powerful possession
   (D) possibly man's most powerful possession

2. (F) NO CHANGE
   (G) effects not only his immediate
   (H) affects not only his immediacy
   (J) affects not only his immediate

3. (A) NO CHANGE
   (B) vehicle to remember and project
   (C) vehicle of remembering and projecting
   (D) vehicle for remembering and projecting

4. (F) NO CHANGE
   (G) the greatest characteristic of language
   (H) the more greater characteristic of language
   (J) the most great characteristic of language

5. (A) NO CHANGE
   (B) inables men to communicate with his fellowmen
   (C) enables man to communicate with his fellowmen
   (D) enables men to communicate with their fellowmen

6. (F) NO CHANGE
   (G) Never before in the history of civilization
   (H) Never, before in the history of civilization,
   (J) Never before, in the history of civilization

7. (A) NO CHANGE
   (B) circumstances; but also, to the folkways and mores
   (C) circumstances but also to the folkways and mores
   (D) circumstances: but also to the folkways and mores

8. (F) NO CHANGE
   (G) information either for education or entertainment,
   (H) information for education or entertainment,
   (J) information, either for education or entertainment,

9. (A) NO CHANGE
   (B) has made him seek, and
       share facts
   (C) has made him seek and
       share, facts
   (D) has made him, seek and
       share facts

10. (F) NO CHANGE
    (G) dawn of history only
    (H) dawn of history—only
    (J) dawn of history: only

11. (A) NO CHANGE
    (B) technologically advanced
        society
    (C) technological advancing
        society
    (D) technologically advance
        society

12. (F) NO CHANGE
    (G) been to participate
    (H) has been made the
        participant
    (J) been made the participant

13. (A) NO CHANGE
    (B) on an instant basis.
    (C) on an instant base.
    (D) on a basis.

14. (F) NO CHANGE
    (G) (local, regional, national,
        or international),
    (H) (local, regional, national or
        international),
    (J) local, regional, national, or
        international

15. (A) NO CHANGE
    (B) even radio, television and
        personal contact
    (C) including radio, television,
        and personal contact
    (D) radio, television, and
        personal contact

Passage 2

During the twentieth century psychological criticism has come to be
                    ‾‾‾‾‾‾‾‾‾‾‾‾‾‾‾‾‾‾‾‾‾‾‾‾‾‾‾‾‾‾‾‾‾‾‾‾‾‾
                              16
associated with a particular school of followers. From this association have

derived most of the abuses' and misunderstandings of the modern psychologi-
        ‾‾‾‾‾‾‾‾‾‾‾‾‾‾‾‾‾‾‾
               17
cal approach to literature. On the one hand, abuses of the approach have

resulted in an excessive of enthusiasm, which has been manifested in several
‾‾‾‾‾‾‾‾‾‾‾‾‾‾‾‾‾‾‾‾‾‾‾‾‾‾‾‾‾‾‾‾‾
               18
ways. First, the practitioners of the Freudian approach often push their

critical theses too far, forcing literature into a bed of psychoanalytic theory at
‾‾‾‾‾‾‾‾‾‾‾‾‾‾‾‾‾
       19
the expense of other relevant considerations, for example the total thematic
          ‾‾‾‾‾‾‾‾‾‾‾‾‾‾‾‾‾‾‾‾‾‾‾‾‾‾‾‾‾‾‾‾   ‾‾‾‾‾‾‾‾‾‾‾‾‾‾‾‾‾‾
                        20   21
and esthetic context of the work. Second, the literary critical of the
‾‾‾‾‾‾‾‾‾‾‾‾‾‾‾‾‾‾‾‾‾‾‾‾‾‾‾‾‾   ‾‾‾‾‾‾‾‾‾‾‾‾‾‾‾‾‾‾‾‾‾‾‾‾‾
            21   22

psychoanalytic extremists <u>has at times degenerate into a special occultism</u>
         22   23
with its own mystique and jargon exclusively for the "in group." Third,

<u>many critic of the "psychological school"</u> have been either literary scholars
            24
who have had an imperfect understanding of <u>psychological principles, or</u>
                                     25
<u>professional psychologists who have had</u> little feeling for literature as art. The
          25
<u>former have abused freudian insights through oversimplification</u> and distor-
                  26
tion; the latter have abused our literary sensibilities.

These abuses <u>had given rise, on the other hand,</u> to a widespread
                          27
<u>mistrust</u> of the psychological approach as <u>a tools for critical analysis.</u> Conser-
 27   28
vative scholars and teachers of literature, often shocked by some of the

terminology and confused by the clinical diagnoses of literary problems, have

rejected all psychological criticism, other than the common sense type. In

some quarters, this reaction goes so far as to brand the approach as not only

<u>"invalid"; but also "indecent."</u> By explaining a few of the principles of
          29
psychology that have been applied to literary interpretation and by providing

some cautionary remarks, we hope to introduce the reader to a balanced

critical <u>perspective that avoid either of these extremes.</u>
                     30

16. (F) NO CHANGE
    (G) twentieth century,
         Psychological Criticism
    (H) twentieth century,
         psychological criticism
    (J) Twentieth Century,
         psychological criticis

17. (A) NO CHANGE
    (B) most of the abuse
    (C) mostly abuses'
    (D) most of the abuses

18. (F) NO CHANGE
    (G) resulted in an excessive of
         enthusiasm
    (H) resulted in, an excessive
         of enthusiasm,
    (J) resulted in an excess of
         enthusiasm,

19. (A) NO CHANGE
    (B) critical theseses too far
    (C) critical thesis too far
    (D) critically theses too far

Peterson's ■ Panic Plan for
the ACT Assessment
      195   www.petersons.com

20. (F) NO CHANGE
    (G) of other relevant consider-
        ations, for example,
    (H) of other relevant consider-
        ations; for example
    (J) of other relevant consider-
        ations; for example,

21. (A) NO CHANGE
    (B) the total theme and
        esthetic context
    (C) the total thematic and
        esthetics context
    (D) the total thematics and
        esthetic context

22. (F) NO CHANGE
    (G) literary critical of the
        psychoanalysis extremists
    (H) literary critical of the
        psychoanalytic extremists
    (J) literary criticism of the
        psychoanalytic extremists

23. (A) NO CHANGE
    (B) has at times degenerate
        into a special occultisms
    (C) has at times degenerated
        into a special occultism
    (D) has at time degenerates
        into a special occultism

24. (F) NO CHANGE
    (G) many critics of the
        "psychological school"
    (H) more critics of the
        "psychological school"
    (J) a critic of the "psychology
        school"

25. (A) NO CHANGE
    (B) psychology principles, or
        professional psychologists
    (C) psychological principles or
        professional psychologists
    (D) psychologically principles or
        professional psychologists

26. (F) NO CHANGE
    (G) have abused freudian
        insight through oversimpli-
        fication
    (H) have abused freudian
        insights, through oversim-
        plification
    (J) have abused Freudian
        insights through oversim-
        plification

27. (A) NO CHANGE
    (B) had given rise on the
        other hand, to a wide-
        spread mistrust
    (C) have given rise, on the
        other hand, to a wide-
        spread mistrust
    (D) had given rise, on the
        other hand to a wide-
        spread mistrust

28. (F) NO CHANGE
    (G) tools for critically analysis
    (H) tool for critical analysis
    (J) tools for critical analyses

29. (A) NO CHANGE
    (B) "invalid" but also "inde-
        cent."
    (C) "invalid;" but also "inde-
        cent."
    (D) "invalid", but also "inde-
        cent."

30. (F) NO CHANGE
    (G) perspective that avoid
        either of these extreme.
    (H) perspective that avoids
        either of these extremes.
    (J) perspective that avoiding
        either of these extremes.

Passage 3

In order to achieve psychic survival, <u>one must cultivate your own</u>
31
<u>memory.</u> Memory does not serve; it is the hub for the <u>sundry spokes of</u>
31 32
<u>random roles, costumes, locales and languages.</u> Memory will verify not just
33
that someone existed through time, <u>but that he was a particular someone</u>
34
whose psychic fingerprint may be the very pattern of his recollections.

<u>Memory is also the strategy for survival.</u> After an episode in which a
35
terrifying incident <u>has been witness, one may become terrified</u> that the same
36
incident will be personally experienced and desperately seek to escape

<u>such an incident, and have flashbacks</u> of that memory throughout a lifetime as
37
a warning to avoid a similar circumstance. <u>The memory is retained.</u>
38
As such, memory is <u>one way out of a divided self hood.</u> One dare not, in
39
the present moment, <u>have the experience as one own self,</u> or even feel
40
<u>that it will occur, however that memory</u> is there as a warning or barrier.
41
Memory may be <u>the way of taking the world in and provides community.</u>
42
It is also the faculty that <u>further isolates one's own memory, the more one is</u>
43
<u>seperated from others.</u> My emotions and senses divide that memory from
44
<u>others as effectively as thick reed screens</u> separate areas of a room from sight
45
and use.

The utilization of memory provides multiple possibilities for explaining

man's actions. It is memory that helps one to trace growth either in a benevo-

lent or belligerent and revengeful manner. Memory helps one to transcend

environment by escaping into what was and to dream of what can be. It is

through memory that one prevents reality from threatening or overwhelming.

The minute registration of detailed impressions serve for all of a lifetime.

31. (A) NO CHANGE
    (B) one cultivates your own memory
    (C) one must cultivate ones own memory
    (D) one must cultivate one's own memory

32. (F) NO CHANGE
    (G) it is the hub, for the sundry spokes
    (H) it is the hub for the sunday spokes
    (J) it is the hub and the sundry spokes

33. (A) NO CHANGE
    (B) roles, costumes, locales, and Languages
    (C) roles, costumes, locales and languages
    (D) roles, costumes, locales, and languages

34. (F) NO CHANGE
    (G) but, that he was a particular someone
    (H) but that one was a particular someone
    (J) but that he was a particular person

35. (A) NO CHANGE
    (B) Memory is also the strategy for survival!
    (C) Memory was also the strategy for survival.
    (D) Memory is also the strategy to survival.

36. (F) NO CHANGE
    (G) has been witness one may become terrified
    (H) had been witness, one may become terrified
    (J) has been witnessed, one may become terrified

37. (A) NO CHANGE
    (B) such an incident; and have flashbacks
    (C) such an incident and have flashbacks
    (D) such an incident: and have flashbacks

38. (F) NO CHANGE
    (G) The memory will have been retained.
    (H) The memory was retained.
    (J) The memories is retained.

39. (A) NO CHANGE
    (B) one way out of a dividing self hood
    (C) one way out of a divided self-hood
    (D) one way out of a divide self hood

40. (F) NO CHANGE
    (G) have the experience as one own self
    (H) have the experience as one's own self,
    (J) have the experience as one's own self

41. (A) NO CHANGE
    (B) it will occur, however, that memory
    (C) it will occur; however that memory
    (D) it will occur; however, that memory

42. (F) NO CHANGE
    (G) taking the world in;
        providing community
    (H) taking the world in and
        providing community
    (J) take the world in and
        provides community

43. (A) NO CHANGE
    (B) further isolates ones own
        memory, the more one
    (C) further isolates one's own
        memory the more one
    (D) further isolates one's own
        memory; the more one

44. (F) NO CHANGE
    (G) seperated from others my
        emotions
    (H) seperated from others, my
        emotions
    (J) separated from others. My
        emotions

45. (A) NO CHANGE
    (B) as effective as thick reed
        screens
    (C) as affectively as thick reed
        screens
    (D) as effectively as thick,
        reed screens

Passage 4

Homework may be twenty minutes of serious studying interspersed with
$\underline{\hspace{2cm}}$
                                                        46
forays to the kitchen or game room. For the student who is a reader, home-
$\underline{\hspace{2cm}}$
          46
work requires careful studying over notes and books so that the lecture in
$\underline{\hspace{2cm}}$
                                                        47
class can sink in.
$\underline{\hspace{2cm}}$
      47
For some students concentration is ruined when more than a momen-
$\underline{\hspace{2cm}}$
                    48
tary break from studying is taken. These are usually the students who are

listeners. Studying with a friend, reading notes aloud, or thinking of questions
$\underline{\hspace{2cm}}$
                    49
that might be asked in class is the best sort of study for the listener. That

student may also retreat to the language lab where the French language that

seems so alien in print come alive through the headphones.
$\underline{\hspace{2cm}}$
                              50
Research has shown that everyone has a unique learning style. While
$\underline{\hspace{2cm}}$
                              51
one may need prodding and encouragement, another may need to
$\underline{\hspace{2cm}}$
                              52
buckle down alone. One may study best in the morning, while another
$\underline{\hspace{2cm}}$
      52   53
prefered afternoon studying. All of this has little to do with moods, but much
$\underline{\hspace{2cm}}$
          53
to do with inborn preferences.

In order to best determine <u>how one studys best,</u> there are many factors
54

to consider. If one gets more out of hearing an explanation <u>than reading it</u>

55

chances are that one will study best by talking about the material or studying

<u>55</u>

with someone else, <u>stopping occasionally to talk about the material.</u> Even

56

imagining that one is hearing the words read will help one who learns best by

hearing.

If one learns best by seeing, then material is absorbed best by reading.

This is the student <u>who after hearing the lecture feels</u> better if the teacher

57

gives the class a printed handout or more examples <u>on the board—something</u>

58

to which the student may relate to visually.

Some students find it almost impossible to sit still and study. These

students are probably miserable <u>setting in a library</u> or at a desk for very long

59

at one time. They need breaks—if only to stretch—every half-hour or so. By

listening to the needs of their bodies, these students can learn even more.

When confined to a desk, the mover needs to practice breathing

exercises—inhale deeply and imagine the air flowing down through the body,

all of the way to the toes. <u>Then exhaling, drawing the air back up.</u> Relax the

60

jaw. Avoid getting up for a snack since eating is a distraction.

46. (F) NO CHANGE
    (G) interspersed with forays to the kitchen, or game room.
    (H) interspersed with a foray to the kitchen or game room.
    (J) interspersing with forays to the kitchen or game room.

47. (A) NO CHANGE
    (B) so the lecture in class can sink in.
    (C) so that the lecture in class will have sunk in.
    (D) so that the lecture in class can be retained.

48. (F) NO CHANGE
    (G) For some students, concentration is ruined
    (H) For some students concentrating is ruined
    (J) For some students concentration will be ruined

49. (A) NO CHANGE
    (B) Study with a friend, reading notes aloud,
    (C) Study with a friend, read notes aloud,
    (D) Studying with a friend, read notes aloud,

50. (F) NO CHANGE
    (G) alien in prints comes alive through the headphones
    (H) aliens in print come alive through the headphones
    (J) alien in print came alive through the headphones

51. (A) NO CHANGE
    (B) Research showed that everyone has a unique learning style.
    (C) Research has shown that everyone have a unique learning style.
    (D) Research has shown that everyone will have a unique learning style.

52. (F) NO CHANGE
    (G) encouragement, another may need buckling down.
    (H) encouragement, another needs to buckle down.
    (J) encouragement another may need to buckle down.

53. (A) NO CHANGE
    (B) another is preferring afternoon studying
    (C) another prefers afternoon studying
    (D) others prefers afternoon studying

54. (F) NO CHANGE
    (G) how one is studying best, there
    (H) how one studies best, there
    (J) how you study best, there

55. (A) NO CHANGE
    (B) than reading it. Chances
    (C) than reading it; chances
    (D) than reading it, chances

56. (F) NO CHANGE
    (G) stopping occasionally, to talk about the material.
    (H) to stop occasionally to talk about the material.
    (J) stopped occasionally to talk about the material.

57. (A) NO CHANGE
    (B) who, after hearing the lecture, feels
    (C) who after hearing the lecture, feels
    (D) that after hearing the lecture feels

58. (F) NO CHANGE
    (G) on the board something
    (H) on the board; something
    (J) on the board. Something

59. (A) NO CHANGE
 (B) setting in a library, or at a desk
 (C) sitting in a library, or at a desk
 (D) sitting in a library or at a desk

60. (F) NO CHANGE
 (G) Then exhaling to draw the air back up.
 (H) Then exhaling drawing the air back up.
 (J) Then exhales, drawing the air back up.

Passage 5

The value of old and rare books is judged by age, scarcity, beauty of
$\overline{}$
61
binding, printing, subject matter and author. But sometimes—very rarely—
$\overline{}$
61
value can rest on another factor, the foreedge painting discovered on the
$\overline{}$
62
leave edges of the volume. This charming and curious art form is little known,
$\overline{}$ 63
62
even among librarians and antiques dealers.
$\overline{}$
63
  It's sad to understand why the paintings are so relativly obscure, and shy
$\overline{}$
64
volumes containing them may pass through dealers' hands without being
$\overline{}$
65
discovered. The watercolored scenes is painted on the exterior edges of the
$\overline{}$
66
pages of a book while it is slightly fanned open. Then, with the book closed,
$\overline{}$
67
the gilt decoration is added to the edges of the closed pages which hides the
$\overline{}$
68
painting until the book is again fanned open.
$\overline{}$
68
  Many people never see a decoration concealed beneath the gilt—people
$\overline{}$
69
to whom the words fore-edge painting mean nothing. This is true even among

people who have known and handle books all of their lives.
$\overline{}$
70
There is many reasons why fore-edge books are little known. First, they
$\overline{}$
71
are expensive, for they must be hand painted. Though practiced for three
$\overline{}$
72
centuries the art has never been a mechanical process but
$\overline{}$
72

always painstakingly, minutely, executed by hand in watercolors worked as
$\overline{73}$
dry as possible.

Secondly those few libraries and museums fortunate enough to own
$\overline{74}$
such volumes realize the delicate nature of such art work and the books are
$\overline{75}$
inaccessible. Wisely, they are stored in dark locked cupboards where careless

fingers cannot ruin the paintings. Never are they circulated by libraries as are

ordinary books. One would need to know of them and to ask for an appoint-

ment to see them.

61. (A) NO CHANGE
    (B) beauty of binding, print, subject matter and author.
    (C) beauty of binding, printing, subject matter, and author.
    (D) beauty of bind, printing, subject matter and author.

62. (F) NO CHANGE
    (G) the foreedge painting discovered on the leave edge
    (H) the fore-edge painting discovered on the leave edges
    (J) the foreedge paint discovered on the leave edges

63. (A) NO CHANGE
    (B) is little known even among librarians
    (C) is little knowed, even among librarians
    (D) is little knowing, even among librarians

64. (F) NO CHANGE
    (G) are so relativly obscure
    (H) are so relative obscure,
    (J) are so relatively obscure,

65. (A) NO CHANGE
    (B) through dealer's hands
    (C) through dealers hands
    (D) through dealers' hand

66. (F) NO CHANGE
    (G) The watercolored scenes was painted
    (H) The watercolored scenes are painted
    (J) The watercolored scenes were painted

67. (A) NO CHANGE
    (B) while it is slight fanned open.
    (C) while it is slightly fanning open.
    (D) while it is slightly faned open.

Peterson's ■ Panic Plan for
the ACT Assessment
203
www.petersons.com

68. (F) NO CHANGE
    (G) edges of the closed pages which hide the painting
    (H) edges of the closed pages, which hides the painting
    (J) edges of the closed pages which hides the painting

69. (A) NO CHANGE
    (B) decoration concealing beneath the gilt—
    (C) decoration concealed beneath the gilt;
    (D) decoration concealed beneath the gilt,

70. (F) NO CHANGE
    (G) who have known and handle books all of their live.
    (H) who have known and handled books all of their lives.
    (J) who know and handle books all of their lives.

71. (A) NO CHANGE
    (B) There is many reason why fore-edge books are little known.
    (C) There are many reasons why fore-edge books are little known.
    (D) There are many reasons why fore-edge books is little known.

72. (F) NO CHANGE
    (G) Though practiced for three centuries, the art
    (H) Though practice for three centuries the art
    (J) Though practiced for three centurys, the art

73. (A) NO CHANGE
    (B) always painstakingly, minutly, executed by hand
    (C) always painstakingly, minutely executed by hand
    (D) always painstakingly minutely executed by hand

74. (F) NO CHANGE
    (G) Secondly, those few libraries
    (H) Second, those few libraries
    (J) Second those few libraries

75. (A) NO CHANGE
    (B) such art work and the book
    (C) such art works and the books
    (D) such art work, and the books

MATHEMATICS TEST—
60 MINUTES
60 QUESTIONS

(Answers and Explanations begin on page 245)

DIRECTIONS: Solve each problem, choose the correct answer, and then fill in the corresponding oval on your answer document.

Do not linger over problems that take too much time. Solve as many as you can; then return to the others in the time you have left for this test.

You are NOT permitted to use a calculator.

Note: Unless otherwise stated, all of the following should be assumed:

1. Illustrative figures are NOT necessarily drawn to scale.

2. Geometric figures lie in a plane.

3. The word *line* indicates a straight line.

4. The word *average* indicates arithmetic mean.

1. Which of the following is the prime factorization of 2,520?

    (A) $2^4 \times 3^2 \times 5 \times 7$
    (B) $2^3 \times 3^3 \times 5 \times 7$
    (C) $2^3 \times 3^4 \times 5 \times 7$
    (D) $2^3 \times 3^2 \times 5^2 \times 7$
    (E) $2^3 \times 3^2 \times 5 \times 7$

2. Simplify the following expression:

    $(3x^4y^5)(5x^6y)^2$

    (F) $75x^{16}y^7$
    (G) $15x^{16}y^7$
    (H) $75x^{12}y^7$
    (J) $15\ x^{12}y^7$
    (K) $75x^{10}y^6$

3. If rectangle R has an area of 36, then the perimeter of R is:

    (A) 8
    (B) 16
    (C) 30
    (D) 40
    (E) It cannot be determined.

4. An insurance agent bought a new computer priced at $1,800. If he made a down payment of $270, what percent of the price was the down payment?

    (F) 10%
    (G) 12%
    (H) 15%
    (J) 18%
    (K) 20%

5. Find the solution of the following set of equations:

$$2x + y = 3$$
$$5x - 2y = 4$$

(A) $\dfrac{10}{9}, \dfrac{7}{9}$

(B) $-\dfrac{10}{9}, -\dfrac{7}{9}$

(C) $\dfrac{10}{9}, -\dfrac{9}{7}$

(D) $-\dfrac{10}{9}, \dfrac{7}{9}$

(E) $\dfrac{9}{10}, \dfrac{7}{9}$

6. At which values of x does the graph of the function $f(x) = -x^2 + 1$ cross the x-axis?

(F) 1
(G) 0 and 1
(H) 0 and −1
(J) 1 and −1
(K) 0, 1, and −1

7. What is the solution of the inequality $3 - 2x \leq 5$?

(A) $x \leq -1$ or $x \geq 1$
(B) $x \leq -1$
(C) $x \leq 1$
(D) $x \geq 1$
(E) $x \geq -1$

8. Five identical printing presses can finish a job in 12 hours. How long would it take 6 such presses to finish the job?

(F) 10.5 hours
(G) 10 hours
(H) 9.5 hours
(J) 8 hours
(K) 6 hours

9. If a line has a slope of 0, then the line

(A) is vertical.
(B) is horizontal.
(C) passes through the origin.
(D) increases as x increases.
(E) decreases as x increases.

10. If (−3, 2) and (4, −1) are two points on the same line, then the slope of the line is:

(F) −3
(G) $-\dfrac{7}{3}$
(H) $-\dfrac{3}{7}$
(J) $\dfrac{3}{7}$
(K) 3

11. $0.0000000913 =$

(A) 9.13×10^{-5}
(B) 9.13×10^{-6}
(C) 9.13×10^{-7}
(D) 9.13×10^{-8}
(E) 9.13×10^{-9}

12. $215(54) + 215(46) =$

(F) 2,150
(G) 4,300
(H) 21,285
(J) 21,500
(K) 43,000

13. If $p + q = 23$, and $2q = 12$, then $p - q =$

(A) 5
(B) 6
(C) 9
(D) 11
(E) 17

14. What is the value of
$$\sqrt{(-3 - 1)^2 - (7 - (-1))}?$$

(F) 0

(G) $2\sqrt{2}$

(H) 4

(J) $4\sqrt{2}$

(K) 8

15.

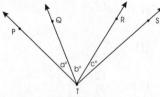

In the drawing above, the measure of angle PTR is the same as the measure of angle QTS. Which of the following statements *must* be true?

(A) $a = c$

(B) $a = b$

(C) $b = c$

(D) $a = b = c$

(E) $a + c = 2b$

16. At a particular college, $\frac{2}{5}$ of the men belong to fraternities, and $\frac{1}{4}$ of the women belong to sororities. If 200 men belong to fraternities, how many women belong to sororities?

(F) 125

(G) 250

(H) 375

(J) 500

(K) It cannot be determined from the information given.

17. Of the following, which is the closest to 1?

(A) $1 + 0.03$

(B) $1 + 0.03^2$

(C) $1 - 0.03^3$

(D) $(1 + 0.03)^2$

(E) $(1 + 0.03)^3$

18. What is the area of square *PQRS*?

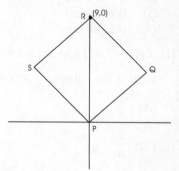

(F) $\dfrac{9\sqrt{2}}{2}$

(G) $\dfrac{27}{2}$

(H) $\dfrac{27\sqrt{2}}{2}$

(J) $\dfrac{81}{2}$

(K) $\dfrac{81\sqrt{2}}{2}$

19. If $\dfrac{ab}{c} = 0.7128$, what is the value of $\dfrac{ab}{2c}$?

(A) 0.0891

(B) 0.1188

(C) 0.1782

(D) 0.3564

(E) 1.4256

20. If used alone, Pipe #1 can fill a tank in 8 minutes, Pipe #2 can fill the tank in 12 minutes, and Pipe #3 can fill the tank in 24 minutes. How long would it take all three tanks, working together, to fill the tank?

- (F) 2.5 minutes
- (G) 4 minutes
- (H) 4.5 minutes
- (J) 6 minutes
- (K) 6.5 minutes

21. If $ax - 7 = 9$ and $bx + 2 = 12$, what is the value of $\dfrac{a}{b}$ if $b \neq 0$?

- (A) $\dfrac{1}{5}$
- (B) $\dfrac{5}{8}$
- (C) $\dfrac{8}{5}$
- (D) 5
- (E) It cannot be determined.

22. If the sum of five numbers is $7x$ and the sum of four other numbers is $2x$, what is the average (arithmetic mean) of all 9 numbers?

- (F) $\dfrac{x}{9}$
- (G) x
- (H) $9x$
- (J) 9
- (K) 1

23. Find the value of $\cos a$ if $\sin a = -\dfrac{5}{13}$, and $\cos a < 0$.

- (A) $-\dfrac{5}{12}$
- (B) $-\dfrac{12}{5}$
- (C) $-\dfrac{13}{5}$
- (D) $-\dfrac{13}{12}$
- (E) $-\dfrac{12}{13}$

24. What is the value of $\dfrac{(-4y)^3}{-4y^3}$?

- (F) -16
- (G) -4
- (H) 1
- (J) 4
- (K) 16

25. If $\dfrac{17q}{11}$ is an integer, then which of the following cannot be a value of q?

- (A) -33
- (B) -11
- (C) 11
- (D) 17
- (E) 121

26. Find the equation of the line that has *x*-intercept −3 and *y*-intercept 4.

(F) $y = -\dfrac{4}{3}x + 4$

(G) $y = \dfrac{4}{3}x + 4$

(H) $y = \dfrac{4}{3}x - 4$

(J) $y = \dfrac{3}{4}x + 4$

(K) $y = -\dfrac{3}{4}x + 4$

27. A quality control officer finds that 3% of the 3,600 pagers inspected are defective. How many pagers are not defective?

(A) 108
(B) 111
(C) 3,489
(D) 3,492
(E) 3,498

28.

The perimeters of which of the figures can be determined from the information given above?

(F) Only A
(G) Only B
(H) Only C
(J) A and B
(K) B and C

29. During the summer season, a swimming pool company increases its number of employees from 2,200 to 2,750. What is the percent of increase in the number of employees?

(A) 15%
(B) 20%
(C) 25%
(D) 30%
(E) 35%

30. At a time 15 seconds after a launching, a ground-control observer located 1.5 km from a launch pad finds that the angle of elevation of a rocket moving vertically upward from the launch pad is 78°. How high, in km, is the rocket at that time?

(F) $\dfrac{\sin 78°}{1.5}$

(G) $\dfrac{\cos 78°}{1.5}$

(H) $1.5 \sin 78°$

(J) $1.5 \cos 78°$

(K) $1.5 \tan 78°$

31. What is the equation of the line through the points (2, 1) and (−4, 6)?

(A) $y = \dfrac{5}{6}x + \dfrac{8}{3}$

(B) $y = -\dfrac{5}{6}x - \dfrac{8}{3}$

(C) $y = -\dfrac{5}{6}x + \dfrac{3}{8}$

(D) $y = -\dfrac{5}{6}x + \dfrac{8}{3}$

(E) $y = \dfrac{5}{6}x + \dfrac{3}{8}$

32. What is the length of a rectangle with an area of $108x^2y^3$ and width $9x^2y$?

(F) $12xy^2$
(G) $12xy$
(H) $9y^2$
(J) $12y^2$
(K) $972x^4y^4$

33. What is the value of $(x^2y^3)^z$ if $x = 2$, $y = 1$, and $z = 3$?

(A) 16
(B) 32
(C) 64
(D) 128
(E) 256

34. A real estate agent receives a commission of $3,625 for selling a house. If this represents 5% of the selling price of the house, what was the selling price of the house?

(F) $38,063
(G) $38,158
(H) $68,875
(J) $72,500
(K) $76,125

35.

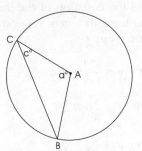

In the figure above, if AC < CB and A is the center of the circle, then which of the following must be true?

(A) $a < c$
(B) $a = c$
(C) $60 < a$
(D) $60 < c$
(E) $a > 2c$

36. 3^3 is what percent of 3^4?

(F) $16\frac{2}{3}\%$
(G) $33\frac{1}{3}\%$
(H) 50%
(J) $66\frac{2}{3}\%$
(K) $133\frac{1}{3}\%$

37. If a circle has a radius of q and an area of 12π, what is the area of a circle with radius $7q$?

(A) $12\sqrt{7}\,\pi$
(B) $28\sqrt{3}\,\pi$
(C) 84π
(D) 294π
(E) 588π

38. A delivery person is paid an hourly wage of $8, and time and a half for all time over 40 hours. How much money did the delivery person earn during a week in which he worked $48\frac{1}{4}$ hours?

(F) $386
(G) $410
(H) $419
(J) $438
(K) $579

39. In the figure below, XY is twice XZ. What is the length of XZ?

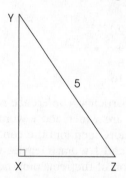

(A) $\sqrt{5}$
(B) $5\sqrt{2}$
(C) $2\sqrt{5}$
(D) 5
(E) 10

40. Simplify the following expression:

$$\sqrt{45} + 7\sqrt{125}$$

(F) $8\sqrt{5}$
(G) $5\sqrt{10}$
(H) $38\sqrt{5}$
(J) $38\sqrt{10}$
(K) $105\sqrt{5}$

41. At the beginning of the week, Beta Utility Organization stock was selling at $47\frac{1}{4}$. By the end of the week, it had lost $6\frac{3}{8}$ points. What was the price of the stock at the end of the week?

(A) $40\frac{3}{4}$
(B) $40\frac{7}{8}$
(C) $41\frac{1}{8}$
(D) $41\frac{3}{8}$
(E) $41\frac{7}{8}$

42.

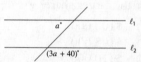

In the figure above, line ℓ_1 is parallel to line ℓ_2. What is the value of a?

(F)   17.5
(G)   20
(H)   35
(J)   40
(K)   70

43. Find the freight charge for transporting 130 cartons of engine parts if each carton weighs 17.6 kg and the charge is $13 per 100 kg.

(A) $96.57
(B) $175
(C) $176
(D) $225
(E) $297.44

44. Express 120% as a fraction.

(F) $\dfrac{1}{5}$

(G) $\dfrac{3}{25}$

(H) $\dfrac{5}{6}$

(J) $\dfrac{28}{25}$

(K) $\dfrac{6}{5}$

45. Last year, the profits for a partnership were shared in a ratio of 7:5. If the total profits for the partnership were $180,000, what was the amount received by the partner who got the larger share?

(A) $100,000
(B) $105,000
(C) $110,000
(D) $120,000
(E) $125,000

46. Solve for x in terms of a, b, and c: $a = \dfrac{b}{1 - cx}$

(F) $\dfrac{b - a}{ac}$

(G) $\dfrac{b}{c}$

(H) $\dfrac{ac}{a - b}$

(J) $\dfrac{ac}{b - a}$

(K) $\dfrac{a - b}{ac}$

47. If $3x^2 - 12 = x(1 + 2x)$, then what is the value of x?

(A) 4
(B) −3
(C) −4 or 4
(D) 4 or −3
(E) 3 or −4

48. If one side of a square is increased by 2, and an adjacent side is multiplied by 3, the rectangle that results has a perimeter that is 4 times the perimeter of the original square. What was the perimeter of the original square?

(F) 1
(G) 2
(H) 4
(J) 8
(K) 16

49. In a particular conference room, there are x men and y women. If 2 more men join the conference and 1 woman leaves, what fraction of the remaining people in the conference room are men?

(A) $x + y + 1$

(B) $\dfrac{x + 2}{x + y + 1}$

(C) $\dfrac{x + y + 1}{x + 2}$

(D) $\dfrac{y - 1}{x + 2}$

(E) $\dfrac{x + 2}{y - 1}$

50. An automobile recall was based on tests that showed 36 brake defects in 1,000 cars. At this rate, how many defects would be found in 35,000 cars?

(F)   878
(G)   972
(H)   1,029
(J)   1,260
(K)   1,352

51. Solve for x: $\dfrac{2}{5}x + \dfrac{x}{3} = 11$

(A)   1

(B) $7\dfrac{1}{2}$

(C)   13
(D)   15
(E)   30

52. N percent of what number is M?

(F)   100MN

(G) $\dfrac{100N}{M}$

(H) $\dfrac{100M}{N}$

(J) $\dfrac{NM}{100}$

(K) $\dfrac{100}{MN}$

53. Find the largest of three consecutive integers such that 10 more than the product of the first and second equals the product of the second and third.

(A)   4
(B)   5
(C)   6
(D)   7
(E)   8

54. What is the solution of the inequality $|y - 5| > 1$?

(F) $y > 6$
(G) $y > 4$
(H) $y < 4$
(J) $y < 6$ and $y > 4$
(K) $y > 6$ or $y < 4$

55. If $3^a = 81$, and $a = b^3 - 4$, then $b =$

(A)   2
(B)   3
(C)   4
(D)   6
(E)   9

56. What is the value of cos 1110°?

(F) $\dfrac{\sqrt{3}}{2}$

(G) $-\dfrac{\sqrt{3}}{2}$

(H) $\dfrac{1}{2}$

(J) $-\dfrac{1}{2}$

(K) $\dfrac{\sqrt{2}}{2}$

57. What is the value of $3 \cos 45° + 3 \sin 30°$?

(A)   1

(B) $\dfrac{2 - 3\sqrt{2}}{2}$

(C) $\dfrac{3\sqrt{2} - 2}{2}$

(D) $\dfrac{-3\sqrt{2} - 2}{2}$

(E) $\dfrac{3\sqrt{2} + 3}{2}$

58. A secretary orders $9,000 worth of office supplies, and receives a discount of 30%, followed by an additional discount of 20%. What single percent discount is the equivalent of the two discounts?

    (F) 42%
    (G) 44%
    (H) 50%
    (J) 56%
    (K) 58%

59. In a group of 30 students, 18 are taking Biology, 15 are taking Chemistry, and 11 are taking both courses. How many students in the group are taking neither Chemistry nor Biology?

    (A) 7
    (B) 8
    (C) 9
    (D) 10
    (E) 11

60. If $\frac{1}{4}a = \frac{1}{3}b = \frac{1}{2}c > 0$, then which of the following is true?

    (F) $a > b > c$
    (G) $b > a > c$
    (H) $c > b > a$
    (J) $a > c > b$
    (K) $b > c > a$

READING TEST—35 MINUTES
40 QUESTIONS

(Answers and Explanations begin on page 265)

DIRECTIONS: There are four passages in this test. Each passage is followed by several questions. After reading a passage, choose the best answer to each question and fill in the corresponding oval on your answer document. You may refer to the passages as often as necessary.

Passage 1

Neutrinos offer an opportunity to measure events taking place inside the sun. Neutrinos are uncharged and, for all practical purposes, massless particles of matter; they very rarely react with anything. A single neutrino can pass through the entire sun with only one chance in a billion of being stopped. Their theoretical properties, however, including a fractional one-half spin quantum number, make them detectable. Even though their brief half-life would lead many to decay in transit, a measurable flux of neutrinos created in the interior of the sun and sent in the direction of Earth should arrive at Earth-based neutrino counters.

Since the number of neutrinos produced varies with the temperature of the specific thermonuclear reaction, scientists counting emitted neutrinos should be able to draw significant conclusions about the reactions taking place in the sun's core. But actually counting these elusive particles is another problem. Not even the most elaborate neutrino traps—including one buried deeply below the earth's surface in the Homestake Mine in South Dakota— have found enough neutrinos to match the number predicted by classical theories of the solar interior.

Many resourceful reasons have been proposed to explain this "neutrino deficit." The measuring instruments may be inadequate. Or, perhaps, at the extreme of astronomers' imaginings, a "sink" of some sort in the sun is altering most of the neutrinos before they can escape. Even the global solar oscillations have been suggested as an explanation: If such oscillations really rock through the sun quickly, perhaps in as short a period as an hour, they could be moving energy out from the center of the sun fast enough to cool the thermonuclear furnace and reduce the production of neutrinos.

But whatever the final explanation, the apparent neutrino deficit poses some hard, fundamental questions. Since astronomy relies fundamentally on an understanding of the sun, the solar neutrino question could very well shake the foundation of astrophysics.

1. Neutrinos are defined by which of the following?

    I.   Positively charged particles

    II. Negatively charged particles

    III. Chargeless particles

    (A) I only

    (B) I and II only

    (C) III only

    (D) II and III only

2. All of the following are FALSE EXCEPT

    (F) Scientists have found more neutrinos than they expected.

    (G) Scientists have found as many neutrinos as they expected.

    (H) Scientists have found far fewer neutrinos than were expected.

    (J) Scientists, on some occasions, have found more neutrinos than expected and, on other occasions, fewer neutrinos than expected.

3. The production of neutrinos varies based on the

    (A) size of the thermonuclear reaction.

    (B) temperature of the thermonuclear reaction.

    (C) number of electrons produced during the thermonuclear reaction.

    (D) number of protons produced during the thermonuclear reaction.

4. One cause of a neutrino deficit may be

    (F) the usage of measuring instruments that are highly reliable.

    (G) a condition in the sun affecting neutrinos before they escape from the sun.

    (H) a reduction in neutrino production due to the moon's increased velocity at periodic times of the year.

    (J) an unusually slow oscillation of solar movements in the sun's center.

5. The writer indicates that one theoretical property of neutrinos that makes them detectable is their

    (A) ability to interact noticeably with other particles.

    (B) massive size in groups.

    (C) one-half spin quantum number.

    (D) activity in the sun's core.

6. In theory, by counting emitted neutrinos, scientists could

    (F) find the age of the sun.

    (G) measure the temperature of the sun.

    (H) draw conclusions about solar reactions.

    (J) improve their measuring instrument.

7. Solar neutrino questions could shake the foundation of which of the following disciplines?

   (A) Astrophysics
   (B) Stellar astronomy
   (C) Astronomy
   (D) Nuclear physics

8. The lack of solar neutrinos could be an indication that something is wrong with which one of the following theories?

   (F) The theory of stellar evolution
   (G) The role of gravity in the universe
   (H) Theory of energy conservation
   (J) The theory of how planets are formed

9. Neutrinos would be useful for measuring

   (A) activity going on in the earth's core.
   (B) activity going on in the sun.
   (C) the energy released in a nuclear fusion reaction.
   (D) the attraction between protons and electrons.

10. The theme or purpose of this selection is to

   (F) describe a phenomenon in space.
   (G) define the neutrino.
   (H) explain the purpose of the neutrino.
   (J) persuade the reader that neutrinos do exist.

Passage 2

Isabel Pervin was listening for two sounds—for the sound of wheels on the drive outside and for the noise of her husband's footsteps in the hall. Her dearest and oldest friend, a man who seemed almost indispensable to her living, would drive up in the rainy dusk of the closing November day. The tram had gone to fetch him from the station. And her husband, who had been blinded in Flanders, and who had a disfiguring mark on his brow, would be coming in from the outhouses.

He had been home for a year now. He was totally blind. Yet they had been very happy. The Grange was Maurice's own place. The back was a farmstead, and the Wernhams, who occupied the rear premises, acted as farmers. Isabel lived with her husband in the handsome rooms in front. She and he had been almost entirely alone together since he was wounded. They talked and sang and read together in a wonderful and unspeakable intimacy. Then she reviewed books for a Scottish newspaper, carrying on her old interest, and he occupied himself a good deal with the farm. Sightless, he could still discuss everything with Wernham, and he could also do a good deal of work about the place—menial work, it is true, but it gave him satisfaction.

They were newly and remotely happy. He did not even regret the loss of his sight in these times of dark palpable joy. A certain exultance swelled his soul.

But as time wore on, sometimes the rich glamour would leave them. Sometimes, after months of this intensity, a sense of burden overcame Isabel, a weariness, a terrible ennui, in the silent house sheltered between a colonnade of tall-shafted pines. Then she felt she would go mad, for she could not bear it. And sometimes he had devastating fits of depression, which seemed to lay waste his whole being. It was worse than depression—a black misery, when his own life was a misfortune to him, and when his presence was unbearable to his wife. The dread went down to the roots of her soul as these black days recurred. In a kind of panic, she tried to wrap herself up still further in her husband. She forced the old spontaneous cheerfulness and joy to continue. But the effort it cost her was almost too much. She knew she could not keep it up. She felt she would scream with the strain and would give anything, anything, to escape. She longed to possess her husband utterly; it gave her inordinate joy to have him entirely to herself. And yet, when again he was gone in a black and massive misery, she could not bear him, she could not bear herself; she wished she could be snatched off the earth altogether, anything rather than live at this cost.

Dazed, she schemed for a way out. She invited friends, she tried to give him some further connection with the outer world. But it was no good. After all their joy and suffering, after their dark, great year of blindness and solitude and unspeakable nearness, other people seemed to them both, shallow, prattling, and rather impertinent. In the presence of their friend, he became impatient and irritated and she was wearied. And so they lapsed into their solitude again. For they preferred it.

11. Isabel Pervin listened for two sounds that symbolize

    (A) antagonism toward her husband.

    (B) anxiety related to a pregnancy.

    (C) a hopeful answer to unhappiness.

    (D) panic about the future.

12. The Pervins lived entirely alone because

    (F) Isabel could not learn to cope with her husband's handicap.

    (G) their farmstead was in an isolated area.

    (H) they were uniquely compatible.

    (J) time and loneliness appeared necessary for adjustment to the husband's blindness.

13. Maurice's life was very full and strangely serene in that first year because of all of the following EXCEPT

(A) He could discuss everything with Wernham.

(B) Blindness did not keep him from work on the farm.

(C) He had a rich and satisfying relationship with his wife.

(D) He developed a belief that God provided compensation for loss of any of the senses.

14. This passage is primarily concerned with Isabel Pervin's

(F) looking forward to a visit from her friend.

(G) realization that she no longer loved Maurice.

(H) anticipation of childbirth.

(J) observations concerning her world.

15. The statement of the narrator, "Yet they had been very happy" is

(A) factual.

(B) ironical and derisive.

(C) critical and caustic.

(D) precise and exact.

16. The word "seemed" in the clause "a man who seemed almost indispensable to her living" indicates that

(F) in the narrator's view, Isabel was not sure of her husband's love.

(G) Isabel knew all would go well.

(H) delusion is a product of unhappiness.

(J) in desperation, people clutch at straws.

17. All of the following made Isabel, on occasion, feel that she would go mad EXCEPT

(A) her desire for children.

(B) the silence.

(C) the boredom.

(D) her weariness and depression.

18. The tone of this passage suggests that the narrator is treating the situation of his characters with

(F) total sympathy.

(G) humor.

(H) honest appraisal.

(J) candor.

19. The narrator tells the reader that "other people seemed to them" to be "shallow, prattling, and rather impertinent." All of the following are true of this statement EXCEPT

(A) The narrator is presenting a subjective opinion.

(B) The reader is expected to accept the narrator's opinion.

(C) The narrator tells the reader that this is the view of Isabel and Maurice.

(D) The narrator has a low opinion of Isabel and Maurice's friends.

20. As the narrator presents it, Isabel's love for Maurice is best characterized as

(F) total and physical.

(G) selfish and consuming.

(H) a mixture of joy and fear.

(J) a frequent yearning to escape.

Passage 3

The language of crisis is commonplace in education. Educators have learned to live with "crises" of finance, curriculum, competence, and confidence.

But there is a genuine crisis in our society and schools that is receiving far too little attention—a crisis in caring.

In schools, the crisis manifests itself in two ways. Students often feel that no one cares for them, and they are not learning how to be carers themselves.

At a time when an already enormous need for caregiving in the larger society is continuing to grow, schools are, for the most part, ignoring the task of preparing people to care. And being cared for may be a prerequisite to learning how to care. The most common complaint of school dropouts against their teachers, according to a recent survey, is "They don't care."

Such concerns are grounds not to blame teachers—who in most cases are trying to care—but rather to look at education from the perspective of caring and to consider changes that might strengthen human relationships as well as intellectual pursuits in schools.

As we consider the term, caring properly refers to relations, not to individuals. We do, certainly, talk about the capacity of individuals to care, and we often praise a particular individual as a "caring person." But in an ethic of caring, both parties—carer and cared for—must contribute in characteristic ways.

People need to learn not only how to care but also how to respond to care extended to them by others. Genuine involvement as the cared-for party in a relationship requires receptivity and discernment.

21. The inference is that the problems of schools include all of the following EXCEPT

   (A) discipline in the classroom.
   (B) curriculum disputes.
   (C) financial problems.
   (D) competence of faculty.

22. Students who drop out of school most often blame it on

   (F) the need for a full-time job.
   (G) disinterested teachers.
   (H) academic concerns.
   (J) poor curriculum.

23. The sense of *care* as demonstrated in this selection indicates

   (A) concern for one's welfare.
   (B) relations between individuals.
   (C) sympathy in times of distress.
   (D) attention to the needs of others.

24. *Caring* involves not only concern for another but also

   (F) the ability to respond to care as well.
   (G) for all of mankind.
   (H) attention to the needs of family.
   (J) an awareness of other cultures.

25. True caring requires both ___ and ___ according to this selection.

   (A) concern . . . responsiveness
   (B) awareness . . . honesty
   (C) receptivity . . . discernment
   (D) giving . . . taking

26. The inference is that the teachers in today's schools are

   (F) thoughtless and insensitive.
   (G) educated and well-trained.
   (H) incompetent and inattentive.
   (J) sincere and well-meaning.

27. The author leaves the impression that a caring atmosphere breeds

   (A) abounding goodwill.
   (B) perceptive thoughtfulness.
   (C) greater intellectual pursuits.
   (D) less crime and violence.

28. According to this passage, lack of caring is a crisis in modern education because

   (F) many students have not been taught to care.
   (G) there is a lack of respect among students.
   (H) time limitations prevent such concerns.
   (J) rules prevent the exercise of caring.

29. In order to teach caring, schools must begin by

   (A) training teachers.

   (B) adopting new curriculum strategies.

   (C) training administrators.

   (D) encouraging human relationships.

30. The theme or main idea of this selection is the need for caring, which demands

   (F) letting others attend to one's needs.

   (G) attending to the needs of others.

   (H) genuine involvement among all parties.

   (J) willingness to sacrifice.

Passage 4

It was not just that World War II and the United States–Soviet Cold War had finally ended in Berlin in 1989. Another war was also winding down. This was a war at once undeclared and yet global. It was a war in which the body count was low but the economic and political impact enormous. It was a war so subtle that leaders everywhere could credibly deny it had ever happened, yet so complex, that the world may need the rest of this century to negotiate the terms of its peace. It was a cold war within the Cold War. It was fought more or less throughout the 1980s. It was from a functional point of view, the Third World War.

The big "winners" of the Third World War were Japan and Germany— the very powers that had been the losers of World War II.

Also among the winners were some of the European and East Asian countries that had been nominal victors in World War II, but only after massive suffering at the hands of Nazi Germany or Imperial Japan. By holding their noses, taking the plunge of geo-realism, and aligning economically with their much-chastened enemies from four decades earlier, Western Europeans as well as East Asians emerged again as winners in the Third World War— with far more to show for their triumph this time around.

The big "losers" of the Third World War were the United States and the Soviet Union—the very powers that not only won World War II but became leaders of vast empires and blocs as a result. The Soviet defeat was obvious and total. Its post-Third World War future looks extremely bleak. America's defeat, on the other hand, was only partial. It left the country in a situation not unlike that of Japan and Germany after World War II. Although sectors of the American economy lay vanquished by foreign competition and in near ruins at the end of the 1980s, the basis for revival was still solid. The necessary condition was an American public- and private-sector leadership willing to pursue in the 1990s policies as farsighted and self-disciplined as those of Germany and Japan in the 1950s and 1960s.

31. The term "Third World War" refers to
    (A) a future time.
    (B) a fictional work.
    (C) the period of the 1980s.
    (D) a legal battle.

32. The winners of this war, according to this selection, include all of the following EXCEPT
    (F) Japan.
    (G) Western Europe.
    (H) East Asia.
    (J) Northern Africa.

33. The Soviet Union, according to this article, is a loser in the described war because
    (A) it could not overcome political strife.
    (B) its defeat was total.
    (C) of poor economic decisions.
    (D) of military dependence.

34. The United States, according to this article, is a loser in this war because of
    (F) political intrigue.
    (G) demilitarization.
    (H) the success of foreign competition.
    (J) lowered performance standards.

35. America's recovery is dependent upon all of the following EXCEPT
    (A) self-discipline.
    (B) isolationism.
    (C) leadership.
    (D) farsighted policies.

36. The victories of Germany and Japan came about because of
    (F) immigration and exportation of goods.
    (G) geo-realism and aligning economically.
    (H) the birth of democracy.
    (J) foreign intervention.

37. According to this article, the Cold War ended
    (A) with a resolution between the United States and the Soviet Union.
    (B) with the taking down of the Berlin Wall.
    (C) in Berlin in 1989.
    (D) with the demise of socialism.

38. Peace following the Third World War, as described in this selection, would
    (F) never come.
    (G) take the rest of the century.
    (H) be immediately available.
    (J) depend upon technological improvements.

39. The winners in World War II had
    (A) to cope with a loss of manpower.
    (B) economic difficulties from arms development.
    (C) to retool factories.
    (D) vast empires and blocs as a result.

40. The inference is that the Third World War concerns
    (F) economic growth and prosperity.
    (G) winning the arms race.
    (H) raising armies.
    (J) progress in social issues.

SCIENCE REASONING TEST—
35 MINUTES
40 QUESTIONS

(Answers and Explanations begin on page 268)

DIRECTIONS: There are seven passages in this test. Each passage is followed by several questions. After reading a passage, choose the best answer to each question and fill in the corresponding oval on your answer document. You may refer to the passage as often as necessary.

Passage 1

Tobacco mosaic virus (TMV) and Holmes ribgrass virus (HRV) are plant viruses that can infect tobacco plants, each producing a readily distinguishable type of injury to the plant. Researchers found that each virus consisted of a specific and unique protein molecule surrounding a specific and unique RNA molecule. The scientists separated the protein coat from the RNA molecule inside and reassembled viruses as follows:

Table 1. Reconstituted combinations of virus protein and RNA

Virus	Type of protein coat	Type of RNA molecule
native TMV	TMV	TMV
native HRV	HRV	HRV
hybrid 1	TMV	HRV
hybrid 2	HRV	TMV

The scientists then applied the four reconstituted viruses to cuts made on the leaves of different tobacco plants, and watched to see whether TMV- or HRV-type injuries resulted. Table 2 presents the results of one of the experiments. A plus (+) sign indicates this type of injury was observed, and a minus (−) sign indicates that this type of injury was not observed.

Table 2. Type of injuries developing on tobacco leaves infected with reconstituted viruses

Virus	TMV-type injury present	HRV-type injury present
native TMV	+	−
native HRV	−	+
hybrid 1	−	+

1. Why were native (same source of protein and RNA) viruses reassembled for the experiment, instead of simply using wild virus?

   (A) As a control
   (B) The scientists just wanted to try doing this
   (C) That was the point of the experiment
   (D) None of the above

2. If native viruses were not reassembled and wild viruses were used instead, how would have the experiment been affected?

   (F) There would have been no effect on the experiment as the outcome would not have been changed
   (G) Without a control, the significance of the experimental results would have been less clear
   (H) There would have been no effect on the experiment, as a control was not needed for such a simple and straightforward experiment
   (J) None of the above

3. According to the results in Table 2, what is the infectious nature of the virus due to?

   (A) The protein coat
   (B) The RNA molecule
   (C) Neither the protein coat nor RNA molecule
   (D) Both the protein coat and RNA molecule

4. What was the point of the experiment?

   (F) To show the reassembled virus was still capable of infecting plants
   (G) To show that disassembling the virus into its constituent parts did not destroy its pathogenicity (ability to cause disease)
   (H) To test virus disassembly as a form of preventing TMV and HRV diseases
   (J) To show that RNA in some cases can, like DNA, carry genetic information

5. If hybrid 2 had been tested in this experiment

   (A) the plant would show TMV-type symptoms.
   (B) the plant would show HRV-type symptoms.
   (C) the results could not be predicted based upon the information given.
   (D) another control would have to be added to determine the effect of hybrid 2 on the plants.

Passage 2

Are high-voltage power lines a possible cancer-causing agent?

Scientist 1
The energy that exists in the photons that are emitted by the 60Hz electro-magnetic radiation is so small that it cannot affect the bonds that hold molecules together or even cause heating effects the way that microwaves do.

Scientist 2
Strong electromagnetic fields, such as those found near high-voltage wires, have been shown to affect the rate of bone growth. Cells exposed to an electric field hold on to calcium ions more than cells not exposed. It is believed this increase in calcium causes cells to divide more often. Cancer growth depends on the rate of cell division.

6. A survey of the incidence of cancer cases among those who live or work near high-voltage lines was conducted. According to Scientist 1, the results should reveal

   (F) a greater incidence of cancer near the power line.

   (G) no greater incidence of cancer near the power line than at other loca-tions.

   (H) bone cells with greater levels of calcium.

   (J) a weak magnetic field.

7. Scientist 2 would predict that the survey will show

   (A) higher electromagnetic fields.

   (B) no breakdown of biomol-ecules.

   (C) fewer 60Hz photons.

   (D) cells that have faster rates of division.

8. Scientist 1 concludes little or no cell changes near high-voltage magnetic fields based on

   (F) 60Hz fields.

   (G) the effect on bone cell growth.

   (H) the way calcium increases the tendency of cells to divide.

   (J) Heisenberg's uncertainty principle.

9. In order to have a more convincing argument, Scientist 2 has to establish a link between

   (A) electromagnetic radiation and emitted photons.

   (B) the rate of cell division and cancer growth.

   (C) high-voltage versus low-voltage electromag-netic radiation.

   (D) an electric current and radiation.

10. Which scientist would ascribe to the theory that cells would be affected by weak pulsating electric and magnetic fields induced in the body by radiation?

(F) Scientist 1
(G) Scientist 2
(H) Both
(J) Neither

11. While cancer is an uncontrolled growth of cells, this does not mean that

(A) 60Hz radiation creates molecular bonds.
(B) photons are emitted by electromagnetic radiation.
(C) an increase of calcium causes cancer.
(D) cells exposed to an electric field have a greater tendency to hold onto calcium ions.

Passage 3

Of the three classical states of matter—solid, liquid, and gas—the latter is the most compressible. This was discovered over 300 years ago by a English chemist and physicist Robert Boyle. Gases can be used in a variety of "cushioning" instances because of their ability to be compressed; their particles are well separated from one another. The most famous demonstration of this property was done by trapping a fixed amount of air in a J-tube using mercury. As more and more mercury was added, the volume of the trapped air was measured. Examine the following table:

Volume of a Trapped Air Sample at 25°C and Different Pressures

Trial	Pressure (atm.)	Volume (cm3)
1	2.40	5.72
2	2.30	5.95
3	2.35	5.84
4	2.50	5.50

12. In the table presented, as the pressure increases, the volume

(F) increases.
(G) decreases.
(H) stays the same.
(J) fluctuates randomly.

13. In order for the relationship between pressure and volume to be true, what property of the gas must remain constant?

(A) Temperature
(B) Volume
(C) Pressure
(D) Density

14. This work is summarized in

 (F) Dalton's Law.
 (G) Charles's Law.
 (H) Le Chatelier's Principle.
 (J) Boyle's Law.

15. What two variables are held constant in this experiment?

 (A) Volume and temperature
 (B) Amount of the gas and temperature
 (C) Pressure and amount of the gas
 (D) Pressure on the gas and temperature

16. How would you answer the question posed by the scientist who originally did this work— "Is there a relationship between the pressure and volume of a gas?"

 (F) Yes, they vary inversely.
 (G) Yes, the variation is direct.
 (H) Yes, the product of the two values is a constant.
 (J) Yes, there is a change in the amount of the gas.

17. Which of the following summarizes the relationship indicated by the data?

 (A) $P_1 \times V_1 = P_2 \times V_2$
 (B) $P_1 \times V_2 = P_2 \times V_1$
 (C) $\dfrac{P_1}{V_1} = \dfrac{V_2}{P_2}$
 (D) $\dfrac{V_1}{P_2} = \dfrac{P_1}{V_2}$

Passage 4

The following experiments were conducted to determine what would happen when a spherical object was dropped onto a hard surface. The rebound height is determined by the total energy in the system. This energy can be present in many different forms. Energy can leave one part of the system and enter another part of the system.

Experiment 1

Three identical balls made of 100 percent rubber are filled with air. Ball number one has a pressure of 30 p.s.i., ball number two has a pressure of 35 p.s.i., and ball number three has a pressure of 40 p.s.i. The balls were released from a height of 5 meters onto a concrete floor. Ball number one rebounded to a height of 1 meter, ball number two rebounded to a height of 1.5 meters, and ball number three rebounded to a height of 2 meters.

Experiment 2

Another experiment was conducted using the same three balls, each having an air pressure of 35 p.s.i. The balls were dropped onto a concrete floor from a height of 5 meters. Each ball was dropped three times in succession. It was noticed that the rebound height increased slightly each time a ball was dropped.

Experiment 3

A third experiment was conducted using the same three balls, each having an air pressure of 35 p.s.i. The balls were dropped onto a hardwood floor from a height of 5 meters. Each ball rebounded to a height of 1.53 meters. The balls were allowed to rest on the floor for a period of 30 minutes before being dropped again. Each ball was dropped a total of three times, with the results being the same each time.

18. What conclusions can be drawn from Experiment 1 alone?

    (F) The higher the air pressure inside the ball, the more energy the concrete floor imparted to it.
    (G) All balls will rebound to a height that is proportional to the air pressure inside the ball.
    (H) The difference in air pressure is responsible for the difference in rebound height.
    (J) G and H are both correct.

19. Using Experiment 2 alone we can conclude

    (A) the concrete floor was imparting energy to the balls.
    (B) something inside the balls was causing the increase in rebound height.
    (C) nothing.
    (D) both A and B could be correct, but further testing needs to be done.

20. Using Experiments 2 and 3, the following conclusion(s) could be made:

    (F) Something inside the balls was causing the increase in rebound height in Experiment 2.
    (G) The concrete floor was responsible for the increase in rebound height in Experiment 2.
    (H) A hardwood floor does not increase the rebound height.
    (J) None of the above.

21. Which experiment served as a control for the other two?

(A) Experiment 1
(B) Experiment 2
(C) Experiment 3
(D) None of the experiments served as a control for the other two.

22. What factor served as a control in all three experiments?

(F) Air pressure
(G) Height
(H) Temperature
(J) None of the above

23. It was decided that the composition of the ball, the temperature of the air inside the ball on rebound, and the surface the ball strike all were involved in the results. To test whether the temperature of the air inside the ball affected the results you would need to

(A) record the air temperature of the room before and after each drop.
(B) record the temperature of the floor before and after each drop.
(C) record the temperature of the ball before and after each drop.
(D) all of the above

Passage 5

In an earth science lab, students were investigating the effect of various factors on the evaporation of water using sponges. Each group had double pan balances from which to hang the sponges. They performed the following experiments.

Experiment 1
Students in this group investigated the effect of the water temperature on evaporation. They cut and weighed sponges until they had two with identical weight. They then filled each with water, one hot and one cold, and hung them on the scales to dry, recording the weights and times.

Experiment 2
This group cut one sponge's edges ragged while ensuring both sponges weighed the same. They then filled the sponges with identical amounts of water, hung them on the scales, and recorded weights and times.

Experiment 3
This group mounted identical sponges on the balances with some water in them and then turned the fan on and directed it at one of the sponges only. They measured the weight over a time period like the other groups did.

24. Which sponge lost water faster in Experiment 1?

(F) The one with cold water

(G) The one with warm water

(H) They lost water at equal rates

(J) None of the above

25. Experiment 2 was attempting to investigate the effect of the

(A) mass of the sponges on evaporation.

(B) size of the sponges on evaporation.

(C) texture of the sponges on evaporation.

(D) surface area on evaporation.

26. Experiment 3 was investigating the effect of

(F) wind patterns

(G) temperature

(H) vapor pressure

(J) none of these

27. The maximum effect would be achieved by

(A) warm water, jagged sponge with no fan.

(B) cool water, fan, jagged edges.

(C) warm water, fan, jagged edges.

(D) jagged edges, no fan, cool water.

28. Which of the following would parallel the second experiment?

(F) Surface water in the Caribbean

(G) Gentle waves striking a beach in the North Sea

(H) Deep water currents in the Gulf Stream

(J) Waves crashing against a California coast

29. Use of warm water parallels what natural situation?

(A) Shallow water in tidal marshes

(B) The effect of solar heating

(C) The trade winds

(D) The water surrounding icebergs

Passage 6

Some plants exert an inhibitory, even lethal effect on the growth of other nearby plants. Since Roman times, gardeners and farmers have noted that many plants such as pine seedlings, many vegetables (such as lettuce), and various cereals (basically domesticated grasses) are unable to grow near walnut trees (*Juglans nigra*). A series of experiments have been carried out to investigate this phenomenon.

Experiment 1

Tomato and alfalfa seedlings are planted at 0.25 meter intervals from 0.5 to 27 meters from the trunk of a walnut tree. Ninety percent of the tomato seedlings and 92 percent of the alfalfa seedlings placed at 16 meters or closer to the trunk died. Ninety-nine percent of the seedlings planted farther than 16 meters from the tree trunk survived.

Experiment 2

Walnut tree leaves were torn into pieces, crushed and mixed with water. The solution was filtered after 24 hours. Samples of the extract were diluted 2, 10, and 20 times with water, and applied to lettuce seeds on moist filter paper in petri dishes. The rate germination of the seeds was 86 percent, 86 percent, and 87 percent, respectively. Aqueous extracts of walnut tree roots and nuts were similarly prepared and gave similar results when applied to lettuce seeds.

Experiment 3

Soil was removed from within the walnut tree's dripline (the leaf or foliage perimeter) and placed in plastic flats. Lettuce seeds were planted in the flats, and 90 percent of the seeds germinated, and the seedlings grew normally.

30. From Experiment 1 it may be concluded that

(F) the closer the seedlings were planted to the walnut tree trunk, the greater the effect on the growth of the seedlings.

(G) something in the environment changed at 16 meters from the tree trunk and beyond.

(H) shade from the tree may have affected the growth of seedlings planted closer to the tree trunk.

(J) no conclusions can be reached from the first experiment alone.

31. From Experiment 2, can it be concluded that the inhibitory chemical is not found in the walnut leaves, roots, or nuts?

(A) Yes, the extracts showed little or no effect on the germination of lettuce seeds.

(B) Yes, but only for a chemical inhibitor that affects lettuce seeds.

(C) No, it is impossible to determine the significance of these rates of germination without a control group to give the normal germination rate for this batch of seeds.

(D) No, since some seeds did not germinate, it means an inhibitory chemical was present.

32. How might it be explained, that most seeds germinated and most seedlings grew normally in Experiment 3, while in the natural setting, lettuce seeds and seedlings cannot readily germinate or grow under walnut trees?

(F) Without a control, it is impossible to determine if any inhibitory effect was being demonstrated.

(G) In nature in the presence of the walnut tree, additional inhibitory chemicals might be constantly added, whereas in the flats, the amount of inhibitor in the soil was limited and eventually depleted.

(H) Lettuce seeds were a poor choice for this experiment

(J) F and G

33. If Experiment 2 were run again, with a control showing an 84 percent to 89 percent rate of germination and otherwise with the same experimental results, how could the lack of inhibition best be explained?

(A) Another factor in the soil or elsewhere in the environment is needed for the inhibitor to work.

(B) A far too low a concentration of extract was used.

(C) Inhibition of germination was in fact clearly shown.

(D) B and C

34. In Experiment 3, why was soil removed from within the dripline of the tree, which was an average of 11 meters from the trunk?

   (F) Since it is where most of the leaves fall, and where rain drips from the leaves.

   (G) Most of the roots of a tree are located within the dripline.

   (H) The dripline is closer than 16 meters to the trunk.

   (J) F, G, and H

35. A good control for Experiment 3 would be

   (A) soil taken from an area between 16 and 27 meters from the walnut tree.

   (B) soil from another area with no walnut trees.

   (C) soil taken at 16 meters or closer to the trunk.

   (D) sterilized commercial potting soil.

Passage 7

Several groups of students were given a clear unknown liquid, asked to perform several tests on it, and record their results. After their tests were performed, the groups were to compile their data and try to conclude what the unknown liquid was.

Experiment 1

Students in Group A added Manganese dioxide [MnO_2], a black powdery chemical, to the unknown liquid causing it to fizz. The gas that was given off caused a glowing splint to burst into flames. The group filtered out the MnO_2 to see if it would cause the liquid to fizz again and it did. They repeated this on their sample until the sample fizzed no more. The result was still a clear liquid. The students then placed this sample in their electrolysis apparatus and passed an electric current through the liquid and got a gas at each electrode; one was twice the volume of the other. The larger volume of gas burned when ignited and the smaller volume caused a glowing splint to burst into flames. When they placed some of the "leftover" MnO_2 in a fresh sample of the liquid, the fizzing was as strong as the original had been.

Experiment 2

Students in Group B were given the unknown liquid and several raw chicken livers. When they dropped small pieces of the liver into the unknown liquid, it fizzed. They decided to grind up the liver samples using a mortar and pestle and a little sand. The ground up liver made a fresh sample of the unknown liquid fizz more. They tested the gas and it caused a glowing splint to burst into flames. They then boiled some of the liver and placed it in the unknown liquid; it failed to fizz.

Experiment 3

The students in Group C added MnO_2 to a sample of fresh tap water and it did not fizz. They placed samples of the sand alone in the unknown liquid and it did not fizz. They placed a sample of liver in tap water and it did not fizz. A piece of boiled liver placed in a sample of water caused no fizzing.

36. Which group did the most to establish controls for this series of experiments?

(F) Group A
(G) Group B
(H) Group C
(J) None of the groups established controls.

37. In this series of experiments, MnO_2 acts like a(n)

(A) base.
(B) conjugate acid.
(C) aromatic.
(D) catalyst.

38. Liver contains an organic substance similar to the MnO_2 known as a(n)

(F) enzyme.
(G) lipid.
(H) inhibitor.
(J) carrier molecule.

39. Why did Group A use the MnO_2 on a fresh sample of the unknown liquid after the original sample would not react any more?

(A) In order to revive the original sample
(B) To see if the MnO_2 had been altered in its activity
(C) To see if water reacted in the same way
(D) To make sure no one switched the unknown liquid with water

40. The liquid placed in the electrolysis apparatus was most likely

(F) water.
(G) hydrogen peroxide.
(H) carbon disulfide.
(J) a hydrocarbon.

QUICK SCORE ANSWERS

English Test

1. D	26. J	51. A
2. H	27. C	52. F
3. A	28. H	53. C
4. G	29. B	54. H
5. D	30. H	55. D
6. F	31. D	56. F
7. C	32. F	57. B
8. J	33. D	58. F
9. A	34. H	59. A
10. F	35. A	60. J
11. B	36. J	61. C
12. J	37. C	62. H
13. A	38. F	63. A
14. G	39. C	64. J
15. D	40. J	65. A
16. H	41. D	66. H
17. D	42. H	67. A
18. J	43. C	68. H
19. A	44. J	69. A
20. G	45. A	70. H
21. A	46. F	71. C
22. J	47. D	72. G
23. C	48. G	73. C
24. G	49. A	74. G
25. C	50. H	75. D

Mathematics Test

1. E	21. C	41. B
2. F	22. G	42. H
3. E	23. E	43. E
4. H	24. K	44. K
5. A	25. D	45. B
6. J	26. G	46. K
7. E	27. D	47. D
8. G	28. G	48. G
9. B	29. C	49. B
10. H	30. K	50. J
11. D	31. D	51. D
12. J	32. J	52. H
13. D	33. C	53. C
14. G	34. J	54. K
15. A	35. C	55. A
16. K	36. G	56. F
17. C	37. E	57. E
18. J	38. H	58. G
19. D	39. A	59. B
20. G	40. H	60. F

Reading Test

1. C	15. A	28. F
2. H	16. J	29. D
3. B	17. A	30. H
4. G	18. J	31. C
5. C	19. D	32. J
6. H	20. H	33. B
7. A	21. A	34. H
8. F	22. G	35. B
9. B	23. B	36. G
10. G	24. F	37. C
11. C	25. C	38. G
12. J	26. J	39. D
13. D	27. C	40. F
14. J		

Science Reasoning Test

1. A	15. B	28. J
2. G	16. F	29. B
3. B	17. A	30. G
4. J	18. J	31. C
5. A	19. D	32. J
6. G	20. J	33. A
7. D	21. D	34. H
8. F	22. G	35. A
9. B	23. D	36. H
10. G	24. G	37. D
11. C	25. D	38. F
12. G	26. F	39. B
13. A	27. C	40. F
14. J		

Now you are ready to review your work.

- First, for each question you answered incorrectly, read the explanation below.

- Second, try to explain why the book's answer is better than your answer. Remember, the instructions for the ACT test ask you to choose the **best** answer for each question. While your answer may have some merit, look closely to understand why it is not the best answer.

- Third, analyze what kind of errors you are making. Refer to the charts at the end of the solutions for English and Mathematics Tests.

ENGLISH TEST ANSWERS AND EXPLANATIONS

1. **The correct answer is (D).** In order to make a noun possessive, an apostrophe must precede the *s*. **(Usage/Mechanics—Punctuation)**

2. **The correct answer is (H).** The word *effect* and the word *affect* are often used incorrectly. Effect is a noun; affect is a verb. **(Rhetorical Skills—Strategy)**

3. **The correct answer is (A).** No change is needed. Word choice is the writer's reflection of his or her style. **(Rhetorical Skills—Style)**

4. **The correct answer is (G).** When forming the superlative degree of a one-syllable word, *-est* is added, and *most* is not used. **(Usage/Mechanics—Basic Grammar and Usage)**

5. **The correct answer is (D).** Pronouns must agree with their antecedent in gender and in number. You have plural *men*, therefore, you must have plural pronouns throughout the rest of the sentence. **(Usage/Mechanics—Basic Grammar and Usage)**

6. **The correct answer is (F).** A comma must follow an introductory phrase. **(Usage/Mechanics—Punctuation)**

7. **The correct answer is (C).** Do not use a comma to separate a phrase that is essential to the meaning of the sentence. **(Usage/Mechanics—Sentence Structure)**

8. **The correct answer is (J).** Within the body of a sentence, information not necessary to the sentence meaning is set off with commas. **(Usage/Mechanics—Sentence Structure)**

9. **The correct answer is (A).** Commas may not be used between parts of the predicate. **(Usage/Mechanics—Sentence Structure)**

10. **The correct answer is (F).** For organization, an author will often introduce new subject material with a long introductory phrase. **(Rhetorical Skills—Organization)**

11. **The correct answer is (B).** An adverb modifies an adjective; therefore, *-ly* must be added to the word. **(Usage/Mechanics—Basic Grammar and Usage)**

12. **The correct answer is (J).** An author will use verb forms as nouns in an effort to show style. **(Rhetorical Skills—Style)**

13. **The correct answer is (A).** An author will choose startling words to make a point. This is an organizational tool. **(Rhetorical Skills–Organization)**

14. **The correct answer is (G).** Material not vital to the subject is enclosed in parenthesis, and items in a series must have a comma before *and*. **(Usage/Mechanics—Basic Grammar and Usage)**

15. **The correct answer is (D).** When items are listed, all objects of the same verb, the word *even* is not necessary. **(Rhetorical Skills—Strategy)**

16. **The correct answer is (H).** An introductory phrase must be followed by a comma. **(Rhetorical Skills—Sentence Structure)**

17. **The correct answer is (D).** A compound subject or object must be of the same number. If one is plural, both must be plural. Possession is not needed. **(Rhetorical Skills—Sentence Structure)**

18. **The correct answer is (J).** When constructing a sentence, an adjective must describe a noun. The word *excessive* is an adjective; however, there is no noun that it modifies. A noun is needed. **(Usage/Mechanics—Basic Grammar and Usage)**

19. **The correct answer is (A).** No change is needed. The plural of *thesis* is *theses*. **(Usage/Mechanics—Basic Grammar and Usage)**

20. **The correct answer is (G).** When adding an example that is not a complete sentence, the semicolon is not needed. The example is NOT an independent clause. Do set off the transitional expression with commas. **(Rhetorical Skills—Sentence Structure)**

21. **The correct answer is (A).** Modifiers within a sentence must be consistent. Both *thematic* and *esthetic* are adjectives. **(Rhetorical Skills—Style)**

22. **The correct answer is (J).** The object of this sentence is *criticism,* which is a noun. The use of *critical,* an adjective, is incorrect. **(Rhetorical Skills—Strategy)**

23. **The correct answer is (C).** Use the participle form of the verb with "has" to form the present perfect tense. **(Usage/Mechanics—Basic Grammar and Usage)**

24. **The correct answer is (G).** The word *many* indicates more than one; therefore, the word it describes or modifies must be plural. Adjectives must agree in number with the nouns they modify. **(Rhetorical Skills—Sentence Structure)**

25. **The correct answer is (C).** No comma is needed before the *or* when only two items are used. **(Usage/Mechanics—Basic Grammar and Usage and Punctuation)**

26. **The correct answer is (J).** A proper adjective must always be capitalized. *Freudian* comes from the name Freud and must begin with a capital letter. **(Usage/Mechanics—Basic Grammar and Usage)**

27. **The correct answer is (C).** The parenthetical phrase is correctly set off by commas; however, the verb tense must be present perfect to be consistent with the tense of the passage. **(Usage/Mechanics—Basic Grammar and Usage and Punctuation)**

28. **The correct answer is (H).** The article *a* is singular and must precede a singular noun. **(Usage/Mechanics—Sentence Structure)**

29. **The correct answer is (B).** Punctuation is not used to separate the correlative conjunctions *not only . . . but also.* **(Usage/Mechanics—Punctuation)**

30. **The correct answer is (H).** The subject of a sentence must agree with the verb of a sentence in number. **(Usage/Mechanics—Sentence Structure)**

31. **The correct answer is (D).** A pronoun must agree with its antecedent in person, gender, and number. The word *one* is a third-person antecedent; therefore, *you*, a second-person pronoun, is not consistent in person. **(Usage/Mechanics—Basic Grammar and Usage)**

32. **The correct answer is (F).** No change is needed. **(Rhetorical Skills—Style)**

33. **The correct answer is (D).** Use commas to separate more than two items in a series. A comma is needed after the item that precedes the conjunction. **(Usage/Mechanics—Punctuation)**

34. **The correct answer is (H).** The pronoun *he* does not agree with the antecedent *someone*. The change to the word *one* provides agreement. **(Usage/Mechanics—Basic Grammar and Usage)**

35. **The correct answer is (A).** The writer has used this simple sentence as a transitional device to move from one thought to another. **(Rhetorical Skills—Organization)**

36. **The correct answer is (J).** Since the verb tense is set in the past, this must be continued. Verb formation must be uniform. **(Usage/Mechanics—Basic Grammar and Usage)**

37. **The correct answer is (C).** Do not separate a subject and its verb. **(Usage/Mechanics—Punctuation)**

38. **The correct answer is (F).** The verb tense is consistent with that of the paragraph. **(Usage/Mechanics—Basic Grammar and Usage)**

39. **The correct answer is (C).** A hyphen is used to separate parts of a compound noun. **(Usage/Mechanics—Punctuation)**

40. **The correct answer is (J).** An apostrophe is used to indicate possession. The comma after *self* is not needed. The sentence has a compound verb. Do not separate a subject and its verb. **(Usage/Mechanics—Punctuation)**

41. **The correct answer is (D).** When two independent clauses are joined with a transitional word, a semicolon should follow the first clause. A comma is placed after the transitional word. **(Usage/Mechanics—Sentence Structure)**

42. **The correct answer is (H).** The author chooses expressions as a strategy to hold the reader's attention. Both verbs must end in *-ing*. **(Rhetorical Skills—Strategy)**

43. **The correct answer is (C).** The comma is incorrect because it separates an essential clause from the rest of the sentence. This sentence is incorrectly structured. **(Usage/Mechanics—Sentence Structure)**

44. **The correct answer is (J).** The word *separated* is often misspelled. **(Usage/Mechanics—Basic Grammar and Usage)**

45. **The correct answer is (A).** The author's choice of words are used for comparison and is a matter of style. **(Usage/Mechanics—Style)**

46. **The correct answer is (F).** An author's choice of images and expressions can strengthen writing and set the purpose. In this case, the author is making homework seem like a battle. **(Rhetorical Skills—Strategy)**

47. **The correct answer is (D).** Generally, a sentence should not end with a preposition because a preposition must have an object. **(Usage/Mechanics—Sentence Structure)**

48. **The correct answer is (G).** A comma should follow an introductory word, phrase, or clause. **(Usage/Mechanics—Punctuation)**

49. **The correct answer is (A).** Proper writing requires parallel structure: reading and *studying* must therefore have the same formation. **(Usage/Mechanics—Sentence Structure)**

50. **The correct answer is (G).** A subject and a verb must agree in number; therefore, *language*, which is singular, requires a singular verb. **(Usage/Mechanics—Basic Grammar and Usage)**

51. **The correct answer is (A).** A writer inserts a fact-like sentence in order to provide transition from one thought to another. **(Rhetorical Skills—Organization)**

52. **The correct answer is (F).** The word choice of a writer sets the tone for a selection. The words *buckle down* maintain the warlike tone the author is using. **(Rhetorical Skills—Style)**

53. **The correct answer is (C).** A subject must agree with its verb in number. The subject *another* is singular and requires a singular verb. **(Usage/Mechanics—Basic Grammar and Usage)**

54. The correct answer is (H). The subject and verb must agree in number. The subject *one* is singular and needs a singular verb. The verb *study* has a consonant before the ending *-y* and must have the letters *-ie* inserted before the *-s*. **(Usage/Mechanics—Basic Grammar and Usage)**

55. The correct answer is (D). An introductory dependent clause must be followed by a comma. **(Usage/Mechanics—Sentence Structure)**

56. The correct answer is (F). The writer's construction and choice of descriptive words provides the reader with the chance to make decisions and follow the order. **(Rhetorical Skills—Organization)**

57. The correct answer is (B). An idea not essential to the meaning of the sentence is set off with commas and called a *parenthetical phrase.* **(Usage/ Mechanics—Sentence Structure)**

58. The correct answer is (F). A dash (in typing, this is two hyphens with no space before, between, or after) is used to set off a phrase or a clause that summarizes or emphasizes what has preceded it. **(Usage/ Mechanics—Punctuation)**

59. The correct answer is (D). The words *sit* and *set* are often confused. *To sit* is to place the body on a surface; *to set* is to place an object. **(Usage/ Mechanics—Basic Grammar and Usage)**

60. The correct answer is (J). Use the same tense and form of verbs throughout the paragraph to create unity. **(Rhetorical Skills—Style)**

61. The correct answer is (C). When items are in a series, a comma must precede the word *and.* **(Usage/Mechanics— Punctuation)**

62. The correct answer is (H). When two words are combined to make a compound word, a dash should be placed between them. This needs to be *fore-edge.* **(Usage/Mechanics— Punctuation)**

63. The correct answer is (A). When formulating the past tense of the verb *know*, an *-n* is added. **(Usage/Mechanics— Basic Grammar and Usage)**

64. The correct answer is (J). When adding *-ly* to make a word in to an adverb, if the word ends in a vowel preceded by a consonant, the vowel is dropped. **(Usage/Mechanics— Basic Grammar and Usage)**

65. **The correct answer is (A).** When making a plural word possessive, the -*s* is added before the apostrophe is added. **(Usage/Mechanics—Punctuation)**

66. **The correct answer is (H).** A subject and a verb must agree in number. Because the word *scenes* is plural, the verb must also be plural. **(Usage/Mechanics—Basic Grammar and Usage)**

67. **The correct answer is (A).** When adding -*ing* to a short verb that ends in a consonant, the ending consonant must be doubled. **(Usage/Mechanics—Basic Grammar and Usage)**

68. **The correct answer is (H).** When a dependent clause follows an independent clause, they should be separated by a comma. **(Usage/Mechanics—Sentence Structure)**

69. **The correct answer is (A).** A dash (in typing, this is two hyphens with no space before, between, or after) is used to set off a phrase or a clause that summarizes or emphasizes what has preceded it. **(Rhetorical Skills—Strategy)**

70. **The correct answer is (H).** When two verbs are used they must be parallel—of the same tense. **(Rhetorical Skills—Organization)**

71. **The correct answer is (C).** A subject and verb must agree in number. The subject of the verb is *many*; therefore, the verb must be plural. **(Usage/Mechanics—Sentence Structure)**

72. **The correct answer is (G).** An introductory word, phrase, or clause must be followed by a comma. **(Usage/Mechanics—Punctuation)**

73. **The correct answer is (C).** Adverbs preceding the verb in a series are followed by commas EXCEPT for the one preceding the verb. **(Usage/Mechanics—Punctuation)**

74. **The correct answer is (G).** An introductory word should be followed by a comma. **(Rhetorical Skills—Organization)**

75. **The correct answer is (D).** Two independent clauses should be separated by a comma and a conjunction. **(Rhetorical Skills—Strategy)**

English Review Chart

Circle the item numbers you answered incorrectly. Then review the instruction on the indicated pages.

Item Numbers	Concepts	Pages of Instruction
1, 17, 19, 40, 65	Singular, Plural, and Possessive Nouns	73–76
5, 31, 34	Pronoun Usage	76–81
4, 18, 21, 28, 44	Adjective Usage	81–82
2, 23, 24, 27, 30, 36, 50, 53, 54, 59, 63, 66, 67, 71	Verb Usage: Tenses and Agreement	93–102
11, 47, 64, 73	Adverb, Conjunction, and Preposition Usage	112–117
8, 12, 16, 35, 41, 43, 57, 68	Sentence Elements: Verbals, Phrases, and Clauses	129–131
20, 37, 38, 49, 60, 70, 75	Common Sentence Errors	132–133
6, 7, 9, 14, 25, 26, 29, 33, 39, 48, 55, 58, 61, 62, 69, 72, 74	Capitalization and Punctuation	143–146
3, 10, 13, 15, 22, 32, 42, 45, 46, 51, 52, 56	Style and Organization	171–174

MATHEMATICS TEST ANSWERS AND EXPLANATIONS

1. **The correct answer is (E).** The best first step to make is to note that 2,520 is equal to 252 × 10. Thus, we simply need to prime factor 10 and then 252, and multiply the results. 10, of course, is equal to 2 × 5. As for 252,

$$252 = 2 \times 126 = 2 \times 2 \times 63 = 2 \times 2 \times 3 \times 21 = 2 \times 2 \times 3 \times 3 \times 7.$$

This tells us that

$$2,520 = 2 \times 2 \times 2 \times 3 \times 3 \times 5 \times 7 = 2^3 \times 3^2 \times 5 \times 7$$

2. **The correct answer is (F).** Two of the fundamental properties for working with exponents are needed to simplify the given expression. Recall:

$$x^n \times x^m = x^{n+m} \qquad \text{and}$$

$$(x^n)^m = x^{nm} \qquad \text{Thus,}$$

$$(3x^4y^5)(5x^6y)^2 = (3x^4y^5)(25x^{12}y^2) = 75x^{16}y^7$$

3. **The correct answer is (E).** This is a question with which you must be very careful. Note that while you *do* know the area of the rectangle, you are *not* told the lengths of the sides. Since the area of a rectangle is given by A = LW, a rectangle with area 36 could have sides of many different lengths. For example, the rectangle could be 12 × 3, 6 × 6, 18 × 2, 36 × 1, etc. All of these rectangles have different perimeters. Thus, it really is not possible to find the perimeter of the rectangle.

4. **The correct answer is (H).** In this problem, we are given the *whole* price of the computer, and the *part* that represents the down payment. Thus,

$$\text{Percent of down payment} = \frac{\$270}{\$1,800} = 15\%.$$

5. **The correct answer is (A).** There are two common methods for solving a system of equations, the addition method and the substitution method. To set up for the addition method, you can multiply both sides of the first equation by 2. Thus,

$2(2x + y) = 2(3)$

$5x - 2y = 4$ which leads to

$4x + 2y = 6$

$5x - 2y = 4$ Adding the two equations together gives us

$9x = 10$ Divide by 9

$x = \dfrac{10}{9}$. Now, to find y, plug the value for x into one equation or the other. Let's choose the first one. Then, $2x + y = 3$ so that

$2\left(\dfrac{10}{9}\right) + y = 3$

$\dfrac{20}{9} + y = 3$

$y = 3 - 209 = 279 - 209 = 79$. Thus, the common solution is $\left(\dfrac{10}{9}, \dfrac{7}{9}\right)$.

6. **The correct answer is (J).** The given function will cross the x-axis whenever it is equal to 0. Thus, we need to solve the quadratic equation $-x^2 + 1 = 0$.

   While this equation can be solved via factoring, the easiest way to proceed is to simply observe that the equation is solved for all values of x such that $x^2 = 1$. There are two such values, $x = 1$ and -1.

7. **The correct answer is (E).** Remember that solving inequalities is exactly the same as solving equations with one exception: whenever you multiply or divide by a negative number, you must change the direction of the inequality. Thus,

$3 - 2x \leq 5$ Subtract 3 from both sides.

$-2x \leq 2$ Divide by -2; change the direction of the inequality

$x \geq -1$

8. **The correct answer is (G).** If N_1 machines can do a job in H_1 hours, and N_2 machines can do the job in H_2 hours, then $N_1 \times H_1 = N_2 \times H_2$

   If 5 presses need 12 hours to complete the job, there must be $5 \times 12 = 60$ hours of work to be done. The question then becomes, "How long would it take 6 presses to complete 60 hours of work?" It is easy to see that if each press works $\dfrac{60}{6} = 10$ hours, the job would be finished.

9. **The correct answer is (B).** If a line has a slope of 0, then the line neither increases nor decreases, but stays "flat." Such a line is horizontal. Note that a line with a slope of 0 *may* pass through the origin (if it is the *x*-axis), but it certainly does not have to.

10. **The correct answer is (H).** Since we are given the coordinates of two of the points on the line, we simply need to use the formula for the slope of a line to compute the slope. Recall that if (x_1, y_1) and (x_2, y_2) are two points on a line, then the slope is given by

    $$\text{slope} = \frac{y_2 - y_1}{x_2 - x_1}$$

    For the two given points, $(-3, 2)$ and $(4, -1)$, the slope is

    $$\text{slope} = \frac{y_2 - y_1}{x_2 - x_1} = \frac{2 - (-1)}{-3 - 4} = \frac{2 + 1}{-7} = -\frac{3}{7}$$

11. **The correct answer is (D).** The quickest way to solve this problem is to remember that 10^{-n} can be viewed as a "code" which tells you to move the decimal point n places to the left. To change 9.13 into 0.0000000913, the decimal point must be moved 8 places to the left. Thus, $0.0000000913 = 9.13 \times 10^{-8}$.

12. **The correct answer is (J).** Of course, this problem can be solved by performing the indicated multiplication and addition, but there is a much easier, quicker way. Noting that both 54 and 46 are multiplied by the same number, 215, it can be seen that the expression can be condensed by applying the distributive property.

    $$215 \times 54 + 215 \times 46 = 215 \times (54 + 46) = 215 \times 100 = 21,500$$

13. **The correct answer is (D).** Begin by noting that we can easily determine the value of q from the equation $2q = 12$. The value of q is 6. Since $p + q = 23$, we have $p + 6 = 23$, or $p = 17$. Finally, $p - q = 17 - 6 = 11$.

14. **The correct answer is (G).** This is a straightforward problem; simply evaluate the radical, being careful to follow the rules of sign and the order of operations.

$$\sqrt{(-3-1)^2 - (7-(-1))} = \sqrt{(-4)^2 - (7+1)}$$
$$= \sqrt{16-8} = \sqrt{8} = 2\sqrt{2}$$

15. **The correct answer is (A).** We are given that the measure of angle *PTR* is the same as the measure of angle *QTS*. This tells us that $a + b = b + c$. Subtracting *b* from both sides of this result gives us $a = c$. Thus it appears as if choice (A) must be true.
Let's consider the other possible answers for a moment. There is no reason that *b* has to be the same as *a* or *c*, so choices (B), (C), and (D) are not necessarily true. As far as choice (E) is concerned, since we already know that $a = c$, this statement boils down to telling us, once again, that $a = b = c$, which we know is not true. Thus, only choice (A) is correct.

16. **The correct answer is (K).** Reading the problem carefully, it can be seen that all we know about the women at the college is that $\frac{1}{4}$ of them belong to sororities. The other two numbers we are given relate to the number of men at the college. Using the information in the problem, we can determine that there are $\frac{5}{2} \times 200 = 500$ men at the college, but this is as far as we can go.

17. **The correct answer is (C).** One way to solve this problem would be to evaluate all five expressions, but this would take a very long time. It is easier to simply look at the numbers and consider how much each of them differs from 1. The number that differs from 1 by the smallest amount is the answer.

Thus, the first number, $1 + 0.03$, differs from 1 by 0.03.

The second number, $1 + 0.03^2 = 1 + 0.0009$, differs from 1 by 0.0009. Since 0.0009 is smaller than 0.03, $1 + 0.03^2$ is closer to 1 than $1 + 0.03$ is.

The third number, however, only differs from 1 by $0.03^3 = 0.000027$, so this number is the closest to 1 so far.

Finally, consider choices (D) and (E). Since when you square or cube a number bigger than 1 the number gets bigger still, these two numbers differ from 1 by more than 0.03, and thus cannot be the closest.

18. **The correct answer is (J).** In a 45-45-90 triangle, if H = hypotenuse,

legs = $\dfrac{H}{\sqrt{2}}$. Since point P is at the origin, and point R is at (9, 0), we

can see that the diagonal of the square has a length of 9. Next, note that RPQ is a right triangle, and that RP is the hypotenuse of length 9. Further, since $RQ = PQ$, triangle RPQ is a 45-45-90 triangle, with sides of

length $\dfrac{9}{\sqrt{2}} = \dfrac{9\sqrt{2}}{2}$.

The area of a square is the length of the side squares, so

$$A = \left(\dfrac{9\sqrt{2}}{2}\right)^2 = \dfrac{81 \times 2}{4} = \dfrac{81}{2}$$

19. **The correct answer is (D).** This problem can be solved very simply by

noticing that $\dfrac{ab}{2c} = \dfrac{1}{2}\left(\dfrac{ab}{c}\right)$. Since $\dfrac{ab}{c} = 0.7128$, we have

$$\dfrac{ab}{2c} = \dfrac{1}{2}\left(\dfrac{ab}{c}\right) = \dfrac{1}{2}(0.7128) = 0.3564$$

20. **The correct answer is (G).** Fraction of Work Done by Pipe #1 + Fraction of Work Done by Pipe #2 + Fraction of Work Done by Pipe #3 = 1

Let x = the amount of time the three pipes need to fill the tank working together. Since Pipe #1 can fill the tank in 8 minutes, in one minute it

can fill $\dfrac{1}{8}$ of the tank, and, in general, in x minutes it can fill $\dfrac{x}{8}$ of the

tank. Similarly, in x minutes, Pipe #2 can fill $\dfrac{x}{12}$ of the tank, and Pipe #3

can fill $\underline{x}$ of the tank. Thus,

$$\dfrac{x}{8} + \dfrac{x}{12} + \dfrac{x}{24} = 1$$

The quickest way to solve this problem is to eliminate the fractions by multiplying both sides of the equation by the LCD of 24. Then,

$$24\left(\dfrac{x}{8}\right) + 24\left(\dfrac{x}{12}\right) + 24\left(\dfrac{x}{24}\right) = 1(24) \qquad \text{or}$$

$$3x + 2x + x = 24$$

$$6x = 24$$

$$x = 4$$

21.　**The correct answer is (C).** If $a = b$, and $c = d$, then $ac = bd$ ($cd \neq 0$).

Note that in this problem you are given only two equations that contain three unknowns. Typically, this means that it is not possible to solve for the unknowns, and this leads many people to choose (E) as the answer to the problem. The trick here, however, is that you are never actually asked to find the values of a and b, but simply the ratio between the two. And it may be possible to find the ratio without actually knowing the values of a and b.

The first equation, $ax - 7 = 9$, tells you that $ax = 16$. The second equation, $bx + 2 = 12$, tells you that $bx = 10$. If you take the two equations $ax = 16$ and $bx = 10$ and divide the former by the latter, you get

$$\frac{ax}{bx} = \frac{16}{10} \quad \text{or}$$

$$\frac{a}{b} = \frac{16}{10} = \frac{8}{5}$$

22.　**The correct answer is (G).** The average (arithmetic mean) of a group of nine numbers would be the sum of the nine numbers divided by 9. Since five of the numbers add up to $7x$ and the other four numbers add up to $2x$, the sum of all nine numbers is $9x$. Thus,

$$\text{Average} = \frac{9x}{9} = x$$

23.　**The correct answer is (E).** The sin and cos functions are related by the Pythagorean identity, $\sin^2 a + \cos^2 a = 1$. Since $\sin a = -\frac{5}{13}$, we have

$$\sin^2 a + \cos^2 a = 1$$

$$-\left(\frac{5}{13}\right)^2 + \cos^2 a = 1$$

$$\frac{25}{169} + \cos^2 a = 1 = \frac{169}{169} \qquad \text{Subtract } \frac{25}{169} \text{ from both sides}$$

$$\cos^2 a = \frac{169}{169} - \frac{25}{169} = \frac{144}{169} \qquad \text{Thus,}$$

$$\cos a = \frac{\sqrt{144}}{169} = -\frac{12}{13} \qquad \text{since we are given } \cos a < 0.$$

24. **The correct answer is (K).** Use the following formula: $(xy)^n = x^n y^n$

    To begin, note that $(-4y)^3 = (-4)^3 y^3 = -64y^3$. Therefore,
    $$\frac{(-4y)^3}{-4y^3} = \frac{-64y^3}{-4y^3} = 16.$$

25. **The correct answer is (D).** For $\frac{17q}{11}$ to be an integer, $17q$ must be
    equal to a number that 11 can divide into evenly. However, the number
    17 is prime. This means that the only way $17q \,/\, 11$ can be an integer is
    if q is a number that 11 can divide into evenly. Thus, to solve the
    problem, all we need to do is find the answer choice that is not divisible
    by 11. All of the choices given are divisible by 11 except choice (D), 17.

26. **The correct answer is (G).** The given line has x-intercept -3, which
    means that it contains the point $(-3, 0)$. It also has y-intercept 4, which
    means that it contains the point $(0, 4)$. If we can determine the slope of
    the line, we can easily write the equation using the slope-intercept form
    for the equation of a line.

    $$\text{slope} = \frac{y_2 - y_1}{x_2 - x_1} = \frac{4 - 0}{0 - (-3)} = \frac{4}{3}$$

    Thus, $y = \frac{4}{3}x + b$, with $b = 4$.   This gives us

    $$y = \frac{4}{3}x + 4$$

27. **The correct answer is (D).** Once again, before beginning this problem,
    it is important to read the question very carefully. Note that while we
    are told that 3% of the pagers are defective, we are asked for the
    number of pagers that are *not* defective. Thus, there are two ways to
    solve this problem. We can either find 3% of 3,600 to get the number of
    pagers that are defective and then subtract this number from 3,600 to
    get the number of pagers that are not defective, or we can simply notice
    that if 3% of the pagers are defective then 97% of the pagers are good.
    Thus all we really need to do is find 97% of 3,600. Let's proceed using
    this second method.

    Thus, in this percent problem, we have the *whole* (the total number of
    pagers—3,600), and the *percent* (97%). We are looking for the *part* of
    the pagers that are not defective. A *part* is always found by multiplying
    the *percent* times the *whole*. Thus, 3,600 × 97% = 3,600 × .97 = 3,492.

28. **The correct answer is (G).** Let's consider the triangles one at a time. As far as triangle A is concerned, it is a right triangle with hypotenuse 7. If we let the legs be called X and Y, we have, from the Pythagorean theorem, $X^2 + Y^2 = 49$. This single equation with two unknowns can be solved for an infinite number of combinations of values of X and Y. Thus, we cannot uniquely determine the values of X and Y, and therefore cannot find the perimeter of triangle A.

    As far as Triangle B is concerned, the unlabeled angle must be 60° to make the three angles total up to 180°. Thus, the triangle is equilateral, and thus all sides are of length 12. The perimeter, then, is 36.

    In Triangle C, we know all three angles, but have no information about the lengths of the sides. There are an infinite number of triangles of different sizes containing these three angles. Thus, we cannot determine the perimeter of the triangle.

29. **The correct answer is (C).** Percent of increase can be easily computed as the amount of change divided by the original value. In this problem, we know the amount of increase is 2,750 − 2,200 = 550.

    Then, Percent of increase $= \dfrac{\text{Change}}{\text{Original}} = \dfrac{550}{2,200} = \dfrac{1}{4} = 25\%.$

30. **The correct answer is (K).** Begin by making a sketch of the situation. Let b = the height of the rocket.

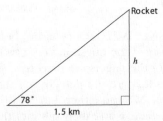

Since we know the length of the side adjacent to the 78° angle, and are looking for the side opposite, we can use the tangent function.

$\tan 78° = \dfrac{b}{1.5}$ Thus,

$1.5 \tan 78° = b$

31. **The correct answer is (D).** The first step in finding the equation of a line is to find the slope of the line. Since you are given two points on the line, you simply need to plug into the slope formula to find the slope.

For the two given points, (2, 1) and (–4, 6), the slope is

$$\text{slope} = \frac{y_2 - y_1}{x_2 - x_1} = \frac{1 - 6}{2 - (-4)} = \frac{-5}{2 + 4} = -\frac{5}{6}$$

There are several ways to proceed from here. One is to use the slope-intercept form for the equation of a line, $y = mx + b$, where m represents the slope, and b the y-intercept. Since you know $m = -\frac{5}{6}$, you have

$$y = -\frac{5}{6}x + b$$

Next, you need to determine the y-intercept. All you need to do to determine b is to take one of the points you are given, say (2, 1), plug it into the equation, and solve for b. Thus,

$$y = -\frac{5}{6}x + b$$

$$1 = -\frac{5}{6} \times 2 + b$$

$$1 = -\frac{10}{6} + b$$

$$b = 1 + \frac{10}{6} = \frac{16}{6} = \frac{8}{3}$$

Thus, the equation of the line is

$$y = -\frac{5}{6}x + \frac{8}{3}$$

32. **The correct answer is (J).** Use the following formula:

$$\frac{x^m}{x^n} = x^{m-n}$$

Since the area of a rectangle is given by A = LW, the length of a rectangle can be computed as L = A/W. Plugging in the values we are given for the area and the width, we obtain

$$L = \frac{108\,x^2 y^3}{9x^2 y} = 12x^{2-2} y^{3-1} = 12y^2.$$

33. **The correct answer is (C).** Two of the fundamental properties for working with exponents are needed to simplify the given expression. Recall:

$(xy)^n = x^n y^n$ and

$(x^n)^m = x^{nm}$ Thus,

$(x^2 y^3)^z = x^{2z} y^{3z} = (2)^{(2 \times 3)} (1)^{(3 \times 3)} = 2^6\,1^9 = (64)(1) = 64$

34. **The correct answer is (J).** Recall that every percent problem involves three quantities, a *whole* (in this case selling price of the house), a *part* (the part of the selling price that the agent receives in commission, that is, $3,625), and a *percent* (in this problem, 5%). Thus, in this problem, you know the part and the percent and you are looking for the whole. The whole is equal to the part divided by the percent. Thus,

$$\text{Selling Price} = \frac{\text{Part}}{\text{Percent}} = \frac{\$3,625}{5\%} = \$72,500$$

35. **The correct answer is (C).** See what you can deduce from the figure above. First of all, you are given that AC < CB. This tells you that $a > c$. You also know that AC = AB (since they are both radii of the same circle), and this tells you that angle ACB = angle ABC. Thus, both of these angles measure $c°$.

Right away, then, you can eliminate choices (A) and (B) as solutions. You can also eliminate choice (E), since other than the fact that $a > c$, you know nothing about their relative sizes.

Now, if you recall that there are 180° in a triangle, you can see that $a + c + c = 180$, or $a + 2c = 180$. If a and c were the same, then, they would both be equal to 60. However, since $a > c$, a must be more than 60. Thus, choice (C) is true, but choice (D) is not.

36. **The correct answer is (G).** In every problem in which a percent needs to be found, you must have two other numbers: the whole and the part. In this problem, the whole is 3^4 and the part is 3^3. The percent is found by dividing the part by the whole. Thus,

$$\frac{3^3}{3^4} = \frac{1}{3} = 33\frac{1}{3}\%$$

37. **The correct answer is (E).** The formula for the area of a circle is $A = \pi r2$. For the circle with radius q, then, $12\pi = \pi q^2$. This means that $q^2 = 12$, or $q = \sqrt{12}$.

Thus, the area of a square with radius $7q$ is $A = \pi r^2 = \pi(7q)^2$
$= \pi(7\sqrt{12})^2 = \pi(49 \times 12) = 588\pi$.

38. **The correct answer is (H).** Use the following formula:

Time Worked × Hourly Salary = Total Salary

First of all, for working the first 40 hours, the employee made $40 \times 8 = \$320$. Then, for 8.25 hours of overtime, the employee earned time and a half, which is $8 \times 1.5 = \$12$ an hour. The amount of money earned is thus $8.25 \times 12 = \$99$.

The total amount earned is, then, $\$320 + \$99 = \$419$.

39. **The correct answer is (A).** Let us call the length of XZ, N. Then, the length of XY is 2N. Next, via the Pythagorean theorem, $a^2 + b^2 = c^2$

$$N^2 + (2N)^2 = 5^2 \qquad \text{This tells us that}$$

$$N^2 + 4N^2 = 25$$

$$5N^2 = 25 \qquad \text{Divide by 5}$$

$$N^2 = 5$$

$$N = \sqrt{5}$$

Since N is the length of XZ, this is the answer to the problem.

40. **The correct answer is (H).** Use the following formulas:

$$\sqrt{a^2 b} = a\sqrt{b}, \qquad \sqrt{a} + \sqrt{a} = 2\sqrt{a}$$

First of all, the only way these two terms can possibly be combined is if they can be simplified so as to have the same number under the radical sign. So, let's begin by simplifying the terms.

$$\sqrt{45} = \sqrt{9 \times 5} = 3\sqrt{5}$$

$$\sqrt{125} = \sqrt{25 \times 5} = 5\sqrt{5}$$

Thus,

$$\sqrt{45} + 7\sqrt{125} = 3\sqrt{5} + 7(5\sqrt{5}) = 3\sqrt{5} + 35\sqrt{5} = 38\sqrt{5}$$

41. **The correct answer is (B).** This question just asks you to subtract mixed numbers. Since the final price of the stock is the original price less the amount of the decline,

$$\text{Final Price} = 47\frac{1}{4} - 6\frac{3}{8} = 47\frac{2}{8} - 6\frac{3}{8}.$$

To perform this subtraction, we must first rewrite $47\frac{2}{8}$ as $46\frac{10}{8}$ (this is what they called "borrowing" in grade school). Then,

$$46\frac{10}{8} - 6\frac{3}{8} = 40\frac{7}{8}.$$

42. **The correct answer is (H).** Note that the angle that forms a vertical angle with the angle labeled $(3a + 40)$ is also equal to $3a + 40$. Now, observe that the angle labeled a and the angle vertical to the angle labeled $3a + 40$ are interior angles on the same side of a transversal. Thus, the two angles are supplementary. This means that

$$3a + 40 + a = 180$$

$$4a + 40 = 180$$

$$4a = 140$$

$$a = 35$$

43. **The correct answer is (E).** If $\dfrac{a}{b} = \dfrac{c}{d}$ then $ad = bc$. The first step is to find out the total weight we wish to ship. Since we have 130 cartons, each weighing 17.6 kg, the total weight is $130 \times 17.6 = 2{,}288$ kg. From here, we can write a proportion to find out the cost, based on the fact that it costs $13 to send 100 kg.

$\dfrac{\$13}{100 \text{ kg}} = \dfrac{\$x}{2{,}288 \text{ kg}}$ Cross multiply

$29{,}744 = 100\,x$ Divide by 100

$x = \$297.44$

44. **The correct answer is (K).** To solve this problem, simply note that percent means per hundred, and that A% is always equal to $\dfrac{A}{100}$.

Thus, in this problem, $120\% = \dfrac{120}{100}$. This reduces to $\dfrac{120}{100} = \dfrac{12}{10} = \dfrac{6}{5}$

45. **The correct answer is (B).** While it is possible to solve this problem algebraically, it is a lot easier to proceed arithmetically. To proceed arithmetically, one must simply understand that one way to picture a ratio of 7:5 is to consider the money divided up into 12 equal pieces ($12 = 7 + 5$).

The largest share is equivalent to 7 of these 12 parts, that is, $\dfrac{7}{12}$ of the total amount. Then,

$\$180{,}000 \times \dfrac{7}{12} = \$105{,}000$

46. **The correct answer is (K).** The procedure for solving this equation calls for you to hold a, b, and c constant and solve for x in the usual way. Thus,

$a = \dfrac{b}{1 - cx}$ Multiply both sides by $1 - cx$

$a\,(1 - cx) = b$ Distribute

$a - acx = b$ so that

$-acx = b - a$ and, dividing by $-ac$

$x = -\dfrac{b - a}{ac} = \dfrac{a - b}{ac}$

47. **The correct answer is (D).** Use the following formula: If AB = 0, then either A = 0 or B = 0.

The first step in solving any quadratic equation (an equation in which the variable is raised to the second power), is to combine like terms and rewrite the equation set equal to 0. Therefore,

$$3x^2 - 12 = x(1 + 2x) \quad \text{Distribute.}$$

$$3x^2 - 12 = x + 2x^2 \quad \text{Set equal to 0.}$$

$$x^2 - x - 12 = 0 \quad \text{Factor the left-hand side.}$$

$$(x - 4)(x + 3) = 0 \quad \text{Set each factor equal to 0 and solve.}$$

$$x = 4$$

$$\text{or } x = -3$$

48. **The correct answer is (G).** Use the following formulas:

$$A = LW, \qquad P = 2(L + W)$$

Begin by making a sketch of the situation, letting x = the length of the side of the original square.

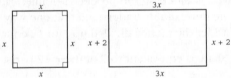

The original perimeter is $4x$ and the new perimeter is $8x + 4$. We have, thus,

$$4(4x) = 8x + 4 \quad \text{Solving for } x,$$

$$16x = 8x + 4$$

$$8x = 4$$

$$x = \frac{1}{2} \quad \text{Thus, the original perimeter is } 4\left(\frac{1}{2}\right) = 2.$$

49. **The correct answer is (B).** Fraction of Men $= \dfrac{\text{Number of Men}}{\text{Total People}}$. Initially, there are x men in the room; when 2 more men enter, there are $x + 2$. Initially, there are y women in the room; when 1 leaves, there are $y - 1$.

At this point in time, the total number of people in the room is $(x + 2) + (y - 1) = x + y + 1$. Thus, the fraction that represents the number of men in the room is

$$\frac{x + 2}{x + y + 1}$$

50. The correct answer is (J). This problem can easily be solved by setting up a proportion relating brake defects to cars, using the following formula:

If $\dfrac{a}{b} = \dfrac{c}{d}$ then $ad = bc$.

$\dfrac{36 \text{ defects}}{1,000 \text{ cars}} = \dfrac{x \text{ defects}}{35,000 \text{ cars}}$ Cross multiply

$1,260,000 = 1,000x$ Divide by 1,000

$x = 1,260$

51. The correct answer is (D). The "safest" way to deal with an equation containing fractions is to get rid of the fractions in the first step. This can be accomplished by multiplying both sides of the equation by the LCD of the fractions. Since in this problem the LCD is 15 (the least common denominator of 3 and 5), we multiply by 15.

$$\frac{2}{5}x + \frac{x}{3} = 11$$

$$15\left(\frac{2}{5}x + \frac{x}{3}\right) = 11 \times 15$$

$$6x + 5x = 165$$

$$11x = 165$$

$$x = 15$$

52. The correct answer is (H). $\text{N\%} = \dfrac{\text{N}}{100}$

There are several ways that can be used to solve this problem; perhaps the most straightforward is to let X equal the unknown and translate the problem statement into an equation that can be solved.

The problem statement tells us that

$(\text{N\%}) \text{X} = \text{M}$ Divide by N%

$\text{X} = \dfrac{\text{M}}{\text{N\%}}$ Substitute $\text{N\%} = \dfrac{\text{N}}{100}$

$\text{X} = \dfrac{\text{M}}{\text{N}/100} = \dfrac{100\text{M}}{\text{N}}$

53. **The correct answer is (C).** Three consecutive integers can be expressed as x, $x + 1$, $x + 2$. Let x equal the first of the three integers. Then, the second integer is $x + 1$, and the third is $x + 2$.

The product of the first and second is $x (x + 1)$, and the product of the second and third is $(x + 1)(x + 2)$. Thus,

$x (x + 1) + 10 = (x + 1)(x + 2)$ Performing the indicated multiplications

$x^2 + x + 10 = x^2 + 3x + 2$

Note that x^2 cancels out, so we do not actually have a quadratic equation to solve.

$x + 10 = 3x + 2$

$2x = 8$

$x = 4$

Therefore, 4 is the smallest integer. The largest is 6.

54. **The correct answer is (K).** Inequalities involving absolute values are tricky to solve. You must remember that there are two ways in which $|y - 5|$ can be greater than 1: $y - 5$ is greater than 1, or $-(y - 5)$ is greater than 1. Thus, there are actually two inequalities that we need to solve to finish this problem. First of all:

$y - 5 > 1$ Add 5 to both sides

$y > 6$

Now, let's solve the other inequality.

$-(y - 5) > 1$ This means that

$-y + 5 > 1$ or,

$-y > -4$ and, dividing by -1 and changing the direction of the inequality,

$y < 4$

Thus, the inequality is true whenever $y > 6$ or $y < 4$.

55. **The correct answer is (A).** To begin, we need to find the value of a. Typically, when a variable appears as an exponent in an equation, the equation requires sophisticated algebraic techniques to solve—unless the numbers have been chosen to be very "nice." On this test, whenever you see such an equation, the numbers will be nice, which means that the equation can likely be solved in your head. In this problem, we are given

$3^a = 81$, so a must be the power to which 3 has to be raised to equal 81. Now, since $3 \times 3 \times 3 \times 3 = 81$, we have $3^4 = 81$, and thus $a = 4$.

Moving to the second equation, and substituting $a = 4$, we get $4 = b^3 - 4$, or $b^3 = 8$. Thus, $b =$ the cube root of 8, which is 2.

56. The correct answer is (F). Use the following formula:

$$\cos 30° = \frac{\sqrt{3}}{2}$$

The cosine function is a repeating function, taking on the same values in cycles of 360°. Our goal is to reduce the number 1,110 to some smaller, more manageable number. One way to do this is to keep subtracting 360° from 1,110° until we end up with a number that is less than 360°.

Since $1,110 - 360 = 750$, and $750 - 360 = 390$ and $390 - 360 = 30$, we have

$$\cos 1,110° = \cos 750° = \cos 390° = \cos 30°.$$

Now, 30° is one of the special angles for which you should have the values of the trigonometric functions memorized. In particular,

$$\cos 30° = \frac{\sqrt{3}}{2}.$$

57. The correct answer is (E). Use the following formulas:

$$\cos 45° = \frac{\sqrt{2}}{2}, \qquad \sin 30° = \frac{1}{2}$$

While, in general, the exact values of trigonometric functions can only be determined from tables or with the help of a calculator, there are certain special angles for which it is possible to find exact values of the functions. The values of the trig functions for these angles, which include 45° and 30°, should be memorized for the test.

In this problem, we need to know that $\cos 45° = \frac{\sqrt{2}}{2}$ and $\sin 30° = \frac{1}{2}$.

Then, $3 \cos 45° + 3 \sin 30° = 322 + 3 \left(\frac{1}{2}\right) = 32 + 32$

58. The correct answer is (G). Final Price = Original Price × (100% − first percent of discount) × (100% − second percent of discount)

It makes sense to begin by showing the common error that many people make. Frequently, the thinking is that a discount of 30% followed by a discount of 20% is equivalent to a discount of 50%. Thus, the final price would be 50% of the original.

The reason that this is incorrect is that the 20% discount is taken after the first discount, and is thus a markdown from an already reduced amount. Thus, the markdowns must actually be taken in two steps. First, find the price after the 30% discount (which is 70% of the original price), then reduce this price by 20%. After we do this, we can determine the single discount that is the equivalent of the two given discounts.

Then, $9,000 × 70% = $6,300. Therefore, the price after the first discount is $6,300. Now, this price must be reduced by 20% (which will make it equal to 80% of the $6,300).

$6,300 × 80% = $5,040.

Thus, overall, the original price of $9,000 is marked down to $5,040. To find the single discount that this represents is equivalent to finding the percent of decrease as $9,000 goes down to $5,040. This is found by computing the amount of the discount divided by the original price. The amount of the discount is $9,000 − $5,040 = $3,960. Then,

$$\text{Percent of Discount} = \frac{\text{Amount of Discount}}{\text{Original Price}} = \frac{3,960}{9,000} = 44\%$$

Note that the final percent of discount is independent of the dollar value of the supplies.

59. **The correct answer is (B).** Total People = Number in Group A + Number in Group B + Number in Both Groups + Number in Neither Group. To begin, make a Venn Diagram to portray the problem.

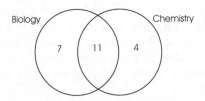

Put 11 in the central portion, which represents the number of people in both courses. This tells us that 7 people are taking Biology only, and 4 people are taking Chemistry only. Call the number of students taking neither course x. We then have

$$11 + 7 + 4 + x = 30$$
$$22 + x = 30$$
$$x = 8$$

60. **The correct answer is (F).** This problem calls for us to determine the relative sizes of a, b, and c. Let's start with a and b. We are given that $\frac{1}{4}a = \frac{1}{3}b$.

Now, we can determine the relative sizes of a and b in several ways. By simply looking at the given equation, we can see $\frac{1}{4}$ of a is the same as $\frac{1}{3}$ of b, and this means that a must be bigger than b. This can also be seen algebraically:

$\frac{1}{4}a = \frac{1}{3}b$ 　　　Multiply by 12

$3a = 4b$ 　　　Divide by $3b$

$\frac{a}{b} = \frac{4}{3}$

Now, since $\frac{a}{b}$ is bigger than 1, it is clear than $a > b$. In the same way, we can show that $b > c$. Thus $a > b > c$.

Peterson's ■ Panic Plan for
the ACT Assessment
263
www.petersons.com

Mathematics Review Chart

Circle the item numbers you answered incorrectly. Then review the instruction on the indicated pages.

Item Numbers	Concepts	Pages of Instruction
1, 12, 38, 41, 43, 59	Whole Numbers and Fractions	51–61
4, 27, 29, 34, 44, 52, 58	Decimals and Percents	63–70
2, 11, 14, 17, 36, 40	Signed Numbers, Exponents, and Roots	85–91
5, 7, 8, 13, 19, 20, 21, 24, 25, 26, 32, 33, 46, 47, 48, 49, 51, 53, 54, 55, 60	Algebra	104–110
16, 45, 50	Ratio and Proportion	138–139
22	Mean and Median	139
6, 9, 10, 31	Coordinate Geometry	150–153
3, 15, 18, 28, 35, 37, 39, 42	Plane Geometry	153–166; 176–182
23, 30, 56, 57	Trigonometry	183–187

READING AND SCIENCE REASONING REVIEW

Now you are ready to review your work.

- First, for each question you answered incorrectly, read the explanation below.

- Second, try to explain why the book's answer is better than your answer. Remember, the instructions for the ACT test ask you to choose the **best** answer for each question. While your answer may have some merit, look closely to understand why it is not the best answer.

- Third, analyze what kind of errors you are making. Reread *Strategies for Taking the Reading Comprehension Test* on pages 28–33. Refer to the chart at the end of the solutions for the Science Test to find out what pages you should review.

READING TEST ANSWERS AND EXPLANATIONS

1. **The correct answer is (C).** The answer can be found in the first sentences "Neutrinos are uncharged . . . massless particles. . . ."

2. **The correct answer is (H).** According to the second paragraph, "Not even the most elaborate neutrino traps . . . have found enough neutrinos to match the number predicted. . . ."

3. **The correct answer is (B).** Paragraph 2 states, "Since the number of neutrinos produced varies with the temperature. . . ."

4. **The correct answer is (G).** The implication of paragraph 3 is that ". . . a 'sink' of some sort in the sun is altering most of the neutrinos before they can escape."

5. **The correct answer is (C).**
Paragraph 1 states: "Their theoretical properties, however, including a fractional one-half spin quantum number, make them detectable."

6. **The correct answer is (H).**
The first sentence of paragraph 2 states that scientists should be able to draw conclusions about solar reactions based on the number of neutrinos emitted.

7. **The correct answer is (A).**
Paragraph 4 indicates that "Since astronomy relies fundamentally on the understanding of the sun, the solar neutrino question could very well shake the foundations of astrophysics."

8. **The correct answer is (F).**
Only choice (F) describes a theory that could relate to the sun.

9. **The correct answer is (B).**
The answer to this question is found in paragraph 1: "Neutrinos offer an opportunity to measure events taking place inside the sun."

10. **The correct answer is (G).**
This article is one of definition with examples.

11. **The correct answer is (C).**
The two sounds were the "sounds of wheels on the drive and . . . her husband's footsteps. . . ." These two sounds reflect her hope for happiness in that her loneliness could be dispelled.

12. **The correct answer is (J).**
Only choice (J) reflects that the couple has chosen their present circumstances despite the difficulties.

13. **The correct answer is (D).**
Paragraph 2 indicates the solitary lifestyle as the result of the things they enjoyed together—talking, singing, and reading.

14. **The correct answer is (J).**
There is no indication that Isabel no longer loves her husband. Rather, the passage shows us her mixed emotions about the world.

15. **The correct answer is (A).**
The narrator offers ample evidence of their shared happiness.

16. **The correct answer is (J).**
The word "seemed" suggests that Isabel is not sure how she would manage without her friend, which indicates desperation.

17. **The correct answer is (A).**
Isabel loves her lifestyle until her depression overtakes her. The narrator never suggests that Isabel equates children with happiness.

18. **The correct answer is (J).**
The narrator gives ample time to all sides of the story focusing on both the joy and misery the character experiences.

19. **The correct answer is (D).** The description as "shallow, prattling, and rather impertinent" represents the characters' view, not the narrator's view.

20. **The correct answer is (H).** Throughout the passage, the narrator focuses on Isabel's mixed emotions.

21. **The correct answer is (A).** The answer is found in paragraph 1: "Educators have learned to live with 'crises' of finance, curriculum, competence, and confidence."

22. **The correct answer is (G).** These students cite teachers who do not seem to care.

23. **The correct answer is (B).** Paragraph 6 states "As we consider the term, caring properly refers to relations, not to individuals."

24. **The correct answer is (F).** Paragraph 7 states "People need to learn not only how to care but also how to respond to care extended to them by others."

25. **The correct answer is (C).** According to this selection, "Genuine involvement as the cared-for party in a relationship requires receptivity and discernment."

26. **The correct answer is (J).** Paragraph 4 describes ". . . teachers—who in most cases are trying to care. . . ."

27. **The correct answer is (C).** The statement is that "Genuine involvement as the cared-for party in a relationship requires receptivity and discernment."

28. **The correct answer is (F).** The author states that ". . . schools are, for the most part, ignoring the task of preparing people to care."

29. **The correct answer is (D).** This article demonstrates the need "to consider changes that might strengthen human relationships as well as intellectual pursuits in schools.

30. **The correct answer is (H).** Throughout this selection, the author underscores the need for involvement on the part of teachers, students, and others.

31. **The correct answer is (C).** According to this selection, the Third World War "was fought more or less throughout the 1980s."

32. **The correct answer is (J).** The writer enumerates the winners including "Western Europeans as well as East Asians" but makes no mention of Africa.

33. **The correct answer is (B).** This article states that "The Soviet defeat was obvious and total."

34. **The correct answer is (H).** The author states that in this period, America "lay vanquished by foreign competition."

35. The correct answer is (B).
According to this selection,
private-sector leadership
together with "policies as
farsighted and self-disciplined as
those of Germany and Japan"
are needed.

36. The correct answer is (G).
The writer tells us that victory
came to Germany and Japan
because of "geo-realism, and
aligning economically."

37. The correct answer is (C).
According to this selection the
"Cold War had finally ended in
Berlin in 1989."

38. The correct answer is (G).
The author states that the world
would "need the rest of this
century to negotiate the terms
of its peace."

39. The correct answer is (D).
According to this selection,
America and the Soviet Union
had "vast empires and blocs as
a result."

40. The correct answer is (F).
Throughout the article, the
author infers that the economic
progress in certain countries
who had lost World War II
exceeded that of the victors of
that war.

SCIENCE REASONING TEST ANSWERS AND EXPLANATIONS

Passage 1

1. The correct answer is (A).
Reassembling the viruses in
their native (natural) form was a
control in that it showed
reassembly did not affect the
ability of the virus to infect the
plant in a characteristic fashion.
That is, reassembled TMV and
HRV still produced characteristic injuries.

2. The correct answer is (G).
Without a control, it would be
impossible to determine if the
disassembly and reassembly
processes affected the viruses in
some fundamental manner.

3. The correct answer is (B).
The type of injury observed on
the plant was associated in
every instance with the
presence of that form of viral
RNA. "Swapping" protein coats
around the RNA had no effect
on the form of the injuries.

4. **The correct answer is (J).**
The experiment demonstrates RNA can code for viral genes. When an experiment similar to this one was carried out in 1957, it was known that DNA usually carried genetic information, but it had not been proven that RNA functioned in a similar fashion in RNA viruses.

5. **The correct answer is (A).**
Hybrid 2 is composed of the HRV protein, but the TMV RNA. As the experiment shows, the nature of the injury is associated with the type of RNA and not the type of protein present in the virus.

Passage 2

6. **The correct answer is (G).**
Scientist 1 believes there to be no connection between high-voltage electromagnetic radiation and the incidence of cancer, making (F) an incorrect choice. Scientist 1 would also not address levels of calcium in bone cells. Finally, this scientist would know that a high-voltage field would produce a strong magnetic field, eliminating choice (J) as an answer.

7. **The correct answer is (D).**
Scientists believe there would be a breakdown of biomolecules and more 60Hz photons causing an increase in the rate of bone growth, and thus, an increase in cell division rates.

8. **The correct answer is (F).**
Scientist 1's statement makes it clear he is basing his conclusions on his knowledge of the effect of 60Hz photons. He will conclude little or nothing relative to choices (G) and (H) and choice (J) relates to the position of an electron in an atom.

9. **The correct answer is (B).**
The connection between the information given in choices (A), (C), and (D) is well established. The rate of growth of cells has not been demonstrated to be a cause of cancer, although cancer cells are known to divide rapidly. The rapid division is a function of their being cancerous.

10. **The correct answer is (G).**
This is in direct agreement with Scientist 2's feeling that the radiation from electromagnetic fields is the cause of cell changes. Scientist 1 does not agree with this at all.

11. **The correct answer is (C).**
The increased tendency of cancer cells to divide is a result of their being cancer, not something that has been demonstrated to be a cause of cancer. Of course 60Hz radiation is not strong enough to break, nor create, molecular bonds. Choices (B) and (D) are true statements.

Passage 3

12. **The correct answer is (G).** If one lines up the pressure figures in order from smaller to larger, the volume figures line up correspondingly from larger to smaller in the classic inverse relationship between pressure and volume for a fixed sample of air at a constant temperature.

13. **The correct answer is (A).** In order for this relationship to work, the temperature must be held constant. The addition of more energy will add to the molecular motion of the gases beyond what would result from additional pressure. The effect of more energy would also reverse the effect on volume that the pressure will have and lead to misleading results. In addition, not keeping temperature constant would introduce a second variable making the results difficult to interpret.

14. **The correct answer is (J).** Charles's Law summarizes the relationship between temperature-volume, Dalton's Law is that of partial pressures adding up to the total pressure when collecting more than one gas, and Le Chatelier's Principle involves equilibrium in a chemical reaction.

15. **The correct answer is (B).** This is a "trapped air sample" so no particles can enter or leave, and while the results indicate that the volume changes, the amount of air cannot. In addition, the title of the chart says the trials occur at 25° C. The chart indicates that both the volume and the pressure change.

16. **The correct answer is (F).** The variation is not direct, it is inverse; as the pressure increases, the volume decreases. The fact that the product of the two is a constant is the result of them being inversely related. Finally, the amount of gas is not relevant, what happens to it—the volume changes with pressure changes—is the key relationship.

17. **The correct answer is (A).** Choice (A) is the correct indication of the inverse relationship that is true here. Choice (B) illustrates a direct relationship and choices (C) and (D) do not indicate a relationship between pressure and volume, e.g., choice (C) translates as follows: $P_1P_2 = V_1V_2$.

Passage 4

18. **The correct answer is (J).**
The only thing that was varied in Experiment 1 was the air pressure. Both choices (G) and (H) say this using different words.

19. **The correct answer is (D).**
The increase in rebound height had to be due to an increase in energy inside the ball. This increase in energy could have been from the floor, or the temperature inside the ball could have been caused by air friction as the ball fell. In either case more testing is required to make a definite conclusion.

20. **The correct answer is (J).**
Without further testing, you can not draw any of these conclusions.

21. **The correct answer is (D).**
None of the experiments served as a control for the other two experiments. In each case the only constant was the height of the drop, while the other experimental conditions changed.

22. **The correct answer is (G).**
The height from which the ball was dropped served as a control in all three experiments, and it was the same in all three experiments.

23. **The correct answer is (D).**
You would need to see if the floor surface became colder, which would mean that energy in the form of heat could have been given to the ball. If the room temperature became colder it could also have given heat energy to the ball. The temperature of the ball has to be recorded before and after to see if there was an increase or decrease in temperature.

Passage 5

24. **The correct answer is (G).**
The higher temperature water particles would, according to the law of kinetic molecular motion, move faster and escape the sponge. The water particles in the other sponge just don't have enough energy to match the motion of the warmer water particles.

25. **The correct answer is (D).** By cutting the edges of one sponge jagged, this group greatly increased the surface area of the sponge. The feel, the mass, and the size of the sponge were not mentioned in the experimental design.

26. **The correct answer is (F).**
The use of the fan obviously relates directly to worldwide wind patterns.

27. The correct answer is (C). The maximum effect for all three variables would be a sponge with warm water—it has more energy in its particles than cool water—jagged edges to increase the surface area, and a fan to add more energy to the particles.

28. The correct answer is (J). This action would send sprays of water for significant distances into the air. Each bubble of water presents an increased surface area compared to calm water or even mild waves. Of course, water in deep underwater currents would not evaporate.

29. The correct answer is (B). The water being warmed would most parallel the effect of solar heating. While the shallow water in the tidal marshes sounds like an attractive choice, it is the solar heating of that small amount of water that would increase evaporation.

Passage 6

30. The correct answer is (G). The effect on seedlings is clearly demarcated at 16 meters distance from the trunk. At 16 meters or closer, only 10 percent of the tomato and 8 percent of the alfalfa seedlings survived, while beyond 16 meters almost all the seedling survived. The information given, however, does not allow any conclusions to be made about an effect of closeness to the tree trunk at any distance other than 16 meters. Choice (F) states that the effect is proportional to the distance from the trunk; the data does not support that interpretation. According to the information given, shade was not tested as an experimental variable and not controlled.

31. The correct answer is (C). Without a control group to demonstrate what is the normal germination rate for these lettuce seeds, the significance of the germination rates obtained in this experiment cannot be evaluated. While it is true that only lettuce seeds were tested, without a control it cannot be stated even whether lettuce seeds were affected or unaffected. If normal germination for these seeds is 98 percent, an inhibitory effect may be present. Conversely, if normal germination is lower, perhaps 85 percent, then no effect is demonstrated. As it stands, there is nothing (no control) to compare the results to, and the experiment is incomplete and therefore inconclusive.

32. The correct answer is (J). Again, a proper control is a vital component in the success of any experiment. Additionally, it is possible or even likely that the tree continuously releases more inhibitory chemical(s).

33. The correct answer is (A).
While choice (B) is a possibility, it is not likely, as a dilution of two times does not seem to be *"far* too low a concentration." If the inhibitory chemical is released into the soil around the tree from leaves or roots, some dilution would be expected in the volume of soil, yet inhibition of germination and growth is seen. Choice (C) is wrong— inhibition of germination was not clearly shown—the germination rates obtained from the experimental groups fell into the range of normal germination rates (84–89 percent) obtained when the experiment was repeated. This rules out both choices (C) and (D). The best, and sole remaining choice is (A).

34. The correct answer is (H).
Choices (F) and (G) make untested assumptions about the source of the inhibitor, whereas Experiment 1 established that inhibition was seen within 16 meters of the trunk. If inhibitor is present in the soil, the soil taken from 16 meters or closer to the trunk would be more likely to be inhibitory than soil samples taken farther away.

35. The correct answer is (A).
The soil from an area around the walnut tree would be more likely to be similar to the experimental soil from under the walnut tree, yet by picking it from a region between 16 and 27 meters from the trunk it would be soil that has no demonstrated effect on germination or growth of seedlings. Such soil would be more likely to differ from the experimental soil sample in only one variable, proximity to the trunk of the walnut tree.

Passage 7

36. The correct answer is (H).
While the other groups performed various tests on the sample, Group C performed tests on various elements of the tests Groups F and G performed. For example, when Group B ground up some liver with sand, Group C tested sand alone in the liquid to see the result of only one of the elements—sand—being added to the unknown liquid. If the sand caused fizzing, then it was not the ground liver alone that caused the increase in fizzing.

37. The correct answer is (D).
The fact that the MnO_2 can be used over and over with no apparent change in its properties suggests that it is acting like a catalyst, a substance that can change the rate of a reaction without getting involved in the reaction itself. None of the other answers qualifies for the action exhibited by the MnO_2. It possesses neither hydrogen nor hydroxide and is a powder, making it an unlikely aromatic.

38. **The correct answer is (F).**
The word meaning organic catalyst is enzyme. Lipid refers to the group of organic compounds that includes fats, oils, and waxes; enzymes are proteins. While a catalyst can be an inhibitor, the ones discussed here are enablers and a carrier molecule facilitates the movement of other molecules.

39. **The correct answer is (B).**
One property of a catalyst is that it does not change as it changes the rate of a chemical reaction. Reviving the original sample will only come by putting back what was released. In order to see if the water reacted the same way, they would have used water. This is not a way not see if the liquids were switched.

40. **The correct answer is (F).**
The properties of the constituents of the liquid placed in the electrolysis are consistent with that of water. One volume of gas to two volumes of gas. The two volumes of gas burn and the one volume supports burning. Choices (H) and (J) would not dissociate in an electric current and hydrogen peroxide would yield equal volumes if it dissociated in this way.

Science Review Chart

Circle the item numbers you answered incorrectly. Then review the instruction on the indicated pages.

Item Numbers	Concepts	Pages of Instruction
1, 2, 3, 4, 5, 6, 7, 8, 9, 10, 11, 30, 31, 32, 33, 34, 35	Biology Review	42–43
12, 13, 14, 15, 16, 17, 36, 37, 38, 39, 40	Chemistry Review	44–45
18, 19, 20, 21, 22, 23, 24, 25, 26, 27, 28, 29	Physics, Earth, and Space Science Review	46–48

NOTES

NOTES

NOTES